The Political Economy of Migration and Post-industrialising Australia

During the 1980s and 1990s, Australia's migration intake turned rapidly towards recruiting business professionals, managers and entrepreneurs to support the country's entry into an economic system marked by global value chains. This book analyses the policy idea termed Productive Diversity, introduced by the Australian government as a way of conceptualising the belief that migrants would bring business acumen and a global outlook to help Australia compete as a trading nation.

The book examines this germinal period of Australia's economic reorientation through a close inspection of policy documents, parliamentary hearings, economic and migration statistics, and interviews with the architects of the policy. It provides a comprehensive account of how the policy framework emerged, how it was implemented, and studies the rationale in recruiting self-starters and managers to connect with global trade flows.

This work will be of interest to students and researchers of migration studies, especially Australian migration, diversity policies, sociology, multiculturalism, economics, development studies, and Asia-Pacific studies. The methods and data will also be of value to political economists and policy makers.

Patrick Brownlee is Director of Research Partnerships in Education and Social Work, University of Sydney, Australia. His research into migration and policy stems back decades as a result of coordinating a research program on Asia-Pacific migration, funded by UNESCO's Management of Social Transformations initiative. He also publishes in the field of education and knowledge production. He has a PhD in Political Economy from the University of Sydney.

The Political Economy of Migration and Post-industrialising Australia

Valuing diversity in globalised production

Patrick Brownlee

LONDON AND NEW YORK

First published 2021
by Routledge
2 Park Square, Milton Park, Abingdon, Oxon OX14 4RN

and by Routledge
52 Vanderbilt Avenue, New York, NY 10017

Routledge is an imprint of the Taylor & Francis Group, an informa business

© 2021 Patrick Brownlee

The right of Patrick Brownlee to be identified as author of this work has been asserted by him in accordance with sections 77 and 78 of the Copyright, Designs and Patents Act 1988.

All rights reserved. No part of this book may be reprinted or reproduced or utilised in any form or by any electronic, mechanical, or other means, now known or hereafter invented, including photocopying and recording, or in any information storage or retrieval system, without permission in writing from the publishers.

Trademark notice: Product or corporate names may be trademarks or registered trademarks, and are used only for identification and explanation without intent to infringe.

British Library Cataloguing-in-Publication Data
A catalogue record for this book is available from the British Library

Library of Congress Cataloging-in-Publication Data
Names: Brownlee, Patrick, author.
Title: The political economy of migration and post-industrialising Australia : valuing diversity in globalised production / Patrick Brownlee.
Description: 1 Edition. | New York : Taylor & Francis Group, 2020. | Includes bibliographical references and index.
Identifiers: LCCN 2020010360 (print) | LCCN 2020010361 (ebook)
Subjects: LCSH: Labor mobility--Australia. | Foreign workers--Australia. | Australia--Emigration and immigration--Government policy. | Australia--Economic policy--20th century.
Classification: LCC HD5717.5.A8 B76 2020 (print) | LCC HD5717.5.A8 (ebook) | DDC 331.6/20994--dc23
LC record available at https://lccn.loc.gov/2020010360
LC ebook record available at https://lccn.loc.gov/2020010361

ISBN: 978-1-138-38666-2 (hbk)
ISBN: 978-1-003-05553-2 (ebk)

Typeset in Sabon
by MPS Limited, Dehradun

For Aki, for Luca and for Sassica: my inspiration

Contents

List of figures	viii
List of tables	ix
Preface and acknowledgements	x
Introduction	1
1 Where did productive diversity come from?	15
2 Surplus value theory and the idea of productive diversity	26
3 Productive diversity, value and the question of cultural capital	39
4 Framing the global political economy since the 1970s	51
5 Global capital and its agents	74
6 The nation on the eve of globalisation	91
7 Terms of engagement I	105
8 Terms of engagement II	128
9 Productive diversity	146
10 The Business Migration Program	172
11 Conclusion	205
References	210
Index	231

Figures

2.1	Comparative mean weekly earnings, Australian-born and selected migrant groups, 1961–70, 1980, 1984 ($A)	30
4.1	GVC growth period: 1990–2017	55
4.2	GVC participation, 1995 and 2009	56
4.3	Gross labour force international comparison – major advanced economies, Australia and New Zealand, 1995–2007, millions of people	61
4.4	Domestic value added embodied in final foreign demand – 1995, 2000, 2005 (USD millions) – advanced economies	62
4.5	Domestic value added for final foreign demand – 1995, 2000, 2005 (USD millions) – Asian developing economies	63
5.1	Australian permanent and long-term arrivals by occupation, July 1997–June 2004	79
5.2	Long-stay business migrants 1999–2000, occupational strata %	81
10.1	Main settler arrivals by visa category 1984–85 to 1994–95	174
10.2	Skilled settler arrival by category (principle and secondary applicants), mid-1984 to mid-1994	175
10.3	Business migrants mid-1984 to mid-1997	176
10.4	Business Migrant Program source countries, 1982–90: proportion of principal applicants	179
10.5	Share of BSC applications versus approvals by country of principal applicant: 17 Feb 1992–31 January 1994	185

Tables

4.1	Majority share of world patents in force by 2012 – top countries	57
6.1	Percentage proportion of professional, management and administration (white collar) migrant arrivals by key source countries – 1962	94
6.2	Labourers as of total workforce intake – permanent arrivals, 1980–96	95
7.1	Real GDP growth (annual % change), 1983–95	108
7.2	South East Asian economies: annual export growth (%), 1980–94	109
7.3	Percentage share of total foreign borrowing from creditors, 1978–92 (7-year intervals)	109
7.4	Comparative immediate interest rates (%) (Call Money & Interbank Rate)	110
7.5	Cumulative level of FDI by country of investor (A$billion – proposed)	112

Preface and acknowledgements

This is a work of political economy. By that, I mean it is concerned with the task of confronting the accumulation of material resources that benefits the few over the many. Migration has long been of interest to political economy. And both of these fields of academic work have also been of interest to me thanks in large measure to an Irish Catholic working-class education and where I grew up. Hence, these words are a personal account as both a preface to how and why I wanted to write this book and an acknowledgement from a personal perspective.

When I first began to read and write about migration and the global political economy I was working on a part-time basis in the Centre for Multicultural Studies at the University of Wollongong. That Centre had developed a tangible relationship with the Office of Multicultural Affairs (OMA), the bureaucracy that is credited with developing and running with the idea of Productive Diversity – a key subject of this book. OMA commissioned the Centre to conduct extensive research on migration and multicultural Australia. These were heady days in the scholarship and debate over Australia's politics of identity, the 'purpose' of migration and the economy (read Mark Lopez's work on multiculturalism to get a sense of it all). During the mid-1990s, the Centre also started work on an international migration research network, focused on the Asia Pacific. All of a sudden, the domestic research agenda was being augmented by research on what was happening globally in terms of mass migration and the links that Australia had forged with countries the Asia Pacific over the last decade or so. I was fortunate to travel in the region and met with migration researchers at a time when the study of migration was also developing its identity as a multidiscipline.

That we worked in and among a city, Wollongong, that was a major coal-mining and steel-making city that then represented the 'old' industrial and migrant-driven economy, made the study of migration and diversity all the more palpable. I grew up there in a family dependent upon the

Preface and acknowledgements xi

steelworks and in a diverse neighbourhood. I lived some 200m from a refugee hostel in the town of Fairy Meadow, which had been a first home to many European migrants postwar and, during the 1970s, had settled hundreds of Vietnamese refugees. These childhood experiences of my neighbourhood were indelible and left me forever curious about the world from where everyone else seemed to have a connection or from where they had fled.

The people I worked with in and through that Centre I have to acknowledge with a heartfelt nostalgia for their brilliant ideas, camaraderie and political purpose. Forever thanks to Director of the Centre, Stephen Castles, most of all for his friendship and for giving me the opportunity to be even a very small part of that Centre and what it represented.

A work of this nature, that is, with the original idea having been in slow and steady fermentation, seemingly over decades, has many more individuals deserving of acknowledgement. Much of the material in this book was eventually brought together in my Doctoral studies and therefore my most emphatic thanks must go to Stuart Rosewarne and Bill Dun, two formidable critics, the likes of whom every PhD student should have. I am grateful for their generosity of spirit most of all.

Four individuals agreed to be interviewed for my Doctoral work and the reflections of two of these, Toni Fedderson and Neil Edwards, are featured extensively in a number of chapters of this book. Toni and Neil were the most thoughtful and accommodating research participants. Their insights were invaluable and challenged my thinking. I hope that their endeavours are remembered as important contributions to a certain moment in Australian policy making. Thanks, then, also to Bill Cope, a former Head of OMA, and to Nick Bolkus, a former Immigration Minister who contributed interviews that informed my further research.

Ellie Vasta (also a member of that same Centre for Multicultural Studies), I have to thank for more recent help: reading and commenting thoughtfully on two chapters of my doctoral work, some of which informs Chapter 2. Likewise, Stephen Brown, who read many chapters and offered his usual unassuming and kind appraisal of my arguments.

Thanks to my close colleagues in my workplace at the University of Sydney, who are always supportive and hence helped me juggle the many daily work demands with organising my thoughts into such a scholarly project. Among these, special thanks are offered to Raewyn Connell and to Sue Goodwin, both of whom, in scholarly and material ways, were exceedingly encouraging of my efforts leading to this book.

To my close friends, I have heartfelt thanks for the encouragement that was always offered in small but meaningful ways. Notably, Damien Cahill and Carol Berry, comrades who have always found the time in their busy lives to offer the kindest words of friendship and intellect that always provided me with emotional sustenance and perspective.

To my children I am indebted most of all, for giving me a reason to complete the task!

Introduction

As aphorisms go, the phrase 'Australia was built on the sheep's back' is by now past its use-by date. Wool was a chief commodity of Australia's pastoralist economy throughout the 19th and 20th centuries. When global competition in the garment industry in the early 1970s put a dent in Australia's foreign income from wool, some in government were becoming uneasy about the real risks that come with reliance on a single primary commodity to underwrite the economy.[1] It was increasingly evident that many of the world's economies were developing and competing at scale and that Australia's protectionist economy might not sufficiently insulate it from growing global competition, especially from countries realising their vast supply of unskilled and low-waged labour. Nowhere was this development becoming more prescient than in the region of the Asia Pacific.

A discussion of sheep might not be a typical introduction to the political economy of migration or of ethnocultural diversity except as a way to demolish that ageing aphorism and instead declare that, if contemporary Australia was built upon anything, it was built first upon the orchestrated and bloody fiction of *terra nullius*, and then upon the work of migrants. What follows is an examination of that second order claim, not in terms of migration simply as an industrial legacy but how a new stream of migrants was envisaged to support Australia's entry into the global market economy.

The period after the Second World War up to the 1980s saw the biggest impact by migrant industrial labour on the Australian economy and society. The textiles industry – responsible for spinning that abundance of wool into export dollars – for example, comprised at least 50% of immigrant labour in the 1960s.[2] However, as the 'sheep's back' began to yield fewer returns, by the 1980s, so had Australia's primary and industrial manufacturing sectors suffered due to tectonic shifts in the global economy, questioning the need for that migrant labour. Australia, however, did not scale back or abandon its migration programme for economic development in the face of persistently high unemployment and an off-shoring of manufacturing that ensued. On the contrary, the Government re-calibrated its intake instruments to attract and select in vastly greater numbers not only the skilled and educated (and their

2   Introduction

families), but also migrants with money capital and those that might facilitate business growth and pursue international trade.

Migration scholars have increasingly acknowledged this shift in Australia's substantive migration intake. The shift is characterised as being away from unskilled and 'blue collar' labour that had powered almost four decades of postwar industrial development and towards skilled and what is nebulously called 'independent' 'labour'. From the turn of the 21st century a further shift occurred, moving Australia away from a historical reliance upon settling migrants as citizens; temporary migration – those engaged in the economy via visas of anywhere between one month and three to four years – has far outstripped those accepted to settle permanently. Globalisation is the convenient lens through which to view this double shift: A global market for talent revealed itself, stoked by the speed and intensity of technological change and of migrant flows noticeably from less developed economies. Labour, meanwhile, seems to be the generic and unquestioned characteristic commodity enduring this shift in Australia, as though a continuum from unskilled to skilled exists as a function of globalisation. Even a cursory glance at Australia's migration occupation classifications and trend data complicates the idea of migrant *labour* and of Australia's apparent need for it in a growing global, market-based economy. From the early 2000s, and enduring the 2007–08 Global Financial Crisis, Managers, Directors and the like – highly skilled market economy professionals – comprised well over 60% of the temporary 'skilled visa' intake.[3] Reconsidering what 'skilled' migration means and analysing the actual occupational classifications of Australia's highly organised skilled and business migration programmes emergent in the 1980s, a compelling case can be made for a distinction between migrant labour as *productive* and *non-productive,* rather than skilled and unskilled. These terms, productive and non-productive, have been used by political economists to refer to labour and its management, to the way value is added to commodities and how profit is gained. By looking at migration programmes in this way we can better understand how internal class-based divisions are created and supported under the guise of skilled migration and agree that migrant work is not always subordinate or singular, or that migration from economically disadvantaged nation-states always represents progressive global economic redistribution.

With this in mind, the origins of Australian government and policy influencers' efforts to engineer a migration shift in response to global economic change in the 1970s and 1980s tell a more calculated story about the role of highly selective migration in and for the emergent global market economy. A unique vignette in this national narrative concerns the multiculturalist policy rubric of **Productive Diversity**, which developed to become inextricably linked to changing the rationale and make up of migrant Australia. How and why an apparent social policy framework became an economic one is revealed in this book.

Introduction 3

The postwar mass migrations, principally from Europe, were governed by a prevailing *social* regime and hegemony that *devalued* ethnocultural difference and diversity. Assimilation to a dominant White, gendered and generally working-class cultural norm was expected and expressed publicly, although it was not easily attained. Australia's protectionist economy, unsurprisingly, included protection for the prevailing social and cultural milieu. At the same time, difference from this norm was *valued* in economic production by virtue of the fact it was a marker of a wage differential – migrant labour provided more value, or yielded more profit! The idea of assimilation into white society was diametrical to the need for ethnic difference on the factory floor. The meaning of the term 'value' is key here.

By the 1970s, things had begun to unravel for *White Australia* and its ability to protect its manufacturing economy was challenged. Industry suffered the shocks of a global recession, the inflation rate ballooned, unemployment in 1975 ran to more than double the average rate of the previous ten years and would spike in 1978 to more than treble that average.[4] Marginalised social and political constituencies were mobilising for social justice with the winds of change illustrated by the removal in 1972 of a conservative government that had been in power for decades. Australia's political economy was entering uncharted waters!

Support for migrant minorities from non-English speaking backgrounds regarding their wage and living conditions took on greater significance in Federal politics, leading to policies geared towards amelioration of decades of social exploitation of this postwar labour force. These policies, only gradually understood and articulated as Multiculturalism, also responded to another migration 'shift' that had further challenged the nation-building hegemony of White protectionism: a whole new era of refugee migration from what was then Indochina, following the Vietnam War and then, a burgeoning of migrants with money capital and experience in trade and business mostly from Hong Kong, Malaysia, Singapore and elsewhere in Asia. Australia's national narrative as an outpost of the British Empire became a millstone as it struggled to connect with economic growth in Asia.

Programmes and policies in support of ethnic diversity quickly became more sophisticated and conceptually progressive in the 1980s but were almost immediately in conflict: not only did social conservatives stoke fears about the loss of identity as a white majority nation; the economy underwent a triple bypass surgery of fiscal and monetary reform towards the global free market. Community and welfare-oriented migrant social policy – multiculturalism – ran counter to the self-reliance and individual responsibility that is purported to drive a market economy and to which Australian governments were turning.

Productive Diversity emanated from within the inner circles of government grappling with this apparent conflict. As a form of 'boosterism' for the global market economy, Productive Diversity grafted a concern for migrants as effective citizens onto the new economic conditions. It was a

4   *Introduction*

unique policy expression of multiculturalism that envisaged a new economic purpose in and for migrant work and corresponded with the significant quantitative *and* qualitative shift in Australia's migration intake towards business people, market economy professionals and entrepreneurs.

The origins and underlying dynamics of the connection between the recruitment of certain migrant occupations and the shift to a specifically market-oriented immigrant diversity policy have been variously understood. It is also the case that most developed economies with a history of mass migration were developing versions of the same approach to immigrant selection: professional-grade skill and talent and economic self-sufficiency were sought out, typically favouring male migrants, along with a penchant for recruiting those from the regions of the world going through industrial growth and with large unskilled labour forces. The 'global race for talent', as Boucher[5] aptly describes it, emerged from a specific moment in the global political economy.

Minority migrant labour has been a central subject in research on ethnicity in Australia not least because it was so visible and tangible in the industrialisation of Australia. Class discrimination and ethnicity consequently have been strongly interlinked, especially in sociological research. Analyses of multicultural or diversity policies in Australia have mostly focused upon issues of minority social and political rights in response to discrimination, social cohesion in the face of social and economic change (often the reason for recruiting migrants), or concerns that migrant labour suffers with sub-standard working conditions.[6] A summary conclusion in much research is that migrant minority labour, and more specifically migrant ethnicity, is a treated as commodity but yet a lesser commodity than *non*-minority labour.[7] Such conclusions may elide whether and how labour in general might also be a commodity, considering, in Marxian terms, how commodities come into existence *as the result of labour*. Earlier analyses of labour migrant ethnicity that emphasise an economic rationale drew upon a 'reserve army of labour' concept.[8] These approaches rely upon a uni-dimensional supply-demand epistemology, where greater supply inevitably produces cheaper labour prices. This has some explanatory power but at a very coarse-grained level. Consideration of whether a labour market actually exists and operates like markets for commodities, especially in relation to entrepreneurs, business owners, skilled professionals and independent migrants, questions the 'reserve army' as a simple binary theorisation. Nevertheless, a global division of productive and non-productive labour, tiered, segmented, stratified, precarious – *valued* – now operates through complex chains of production, distribution and accumulation across and within nation-state jurisdictions.

An analysis divergent from these accounts and intimately related to the policy rubric of Productive Diversity is Cope and Kalantzis's broader theory entitled *Productive Diversity*.[9] Curiously little attention is given to this in the literature as a theorisation of global market dynamics and

Introduction 5

labour. These authors 'celebrate' ethnocultural diversity for perceived personal, workplace, corporate and national economic possibilities in the emergent global market. The Cope and Kalantzis version of Productive Diversity reifies ethnoculture as an object to either create or add value within a workplace or firm's cooperative relations. Ethnoculture tends also to become valorised as an expansive aggregate form, 'diversity', in this market model, suggesting that diversity is a productive capital somehow circulated as a virtuous and reciprocal event. The idea that diversity was a kind of knowledge commodity was contemporaneous with nascent ideas about communicative competency and an information economy. A main problem with the Cope and Kalantzis's theory is its denial of the actually existing contested nature of both value and exchange in market capitalist relations and the actually existing consequences of the historical concentration of accumulated private capital. Bowles and Gintis's idea of 'contested exchange'[10] puts paid to this fancy: The market is brutally competitive with winners and losers determined by their acumen, knowledge and accumulated material resources.

The Cope and Kalantzis analysis is an ideal form presenting the market as benign, where extant inter-firm competition and the transnational division and exploitation of labour are omitted for their real effects. Where Australian Government interpretations of Productive Diversity *as policy* differ from Cope and Kalantzis is in the government's embrace of the competitiveness of markets, and therefore the contestation inherent in capitalist accumulation.

This brings us to the key theoretical concern of this book and one that addresses Marx's original idea of value and social reproduction: Forms of 'commoditising', 'valorising' or 'reifying' ethnocultural diversity – terms that often, mistakenly, are used to mean 'promoting' ethnocultural diversity – do not *increase* exploitation for surplus value in actual production. In other words, ethnicity is not a factor of labour intrinsically useful *in production*, in actual labour power whether productive or nonproductive. The contest over value and its surplus is played out in the way ethnic minorities have historically and continue to be devalued in terms of social living conditions, that is, in the cost to replenish and reproduce themselves for labour daily, yearly and generationally. What this logically implies is that exploitation of value from minority migrant labour, skilled or unskilled, would be diminished relative to (some reduction in) their social marginalisation. In Australia's case, if Productive Diversity and multiculturalism advanced equality and occupational opportunity for ethnic minority migrants, it follows that any surplus value extractable from their labour should be *decreased*.

Moreover, Productive Diversity in real terms was conceived of with the highly skilled, entrepreneurial and so-called 'business migrants' in mind, rather than *labour*. Arguments about the policy's exploitative efforts to surrender more value from migrant labour are difficult to sustain for such

6 *Introduction*

occupational forms, many of which are not creators of value in the first instance, but instead oversee labour or expand market opportunity. These occupations fall largely on one side of a global division of labour and what Duménil and Lévy referred to as 'unproductive labour' or 'profit-rate maximizing labour'[11] – those who control, own or facilitate deliberately the circulation of capital. This includes both global corporate elites and many more migrant entrepreneurs involved in enterprise in the global market economy. Non-productive labour also refers to production management and innovation.[12] Productive labour, on the other hand, is involved in the circulation of capital fundamentally by creating commodities ordinarily, as directed. In organised forms (e.g., trade unions), productive labour is also involved in contesting the amount of money capital which is 'circulated' as wages and that which is not. But labour's *raison d'être* is not deciding the circulation of investment and productive capital for the sake of creating more.

From this theoretical vantage point, we can begin to see if there is any difference in how ethnicity and diversity might be applied or are useful in non-productive occupations, that is, managers, business owners, entrepreneurs, financial investors and advisers, global corporate professionals and the like. Within an abstract notion of a market, ethnoculture and diversity may not have any exclusive, advantageous exchange value over time. Any culturally specific knowledge becomes part of market exchange and equally found or matched, emulated and deployed by all parties to an exchange. The irony that diversity might be thought of as an 'asset' in exchange is evident: diversity's usefulness relies on the predictability of ethnoculture in exchange. It is know-how (language and customs, practices) and trust (identity) that is identifiable, reliable, deployable, anticipated; not internally diverse.

The issue of ethnicity's economic dimension is complicated by some loose and generic applications of the concept of economic agency and especially of the concept of cultural capital – that is, those advantages that are ascribed by and for social grouping and exclusion. Indeed, the epistemology of class in migration and ethnicity has largely been abandoned to measurements of individualistic agency and cultural capital, sometimes as opportunity, sometimes as privilege. It is worth noting some influential and pertinent examples to make the point that scholarship on migrant diversity and value is eclectic. The following passage from Reay et al. (2007), encapsulates just a few of the many scholarly positions on a relationship between ethnocultural diversity and economic value:

> Their value [migrants], or more precisely exchange-value (Skeggs, 2004) lies in their utility as enriching cultures for the host culture. For Skeggs, white middle-class multiculturalism is a practice based on creating and managing an economy of otherness. Hage writes about

'productive diversity' or what he calls *'ethnic surplus value'* (1998: 128) in which the white middle classes further enrich themselves through the consumption of ethnic diversity. ... Ahmed (2004) points out that diversity all too often is not associated with challenging disadvantage but becomes yet another way of doing advantage, while for Gibbons (2002), diversity for the middle classes is primarily about the acquisition of valuable multicultural global capital.[13]

Taksa and Groutsis's analysis of skilled migration examined the shift from industrial to skilled and knowledge workers in Australia as the same commodifying process, and suggesting that racialisation of migrants as sought-after human commodities in knowledge work is a denial of their natural individual agency.[14] History has shown that agency is not guaranteed or ubiquitous and it is only theoretically stable in relation to critical reflection on the processes of socialisation (after Giddens); that is, realising one's own oppression *and* how it is structurally reinforced. In sociological terms, agency is not a 'free-agent' concept! Thus, when scholars talk of 'ethnic business breakout' as agency[15] they are underscoring that ethno-culture can be a means to a wholly different end – agency to extricate oneself from cultural mores and prejudices to instead contest the market. As a term of significance to Marxian political economy, agency pertains experientially to labour's contest with capital over the share of value offered or surrendered. Action is theorised in relation to a political act of 'class consciousness' and classically pertains to mass labour's agency.[16] The term 'consciousness' has proved a distraction to an otherwise important way of understanding agency as coordinated action that must be deliberately shared to effect structural change, at least as far as the economy is concerned.

The idea of agency is raised in a number of chapters in this book because of the tendency in migration research to equate ethnic entrepreneurialism with agency, individual social mobility with agency or, indeed, the act of migrating with agency.[17] There is nothing necessarily emancipatory or consciously political in such notions of agency. Bringing us back to the landscape of this book, market *contest* rather than agency as some liberating force is presented as a prism through which to view this era of Australian migration and diversity policymaking. And as will be detailed, the language of economic competition permeates multicultural policies that were initially built upon notions of community and social equality.

A range of claims clearly exist concerning the economic usefulness of ethnoculture and diversity as the aggregate form of many cultures. In virtually all analyses, however, labour is the presumed target of diversity policy. Principally, and because of their focus on Productive Diversity, the key claims from the above-quoted passages concern: exploitation of 'Ethnic surplus value'; (ethno)cultural capital as either social asset or liability; human skills as capital and agency, and; migrants as commodities of

8 *Introduction*

capital. Deciding a robust epistemology to analyse the idea of value of ethnoculture and Productive Diversity has been complicated by claims upon the idea of 'capital'.

Apart from the treatise on Productive Diversity by Cope and Kalantzis, Bertone[18] remains one of the few scholars strongly engaged with policy concept. An influential Australian critique by Hage about Productive Diversity advanced the phrase 'ethnic surplus value' to analyse migrants' political and social exploitation by dominant 'White' culture.[19] Hage's critique (also cited in the passage by Reay et al., 2007), is unique among Productive Diversity analyses for a claim linking ethnicity with *surplus value* rather than commodification. His idea of how labour derives a value is not elaborated upon. Hage's point, rather, is to eschew government claims about Productive Diversity as a form of social and economic advancement or migrant minority emancipation. Hage's brief analysis on the matter of Productive Diversity and ethnic surplus value is often quoted but poorly analysed or applied, with the concept of Productive Diversity often viewed as a form of managerialism or neoliberal control.[20] Walton-Roberts makes an astute but summary observation of Hage:

> Such criticisms (Hage's) themselves entail contradictions, since they critique the *inclusion,* rather than exclusion, of immigrants into the formal economy. Of course the point of such critical observations is with regard to *how* immigrants are included in economic processes and how the manner of inclusion furthers neoliberal discourses.[21]

Hage's specific criticism of Productive Diversity invokes a decidedly Marxian concept. The 'ethnic surplus value' argument is an exemplar of how the migrant exploitation discourse can obscure: 1) the class differentiation of the migrant intake; and 2) whether ethnoculture is in fact exploitable to render a surplus and, if so, how this might be unique to minority migrant labour. In relation to the first point, data on increasing business migrant recruitment and on professional skilled visas analysed in ensuing chapters suggest that ethnocultural diversity in management and in entrepreneurial talent, not waged productive labour, emerged as the more important rationale for those programmes. In this case a contradiction is apparent: the surplus value argument about ethnic diversity advanced by Hage but generally relevant to adherents of cultural capital exploitation or migrants as commodities, does not solely apply in the case of Australia's Productive Diversity context and policy period. This is because the 're-sources' the policy was most concerned with under the Productive Diversity motif were increasingly and decidedly *non-productive and market-expanding occupations* – not productive waged labour – that, uniquely, do not yield surplus value.

Introduction 9

The most prevalent theories of value relating to migrants are a personified capital, 'human capital' after Becker, or symbolic 'cultural capital', after Bourdieu.[22] Social capital, after Putnam, as the collective or institutional representation of personified material capital is also implicated here.[23] Such 'capitals' have become widespread theoretical constructs in relation to 'agency' and structure. This is especially relevant to analysis of contemporary migrations to Australia of non-productive occupational categories because of assumptions about the degree of agency exercisable by elites and managerial professionals, or 'privileged' migrant labour (after Bauder).

Observing skilled migration and ethnic entrepreneurialism as progress over Australia's industrial past, one could be forgiven for thinking that non-Anglo mass labour, marginalised and yet *valued* for profit making because of this marginalisation, no longer exists. Only through the world of interdependent economic production, that is, through Global Value Chains, however, can we see that work in our postindustrial economy, including the work of some migrants recruited or self-selected into non-productive labour is still connected with ethnocultural segmentations of labour.

Drawing upon Marx's theory of value applied to an international division of labour and non-productive and market expanding occupational forms, the analysis offered in this book explains that ethnoculture or diversity is not a form of capital in production in the strict sense but that it can, as it has historically, affected the value (represented as a price) of productive labour. Finally, however, having established through analysis of economic and migration data that diversity policy in postindustrial Australia really concerned non-productive and market expanding occupations, notably entrepreneurs and self-starters of one sort or another, the conclusion offered is that any *value* intrinsic to ethnoculture is in the realm of exchange or markets, not commodity production; its value concerns types of knowledge deployed in certain competitive markets. It is this reasoning that we return full circle to the defining context of globalisation: That is, the global dispersal of production and exchange and the global concentration of wealth, marked by Global Value Chains with exploitative mass-labour and industrial scale production located in the Global South, and 'value adding' and 'value exchanging' practices of business makers and entrepreneurs, financiers and group managers in closer proximity to the locus of accumulation; writ large, the Global North.[24] And, sometimes, the Global North and South coexist in the same country.

An analysis of an Australian migrant diversity policy bound to the contemporary global economy begs the question of how and why Productive Diversity emerged and has since receded, at least officially. A conservative government elected in 1996 in Australia had rejected the idea of multiculturalism yet Productive Diversity continued to be referred to in government policy and discourse for some time.[25] Namely, is Productive Diversity

10 Introduction

necessarily time-bound, an expression of a policy 'fix' for a renewed migration programme focused on recruiting professionals, entrepreneurs and business people largely to compete with the growth economies of Asia? Was the policy reliant solely on the efforts of a few leading and insightful government bureaucrats? Questions of Productive diversity's half-life, its peak impact and meaningfulness, are made more complex by the second migration shift towards temporary business and skilled professionals, a proliferation under successive conservative and labour governments since 1996 away from attracting citizen nation-building capitalists, large or small. These more recent migrations of mobile capital and corporate specialists and professionals servicing Australia's centres of market activity, nevertheless continued to build Australia's position in the global value chain system of production, circulation and accumulation of wealth.

Structure of this book

This book applies Marxian political economy to the related fields of globalisation, migration and multicultural studies. It ultimately addresses a moral question of value and contemporary global 'skilled' migration – and I leave that to be appreciated fully in the concluding chapter as a reflection on the assemblage of parts that make up this argument. The book is divided into two main parts. In Part I, Theories and Concepts, the first four chapters contend with the conceptual, the theoretical and the epistemological. Chapter 1 explains where Productive Diversity came from as a concept opens this section. The idea of Productive Diversity was a significant conceptual departure formulated within Australia's Office of Multicultural Affairs (OMA), and later co-theorised by a former OMA director concerning the perceived role and value of ethnicity in the workplace in a globally interconnected but cooperative market.[26]

Chapters 2 and 3 establish a theoretical frame for analysing value and occupation-based migration. Value and symbolic forms of capital are discussed in this section. While Marx's surplus value and Bourdieu's cultural capital are well-established tools for analysing what counts as capital, they are at odds when it comes to ethnicity and migrant labour. The idea of economic value of ethnoculture is not a consistent theme of migration research yet in one way or another ethnic minority status is linked to political economy. Mostly this emanates from the historical fact that, in large measure, migrants have traditionally occupied the lower segments or strata of a workforce. However, Chapter 4 discusses the significance of Global Value Chains (GVCs) to explain how and why migration rapidly changed to serve in ways that it hadn't previously a postindustrial landscape of tiered, networked production.

Part II of the book, Australia and Globalisation: Migration for Diversity (Chapters 5 to 11), newly synthesises evidence from policy documents,

Introduction 11

parliamentary hearings and statements, economic and migration statistics, and interviews with architects of Productive Diversity policy, the book offers new explanations about how Australian migration and diversity policies were intertwined from within Government to attract and retain capitalists, entrepreneurs and globally connected market economy professionals. The chapters in this section also reveal how a notion of their agency was constructed and construed within a wider paradigm shift in Australia away from the Keynesian state and social contract to productivity through self-reliance and entrepreneurialism.

I draw on both recent and overlooked migration data to establish the basis for understanding Australia's scaled-up recruitment of business professionals and consultants as befitting the definitive institutions and structures of contemporary global production: transnational corporations and industries and global value chains.

The linking of Productive Diversity and business and skilled migration has hitherto not been systematically undertaken despite the fact migration data has existed to suggest a link for detailed exploration. The politics and planning behind the Business Migration Program has not had a thorough historical review, other than a short article by Birrell *et.al* in the latter 1990s assessing its effectiveness against stated aims. The key source documents including the Australian Senate Estimates Standing Committee on Migration, the 1994 *Deveson Review* into the business migration programmes would appear not to have been previously consulted for such a study. Additionally, Neil Edwards, a former head of the Office of Multicultural Affairs (OMA), jointly responsible for coining the actual term 'productive diversity' was interviewed and provides new insights into the policy making and the role of OMA. A second interview undertaken with a former senior officer within the Committee for the Economic Development of Australia, Toni Fedderson, complements the OMA interview and confirms the close working relationship between these two organisations. That CEDA had a mandate for business development in Asia, as borne out in the interview, provides sure but subtle indications that Productive Diversity in the 1990s became more connected with Australia's strategy for economic engagement with the region.

It is evident that the government of the day pursued migrant economic actors to assist in engaging Asia and the global market economy. Australia, of course, was not alone in its desire to fabricate a nationally directed competitive advantage. What resulted, then, more likely represented a knowledge deficit reduction strategy on behalf of Australia, or a negation of competitive *dis*advantage in a new global market order.

Notes

1 Wilkinson, J. (2000) *Changing Nature of the NSW Economy – Background Paper No. 1.* Sydney: NSW Parliamentary Library Research Service.

12 Introduction

2 Collins, J. (1988) *Migrant Hands in a Distant Land*, Annandale, NSW: Pluto Press. Cashin, P. and McDermott, C.J. (2002) 'Riding on the Sheep's Back: Examining Australia's Dependence on Wool Exports', *The Economic Record*, Vol. 78, No. 242, pp. 249–63. Australia had developed a more diverse commodity base since at least the Second World War.

3 Brownlee, P. (2016) 'Global Capital's Lieutenants: Australia's Skilled Migrant Intake and the Rise of Global Value Chain Production', *Journal of Australian Political Economy*, Vol. 77, pp. 108–35. Tertiary students are the other major category emergent since the early 2000s and are mentioned in later chapters.

4 Warby, M. (1994) *From There to Back Again?: Australian Inflation and Unemployment 1964 to 1993*, Background Paper Number 9, Canberra: Department of the Parliamentary Library, p. 7.

5 Boucher, A. (2016) *Gender, Migration and the Global Race for Talent*. Manchester: Manchester University Press.

6 Jacubowicz, A. and Ho, C. (ed.) (2013) *'For those who came across the seas': Australian Multicultural Theory, Policy and Practice*, North Melbourne: Australian Scholarly Publishing; Jupp, J. (2008) *Social Cohesion in Australia*, Port Melbourne: Cambridge University Press; Lopez, M. (2000a) *The Origins of Multiculturalism in Australian Politics 1945–1975*, Melbourne: Melbourne University Press; Castles, S., Cope, B., Kalantzis, M. and Morrissey, M. (1992) *Mistaken Identity: Multiculturalism and the Demise of Nationalism in Australia*, 3rd edn, Leichhardt: Pluto Press.

7 Taksa, L. and Groutsis, D. (2010) 'Managing Diverse Commodities?: From Factory Fodder to Business Asset', *The Economic and Labour Relations Review*, Vol. 20, No. 2, July, pp. 77–98.

8 Jamrozik, A., Boland, K. and Urquhart, R. (1995) *Social Change and Cultural Transformation in Australia*, Cambridge and New York: Cambridge University Press; Collins, J. (1991) *Migrant Hands in a Distant Land: Australia's Postwar Immigration*, 2nd edn, Leichhardt, NSW: Pluto Press.

9 Cope, B. and Kalantzis, M. (1997) *Productive Diversity: A New Australian Model for Work and Management*, Annandale, NSW: Pluto Press.

10 Bowles, S. and Gintis, H. (1993) 'The Revenge of Homo Economicus: Contested Exchange and the Revival of Political Economy', *Journal of Economic Perspectives*, Vol. 7, No. 1, pp. 83–102.

11 Duménil, G. and Lévy, D. (2011) 'Unproductive Labor as Profit-Rate-Maximizing Labor, Rethinking Marxism: A Journal of Economics' *Culture & Society*, Vol. 23, No. 2, April, pp. 216–25.

12 Hardt, M. and Negri, A. *(2000) Empire*, Cambridge, MA; London: Harvard University Press, pp. 292–93.

13 Reay, D. Hollingworth, S., Williams, K., Crozier, G., Jamieson, F., James, D. and Beedell, P. (2007) 'Inner City Schooling "A Darker Shade of Pale?" Whiteness, the Middle Classes and Multi Ethnic', *Sociology* Vol. 41, No. 6, December, p. 1051 (italics mine). A similar statement from the same authors can be found in Reay, D., Crozier, G., James, D., Hollingworth, S., Williams, K, Jamieson, F. and Beedell, P. (2006) 'Re-invigorating Democracy?: White Middle Class Identities and Comprehensive Schooling', *The Sociological Review*, Vol. 56, No. 2, pp. 238–55.

14 Taksa, L. and Groutsis, D. (2010), p. 7.

15 Lassalle, P. and Scott, J.M. (2018) 'Breaking-out? A Reconceptualisation of the Business Development Process Through Diversification: The Case of Polish New Migrant Entrepreneurs in Glasgow', *Journal of Ethnic and Migration Studies*, Vol. 44, No. 15, pp. 2524–43, DOI: 10.1080/1369183X.2017.1391077; Allen,

R. and Busse, E. (2016) 'The Social Side of Ethnic Entrepreneur Breakout: Evidence from Latino Immigrant Business Owners', *Journal of Ethnic and Racial Studies*, Vol. 39, No. 4, pp. 653–70.

16 Lukács, G. (2000) *History and Class Consciousness: Studies in Marxist Dialectics*. Cambridge, MA: The MIT Press.

17 Cederberg, M. and Villares-Varela, M. (2018) 'Ethnic Entrepreneurship and the Question of Agency: The Role of Different Forms of Capital, and the Relevance of Social Class', *Journal of Ethnic and Migration Studies*, Vol. 45, No. 1, pp. 115–32; Kloosterman, R. and Rath, J. (2001) 'Immigrant entrepreneurs in advanced economies: Mixed embeddedness further explored', *Journal of Ethnic and Migration Studies*, Vol. 27, No. 2, pp. 189–201.

18 Bertone, S. in Jacubowicz, A. and Ho, C. (2013); Bertone, S. and Leahy, M. (2003) 'Multiculturalism as a Conservative Ideology: Impacts on Workforce Diversity', *Asia Pacific Journal of Human Resources*, Vol. 41, No.1. DOI: 10.1177/103841110304 1001026 (accessed 19 June 2012); Bertone, S., Esposto, A. and Turner, R. 1998, *Diversity and Dollars: Productive Diversity in Australian Business and Industry*, Workplace Studies Centre, Victoria University, Melbourne; see also Pyke, K, (2005b) 'Productive Diversity: Which Companies are Active and Why?' Master's thesis, Victoria University, http://vuir.vu.edu.au/386/1/02whole.pdf (accessed 3 December 2010).

19 Hage, G. (2000) *White Nation: Fantasies of White Supremacy in a Multicultural Society*, New York and Annandale, NSW: Routledge and Pluto Press, pp. 128–30.

20 See Reay et al., 2007; For claims about Productive Diversity, managerialism and neoliberalism, see Bertone, S. 'Precarious Bystanders: Temporary Migrants and Multiculturalism', in Jakubowicz and Ho, C. (2014) *For Those Who've Come Across the Seas: Australian Multicultural Theory, Policy and Practice*, Melbourne: Australian Scholarly Publishing; Bertone, M and Leahy, M. 'Social Equity, Multiculturalism and the Productive Diversity Paradigm: Reflections on their Role in Corporate Australia', in Phillips, Scott K. (ed.) (2001) *Everyday Diversity: Australian Multiculturalism in Practice*, Altona, VIC: Common Ground Publishing; Rizvi, F. and Lingard, R. (2010) *Globalizing Education Policy*, Abingdon, Oxon: Routledge. For one summary interpretation of migrants and surplus value emphasising the cost of recreating labour's value as the determinant, see Goh, B.H. and Wong, S. (2004) *Asian Diasporas: Cultures, Identities, Representations*, Hong Kong: Hong Kong University Press, especially pp. 66–7.

21 Walton-Roberts, M. (2009) 'India-Canada Trade and Immigration Linkages: A Case of Regional (Dis)advantage?', *Metropolis Working Paper Series*, No. 09–04, June, Vancouver, Metropolis British Columbia-Centre of Excellence for Research on Immigration and Diversity, p. 10.

22 Bourdieu, P. (1986) 'The Forms of Capital', in Richardson, J. (ed.) *Handbook of Theory and Research for the Sociology of Education*, New York: Greenwood, pp. 241–58, http://www.marxists.org/reference/subject/philosophy/works/fr/bourdieu-forms-capital.htm (accessed 17 February 2020). First published: Bourdieu, P. (1986) 'The forms of capital', in J. Richardson (ed.) *Handbook of Theory and Research for the Sociology of Education*, New York, Greenwood, pp. 241–58; Becker, G.S. (1975) *Human Capital*, 2nd edn, New York: Columbia University Press.

23 Putnam, R. (2000). *Bowling Alone: The Collapse and Revival of American Community*, New York: Touchstone.

14 Introduction

24 Brownlee, P. (2016).
25 Ho, C. 'From Social Justice to Social Cohesion: A History of Australian Multicultural Policy', in Jakubowicz, A. and Ho, C. (2014).
26 Cope, B and Kalantzis, M. (1997) *Op.cit*. Bill Cope was the last Director of OMA from 1994–96. Correspondence and an interview with Bill Cope was undertaken and informs this work.

1 Where did productive diversity come from?

The idea of multiculturalism that took root in many countries of migration around the 1970s remains a contested concept some 40 years later. The marriage or conflation of multiculturalism with immigration in itself has been a site of contestation for almost as long as policies supporting diversity emerged. Separating migration and diversity policy is counter-intuitive as one begs and begets the other, but only in certain economic circumstances. The nation states of Europe, the UK, Australia, Canada and the US, *inter alia,* all have different experiences of migration-induced cultural diversity as a social project with unique vulnerabilities. Yet, multiculturalism, represented for a period in Australia by Productive Diversity has an altogether different political economy in the division of migrant labour and non-productive occupational forms for the global market economy.

Multiculturalism as a state-sponsored project within these mostly Anglophone countries of the Global North varies with the combined and uneven development of each country's history. It has therefore evolved different conceptions, policies and practices in different countries. To that end, some now argue that there is or was no definite era of multiculturalism.[1] Lauter refers to 'that earlier moment of multiculturalism', prior to the post-9/11 era.[2] Other Australian research asks again if there is a 'new era in Australian multiculturalism?'[3] Jacubowicz more specifically cites the global reality of China as world power with a significant transnational community or diaspora becoming politically active in Australia; multiculturalism, he explains, was conceived under very different circumstances.[4]

As a policy framework, multiculturalism is claimed to have been first conceived in Canada in the early 1970s and adopted in principle soon after by Australia to redress racism and cultural discrimination and workplace segmentation. It was later enacted in Canada through constitutional Charter 1982, while in Australia multiculturalism was feted as citizenship-through-'opportunity' in a landmark government framework of 1989, the *National Agenda on a Multicultural Australia.*[5] A decade later the UKs *Parekh Report*[6] attempted to reconcile pluralist social organisation with Westminster rule of law, something that had never been

16   *Where did productive diversity come from?*

quite as controversial with other forms of democratic association, such as trade unionism or what Marshall had termed 'industrial citizenship'.[7] In the USA, meanwhile, diversity policies under the Republic's rubric of *I pluribus Unum* were contextualised by that country's constitutional Bill of Rights to equalise all claims to the nation. America's universalist assimilationist 'model' for diversity is often referred to as the 'melting pot' approach[8] where ethnocultural difference is meant to blend and homogenise. The historical reality is that the USA remains a society stratified economically according to race.

Nevertheless, it is along the lines of individual rights, more consistently associated with the American approach to citizenship, that philosophical origins of multiculturalism would lay claim to a normativity pre-dating the 1970s. These normative claims stem largely from Western European Enlightenment thought on the rights of the individual, from John Locke, Adam Smith, Stuart Mill and Jean-Jacques Rousseau, *inter alia*. At the core is the right to an individual freedom but one that can only be exercised in association with others. Therefore, social relations matter. One key set of social relations that have mattered the most over the last 300–400 years are those of capital, of the mode of production and accumulation. These relations challenge any notion of rights materially where class, but also gender and ethnicity have determined opportunity, and simultaneously where property has become private and quarantined from social and collective forms. A fundamental tension exists in the reciprocal terms of the relationship between individual the state, not in normative rights terms, but in the way the state represents and supports the prevailing relations of production and actual productive forces.

The tension between individual and collective citizenship rights not coincidentally then maps onto the historical contest between capital and labour. That contest over the mode and means of production was reframed by government and industry leaders as a unique association between the market and ethnoculture at the very time that multiculturalism 'emerged' in the 1970s. As with gender, ethnoculture and race were variously transformed from being a restriction on labour supply in industrialised countries of immigration. By the mid-1980s, migrant minorities were being associated with rights and agency as economically productive individuals.[9] This was hard won for many small business ethnic entrepreneurs as Collins and *et al.* have made abundantly clear of Australia's case: while mass-labour industrialisation was increasingly off-shored and partially eclipsed by small and medium enterprise growth, many migrants were pushed into marginal self-employment due to persistent labour market barriers.[10] In all such cases, however, the idea of agency derived from cultural identity is a restrictive one, increasingly tied to economic self-responsibility and private enjoyment of rights rather than class or group defined political efficacy.

Productive Diversity

In the late 1980s, Australia established the Office of Multicultural Affairs (OMA), situated as a special section within the Prime Minister's portfolio. That agency played a pivotal role in conceptualising a new economic dimension to citizenship policy and coining the term Productive Diversity. Former OMA Director, Neil Edwards' account of how Productive Diversity came into being illuminates the importance of the issue within the highest public office. Edwards described a wrestling with 'these two concepts of the economy and cultural diversity'.[11] OMA's political project to ensure cultural diversity, or multiculturalism, had a future in Australia aimed to deliver a deliberate and intellectual advance avoiding the rival 'melting pot' approach to migrant settlement that was supported in some quarters. Indeed, as Edwards recalled in discussions with then Prime Minister Keating, continuing Australia's multicultural project distinct from the US 'melting pot' approach, for example, was 'approved' on the grounds that 'you could do more' with distinct and not-melted-down diversity.[12] That conversation alluded to the government shaping the role of ethnocultural diversity in the economy. There was a clear message that diversity had a utility.

A salient point in Edwards' distinguishing between different models of multiculturalism here is that the melting pot concept, in theory, is largely non-discriminatory in its approach to migrant selection and support, yet is perceived to homogenise or assimilate through direct or indirect hegemonic force. For Hispanic and Black America the reality of the US as an example of an equalising 'melting pot' is markedly different, of course. Edwards' account points to government thinking about diversity as something that can be readily shaped for economic ends; And, that America may have got it wrong – the future it seemed, belonged to a new globally astute world, where homogenisation and assimilation were vestiges of a protectionist past. Australia's immigration and related diversity management from inception ranked culture deliberately within its economic nation building, at times valuing, and at other times devaluing minority cultures. At all times a concept of economic citizenship existed, either as an underclass offering only cheap labour, gradually transforming into individual agency based upon at least two features: economic self-reliance consistent with a neoliberal market economy, and; a distinct appeal to ethnocultural knowledge and practices suited to globalising that market economy.

Productive Diversity tends to be summarised as a neoliberal aberration, an unsuccessful mutation in Australian historical and comparative evolution of multiculturalism, or analysed within the conservative Government period from 1996 to 2007.[13] Neoliberalism broadly speaking is a conceptualisation of the separation of the (market) economy from its social controls.[14] It infers either government powerlessness or cooperation with private property

18 *Where did productive diversity come from?*

interests to achieve this end. Neoliberalism tends to be considered a more enduring feature of Australian society ushered in under both Labor and conservative Liberal governments from at least 1983 to the present. Accounts of neoliberal policy tend to suggest a form of 'economic rationalism', a phrase popular in Australia at the time to characterise concern with efficiency and, as used by the Australian Labor Party in the early 1980s, also referred to economies of scale.[15]

It is clear that Productive Diversity was concerned fundamentally with economic objectives: it addressed microeconomic reform in the form of workplace management and worker communication for productivity;[16] it was articulated in relation to facilitating export trade, particularly to Asia. Specifically, in this respect it conceived of ethnocultures collectively as an asset of the state,[17] as though they could provide a national competitive advantage for Australia's integration into a global economy. Productive Diversity was also considered as an individual asset for self-maximisation in an expanding neoliberal market society. In this case, Productive Diversity is a peculiar amalgam of Laborite statist politics – a form of industrial nation-building – and free market liberalism.

Productive Diversity's emergence paralleled speculation on the authority of the nation-state and the promise of global free market capitalism: the 'free' exchange of goods, services and people. Free exchange has largely been a neoliberal determination of freedom *from* regulation.[18] As a departure from the inclusive civil rights period of the 1960s, ethno-culture subsequently came to be framed within a narrow conception of reciprocity,[19] reflecting a growing deinstitutionalisation of Keynesian-era social organisation. Largely, this has occurred through less state funding for public services (privatisation and marketisation),[20] decreases in welfare support and restrictions upon trade unions.[21] This evokes Harvey's concept of accumulation by dispossession, a process where social forms of organisation are dismantled and reconstituted through market relations with state imprimatur or enforcement to aid the primacy of the flow of capital, its accumulation.[22] Collective 'horizontal' forms of association between groups of people founded on the postwar Keynesian–Marshallian social contract between labour and capital have been eroded or abandoned in such an analysis. Power relations, social risk and reciprocity increasingly represent a 'vertical' contract between state and productive individual citizen, such that governments and business talk increasingly of citizen responsibility rather than rights.[23]

In principle, *Productive Diversity* aligns with the neoliberal shift away from standard rights-based group welfarism to one of responsibility: multicultural policies that were based upon a welfare spending allocation were rapidly outmoded by a new multicultural thinking that focused on the individual, rewarded entrepreneurialism and emphasised market exchange through the mobilisation of culturally specific knowledge. Australian multiculturalism eroded itself as either a social 'politics of

Where did productive diversity come from? 19

transformation',[24] of equal social rights for all organised civic groups, or a welfare-oriented policy through its adoption of a market approach to immigrants and cultural diversity.[25] By the time the conservative Howard government took office in Australia in March 1996, the foundations had already been laid to reduce welfare, including for migrants, by emphasising individual effort through entrepreneurialism and deregulating or outsourcing welfare services.[26] Prime Minister Howard also immediately began to review migration categories and accelerated the intake of skilled and business migrants relative to the family reunion intake. By 2002–03, this 'balance' was about 60–40 in favour of permanent skilled/business migration over family reunion,[27] by 2012, closer to 70% skilled and business.[28] Temporary (up to four years) skilled and business migration also flourished, dwarfing the permanent intake of all categories.

Diversity theory and the global economy

What theories of diversity in multiculturalist nation-states have need to return to is the complexity of class, or migrants' economic class interests as their agency, in a period where such nation-states have come to rely on global supply chains and dispersed production; in other words, the varying international division and circulation of labour and non-productive occupations. A citizen of one nation-state may derive their *class interests* from their economic engagement with in an entirely separate country, for example, as a business leader or production manager facilitating low-wage production for another stage in global circulation and accumulation of capital. Dual and multiple citizenship as a form of identity have been the subject of much research.[29] However, a tension over cause and effect is apparent if the idea of globalisation is only about the compression of time and space, and not about this as an exclusionary device of capitalist production. The formative effects of class or indeed between classes in transnational production contexts remain a difficult subject to analyse. Barnes's analysis of value chain production in India provides a serious guide to this matter.[30] Questions of class interests of wealthy migrants are evident in research. Colic-Peisker's recent analysis is notable for an account of a new social middle-class migrant cohort in Australia, defined largely by their higher educational qualifications. She questions generally the effect of a growing middle class among Australian migrant minorities; the effect on the polity she argues needs further understanding.[31]

An intersection for analysing diversity in and for global capitalist production is found in changed migration patterns globally: from when countries such as Australia were reliant on mass migration for industrial and development and rapid population growth to the present period where government and business are reliant upon migration of non-productive and market expanding occupations to conjoin with the global bulk of low-cost

20 *Where did productive diversity come from?*

productive labour off-shore. Short- and long-term temporary migration, particularly of financial elites and professionals and business people is vital in this form of global production.

The idea that ethnoculture bestows productive use or economic advantage is heavily dependent upon a relationship to the creation or circulation of value in transnational production. It would appear that ethnoculture is less of an economic or social demarcation the closer it is associated with market expanding activity and accumulation of capital – or as if the ethnoculture of global professionals and capitalist elites does not matter. The material connection is often presented as between consumerism (rather than production) and identity formation, summed up neatly by Otis:

> In capitalist societies, consumption is a preeminent means of reproducing culture, class, and status. It is also a terrain where individuals with shared life chances struggle to distinguish themselves from other groups, using the symbols that express, create, and legitimate material hierarchies. Strategies of distinction, as often unintentional as intentional, are based on exclusive access to possessions and practices.[32]

Theories of capitalist elites have explained this in terms of the social reproduction of elite culture. This relationship between ethnoculture and class is not only an issue of consumption and identity. In reality, as other research suggests, ethnocultures as an operative tool of capital have usefulness as a source of low-paid labour globally, as well as aiding the circulation of capital. Often this is expressed as a relationship to foreign direct investment rather than through global value chains;[33] in other words, as a bilateral or state-based dimensional form.

Minority ethnoculture is not useful for *productive labour* as a class, and as will be argued, is a liability in relation to labour's contest over surplus value. This is a vital point in relation to Productive Diversity and theories of diversity in general which claim to argue ethnicity is commodified or reified or represents a form of cultural capital,[34] something of utility the bearer of which is able to realise. The class relations (capital and labour) that play out in transnational production pose fundamental questions for these analytical frames. The central moral and ethical dimensions of multiculturalism and diversity policy at the level of the nation-state, as well as in production or the workplace, are also subject to change consistent with the material reality of an increasingly global and historically unequal market society.

This raises an issue of interpretations of agency or reasoning to act within ethnoculturally diverse and extra-State contexts. In multicultural and diversity research agency is also theorised as citizenship rights. Citizenship in action is not always formally constituted as a direct relationship between individual and State. Delanty explains it as a tiered phenomenon that defines citizenship differently at local, national and global levels.[35] The theoretical construct of *cosmopolitanism* sees individual thought and action

Where did productive diversity come from? 21

as emerging from the means of globalisation, ultimately enabling a global citizen with global political representation formally available.[36] Such ideas in some way connect with the spread but also urban concentration of global capital and infrastructure. A distinct market-functionalist notion of an agency in relation to global diversity is embedded in the theory of *Productive Diversity (the treatise)* advanced by Cope and Kalantzis.[37] In the Australian case, the individual is anticipated as an Australian citizen with multiple ethnocultural identities to be utilised at her or his discretion but still to the benefit of the national economy. Individuals are invited to shape their productive actions to their market milieu or work life, which is claimed to be an instance of culture and multicultures: 'Markets work because they are an instance of culture – the productive play of difference on a common ground in which the negotiation of differences, reciprocity and the creation of mutual interests are keys.'[38] Cope and Kalantzis's version of diversity emphasises a functional or practical application of diversity, but within an idealised context: a harmonious reciprocity flowing through the marketplace.

One challenge with the many versions or typologies of multiple agencies and cultural capital – hybridity, transnationalism, cosmopolitanism – is their application to or situated-ness in competitive capitalist market contexts. A 'transnational actor', such as someone holding a 'business migrant' visa, arguably relies upon or negotiates cultural forms and stereotypes in business transactions. And that same business migrant might also act exactly as is expected of the market, compelled to gain the best available price or result. An understanding is thus required of how competitive markets condition actions and agency, the social relations between actors as representative of their class interests.

Bowles and Gintis explain the relative access to market knowledge as the basis of 'contested exchange': the exchange between buyer and seller contested by differential access to knowledge of market conditions at any point in time.[39] The ability to draw upon one or more cultural identities therefore could be anticipated as useful to gain market advantage, or at least to mitigate disadvantage. It is more than simply a 'productive play of difference' and often not 'common ground' – that is, in other words, the market is not a 'level playing field'. Competition in the circulation and accumulation of capital does not sit comfortably with some virtuous hybridity of cultural exchange suggested in the earlier quote from Cope and Kalantzis; it is still as much conformity to market capitalism, rendering ethnocultural knowledge as competitive and important to processes of accumulation. And this is one of the tensions that Productive Diversity (both the treatise by Cope and Kalantzis and the government policy rubric) unwittingly addresses as a market-based definition of identity. Productive Diversity (treatise and policy) premises the relationship between the State and the individual on one's ability to produce or exchange goods and services utilising a group-derived culture, one which is necessarily a fixed, albeit often intangible, asset.

22 *Where did productive diversity come from?*

In the context of a market economy, the locus in the individual has given attention to ideas of agency, formerly understood in relation to industrial class interests. Agency enacted at the level of the individual has become a main conceptualisation of how power relations are reproduced and is often described as a form of cultural capital, after Bourdieu.[40] Human 'capital' similarly reifies rational decision making as an individual choice against known or given circumstances. The concept of human capital has been especially influential in migration research, as a feature of neoclassical economics and critiqued for a narrow understanding of the dynamics of global population movements.[41] Human and cultural capital have become widespread tools to explain a relationship between ethnoculture, migration and agency.

This *digestif* about rights and agency and the market condition is offered to contextualise how Productive Diversity came into being and would operate in the material world. The chapter argues for a reading of a contemporary global economic change as a principal driver, albeit referenced by a historical presence of migrant minority cultures in Australia. In one respect, Productive Diversity did not depend upon the legacy of postwar labour migration in Australia to come into being because it was fundamentally a market-based policy rubric geared towards and objectifying certain cohorts and classes of new migrants from the mid- to late 1980s engaged in one way or another with transnational forms of production. However, the material reality is that productive diversity was not a universal concept; it is part of the 20th century teleology of multicultural policy making in Australia.

This leads to a point addressed in the chapter concerning neoliberalism as an analytical frame. Productive Diversity has been labelled as neoliberal in Australian diversity research. The chapter does not dispute this as a way of analysing Productive Diversity but argues that a social focus on individual responsibility or consumption, or a denial of such rights, is insufficient criteria to sustain this argument. Neoliberalism is explained in throughout this book as a feature of the global market economy's productive relations. Productive Diversity's relation to the global market economy needs to be thought of in terms of production rather than consumption, applying an economic rather than solely identity-based diagnostic toolset. Consequently, this positions economic class as agency to make an analytical distinction from citizenship, typically the basis of diversity research into rights, philosophy and action.

Notes

1 Lentin, A. and Titley, G. (2011) *The Crises of Multiculturalism: Racism in a Neoliberal Age*, London and New York: Zed Books.
2 Lauter, P. (2009) 'Multiculturalism and Immigration', in Rubin, D. and Verheul, J. *American Multiculturalism After 9/11: Transatlantic Perspectives*, Amsterdam: Amsterdam University Press, 2009, p. 23. '9/11' of course refers to

that date in 2001 after the World Trade Center in New York was attacked by al-Qaeda operatives.

3 Colic-Peisker, V. and Farquharson, K. (2011) 'Introduction: A New Era in Australian Multiculturalism? The Need for Critical Interrogation', *Journal of Intercultural Studies*, Vol. 32, No. 6, pp. 579–86.

4 Jakubowicz, A. (2011) 'Chinese Walls: Australian Multiculturalism and the Necessity for Human Rights', *Journal of Intercultural Studies*, Vol. 32, No. 6, pp. 691–706.

5 Office of Multicultural Affairs (1989) *National Agenda for a Multicultural Australia: Sharing Our Future*, Canberra: Commonwealth of Australia.

6 Parekh, B. (2000) *The Future of Multi-Ethnic Britain: The Parekh Report*, London: Profile Books.

7 In Barbalet, J. (1988) *Citizenship: Rights, Struggle and Class Inequality*, Milton Keynes: Open University Press.

8 Brahm Levey, G., 'Multicultural Political Thought in Australian Perspective', in Brahm Levey, G. (ed.) (2008) *Political Theory and Australian Multiculturalism*, New York: Berghahn Books (see chapter 1).

9 And thereby also as consumers. As gender and race were being addressed in anti-discrimination legal frameworks in a number of countries during the 1970s and 1980s, there is some suggestion the entry of more women and also minority groups to an expanded labour market offered a solution or 'fix' to the over-accumulation crisis of industrialised production or the recessions of the early and late1970s. Peterson, W.C. (1980) 'Stagflation and the Crisis of Capitalism', *Review of Social Economy*, Vol. 38, No. 3, December, http://dx.doi.org/10.1080/00346768000000034 (accessed 18 March 2014). Immediate pressure on unemployment rates was also an effect of an expanded labour force, according to Peterson. The effects of which would be overshadowed by international tariff reductions and gradual off-shoring of industrial production encouraging or forcing more people towards self-employment or SME sector that gradually increased in the wake of deindustrialisation toward more specialised industries and manufactures.

10 Collins, J. Gibson, K, Alcorso, C., Castles, S. and Tait, D. (1995) *A Shop Full of Dreams: Ethnic Small Business in Australia*, Annandale, NSW: Pluto; Collins, J. (1991).

11 Neil Edwards, Interview, 24 January 2012.

12 Ibid. Edwards retailed a conversation with Keating and his advisors utilising an analogy between a stew (i.e the USA) and a salad (i.e Australia).

13 Bertone, S. (2014); Ho, C. (2014); Rizvi, F. and Lingard, R. (2010). Hiebert, D., Collins, J. and Spoonley, P. (2003) 'Uneven Globalization: Neoliberal Regimes, Immigration, and Multiculturalism in Australia, Canada, and New Zealand', *Research on Immigration and Integration in the Metropolis*, Working Papers series, No. 03–05.

14 Harvey, D. (2005) *A Brief History of Neoliberalism*, Oxford: Oxford University Press.

15 Pusey, M. (1991) *Economic Rationalism in Canberra: A Nation-Building State Changes Its Mind*, Cambridge, UK and Melbourne: Cambridge University Press. For an example of the Labor Parry's understanding of the term, see the speech by Minister Barry Jones, who noted that economic rationalism as a way of understanding the allocation of resources among countries was inadequate. Barry Jones in 'Questions Without Notice, Visit to Japan', *Hansard*, 1 December 1983, p. 3167.

16 Bertone, S. et al. (1998).

17 Ho, C. In Jakubowicz, A. and Ho, C. (2014), pp. 35–8.

24 *Where did productive diversity come from?*

18 Edwards, L., Cahill, D. and Stilwell, F. 'Introduction: Understanding Neoliberalism Beyond the Free Market', in Cahill, D., Edwards, L. and Stilwell, Frank (eds) (2012) *Neoliberalism: Beyond the Free Market*, Cheltenham, UK: Edward Elgar; Harvey, D. (2005), p. 20.

19 Hage, G. (2003) *Against Paranoid Nationalism: Searching for Hope in a Shrinking Society*, Annandale, NSW: Pluto Press. For a conception of reciprocity of responsibility that places the onus on the citizen, see also Beck, U. (1992) *Risk Society: Towards a New Modernity*, trans. Mark Ritter, London: Sage.

20 Howard, M.C. and King, J.E. (2008) *The Rise of Neoliberalism in Advanced Capitalist Economies: A Materialist Analysis*, Basingstoke and New York: Palgrave Macmillan; Walker, B. and Con Walker, B. (2001) *Privatisation: Sell off or Sell out: The Australian Experience*, Sydney: ABC Books.

21 Welfare and care industries have been particular targets in many advanced capitalist economies. See, for example, Meagher, G., and Cortis, N. (2009) 'The Political Economy of for-Profit Paid Care: Theory and Evidence', in King, D. and Meagher, G. (eds) *Paid Care in Australia: Politics, Profits, Practices*, Sydney: Sydney University Press, pp. 13–42; Sanger, M.B. (2003) *The Welfare Marketplace: Privatization and Welfare Reform*, Washington, DC: Georgetown University Press; and an illustration on challenges to care sector privatisation in Jeffs, A. (1995) 'Child Welfare Privatization Under Fire', *Calgary Herald*, 22 December, p. A1.

22 See Harvey, D. (2005).

23 Barnett, N. (2003) 'Local Government, New Labour and "Active Welfare": A Case of "Self Responsibilisation"', *Public Policy and Administration*, Vol. 18, No. 25, pp. 25–38.

24 Alibhai-Brown, Y. (2001) *Imagining the New Britain*, New York: Routledge, p. 107.

25 See Bertone, S. In Jacubowicz, A. and Ho, C. (ed.) (2013).

26 Howard, M.C. and King, J.E. (2008); Carney, T., and Ramia, G. (2010) 'Welfare Support and "Sanctions for Non-Compliance" in a Recessionary World Labour Market: Post-Neoliberalism or Not?' *International Journal of Social Security and Workers Compensation*, Vol. 2, No. 1; Wiseman separately points out the government's attempt to build an 'Active Society' of regulated self-responsibility began in a 1986 review of welfare. Wiseman, J. (1998) *Global Nation? Australia and the Politics of Globalisation*, Cambridge, UK: Cambridge University Press, p. 62.

27 DIMIA (2003) *Settler Arrivals 1995–96 to 2005–06 Australia, States and Territories*, Canberra: Commonwealth of Australia, data from tables, see p. 13.

28 Ho, C. In Jakubowicz, A. and Ho, C. (2104), p. 38.

29 Vertovec, S. (2004) 'Migrant Transnationalism and Modes of Transformation', *The International Migration Review*, Vol. 38, No. 3, Fall.

30 Barnes, T. (2018) *Making Cars in the New India*, Cambridge: Cambridge University Press.

31 Colic-Peisker, V. (2011) 'A New Era in Australian Multiculturalism? From Working-Class "Ethnics" to a "Multicultural Middle-Class"', *International Migration Review*, Vol. 45, No. 3, Fall, pp. 561–86.

32 Otis, E.I. (2008) 'Beyond the Industrial Paradigm: Market-Embedded Labor and the Gender Organization of Global Service Work in China', *American Sociological Review*, Vol. 73, No. 1, February, p. 17. http://dx.doi.org/10.1177/000312240807300102; see also McCracken, G. (1986) 'Culture and Consumption: A Theoretical Account of the Structure and Movement of the Cultural Meaning of Consumer Goods', *Journal of Consumer Research*, Vol. 13, No. 1, pp. 71–84.

Where did productive diversity come from? 25

33 Walton-Roberts, M. (2009).
34 For example, Taksa, L. and Groutsis, D. (2010).
35 Delanty, G. 'Theorising Citizenship in a Global Age', in Hudson, W. and Slaughter, S. (eds) (2007) *Globalisation and Citizenship: The Transnational Challenge,* London: Routledge.
36 Miller, T. (2007) *Cultural Citizenship: Cosmopolitanism, Consumerism, and Television in a Neoliberal Age,* Philadelphia: Temple University Press; Held, D. (2013) *Cosmopolitanism: Ideals and Realities,* Oxford: Wiley.
37 Cope, B. and Kalantzis, M. (1997) – note, to distinguish between the theory and policy, Productive Diversity as the treatise by Cope and Kalantzis is italicised in this book while the policy rubric is not; see also Oksenburg-Rorty, A. (1995) 'Rights: Educational Not Cultural', *Social Research*, Vol. 62, No. 1, pp. 161–70; Oksenberg-Rorty, A. (1994) 'The Hidden Politics of Cultural Identification', *Political Theory*, Vol. 22, No. 1, pp. 152–66.
38 Cope, B. and Kalantzis, M. (1997), p. 216.
39 Bowles, S. and Gintis, H. (1993).
40 Bourdieu, P. (1986).
41 Castles, S., De Haas, H. and Miller, M. (2014); see also analysis of Zimmerman and Borjas in later chapters of this book.

2 Surplus value theory and the idea of productive diversity

> In contradistinction therefore to the case of other commodities, there enters into the determination of the value of labour-power a historical and moral element.[1]

What should be made of an analytical claim, originally by Hage, that ethnicity within Australia's Productive Diversity paradigm was realised as a method of extracting 'a kind of ethnic surplus value',[2] an explicitly Marxist formulation? Hage's interpretation is a departure from the way Productive Diversity was conceived by government and business interests concerned with international markets, instead reinforcing a canonical position that migrants as ethnic minorities could only be a factor of the means of production. From the late 1980s, however, as Australian migration trend data and the instruments of recruitment indicates, increasing numbers of settlers and sojourners to Australia might also be useful in facilitating the exploitation of low-waged labour in their countries of origin. Entrepreneurs and professionals engaged in value-adding practices in the global market economy were or could be otherwise implicated in the divisions of labour found in value chain hierarchies, overseeing or reinforcing the work of low-wage economies engaged in the greatest exploitative production of value.

Hage does not go on to present a Marxist value theory analysis of ethnicity and culture based upon a critique of capitalist production. Hage's central theory of 'whiteness' analysed to great effect the discursive practices of the ruling class. His premise that Productive Diversity policy was a discourse reinforcing the position of Anglo-Australians as the managers, as the ruling class thus able to 'yield' surplus value from Australia's immigrant labour force is tenable in principle: Managers aim to 'yield value' from their workforce. Nevertheless, attitudes to minorities historically have often been attended by discriminatory practices that require greater work effort for some and not others. The 'surplus value' claim in relation to ethnic labour then is not unusual. On the other hand, it is not an 'ethnic' surplus in the sense that it adds an ethnic quality to that 'value', or the way ethnicity (e.g. 'whiteness', 'Asian-ness') as cultural capital might be an accumulated value of agreed collective traits and dispositions. There would appear to be a theoretical contradiction implicit in Hage's formulation which is all too easily missed and all too often reproduced by scholars: Productive Diversity is a *celebration* not a *devaluation* of ethnoculture in its societal and workplace context. Even if Productive Diversity did affect surplus value in the way Hage indicates, it should be positive for labour (less surplus surrendered) and negative for capital (less surplus gained). The only other possibility is that migrants in this new era of Productive Diversity were volunteering as Australia's 'Stakhanovites' – always willing to work harder, yet selflessly expecting lesser compensation.

What is surplus value?

To argue whether 'ethnic surplus value' applies as a critique of Productive Diversity, it is first necessary to establish that surplus value, a specifically Marxist concept, derives from the value of *and* value created by labour. Marx's premise is that labour is unique to production because: a) it is essential to transform material resources into goods (commodities); and b) it is socially contingent, meaning it is made available according to the relations of production, those relations in turn reflecting the ownership of the means of production. Capitalist production, Marx distinguished, 'is not merely the production of commodities', which he delineates as the realm of exchange or the market: 'it is essentially the production of surplus-value'.[3] Surplus value accrues from labour put to task against a socially determined price for the labour. Wages become a cost of labour in production but are not directly contingent upon the price returned from sale of any products.

The fundamental point and definitive of Marxism is that profits are held to derive from a surplus of labouring and not from trade of commodities.[4] Specifically, profit is derived from value in the form of the amount of wages paid against the value added or invested in the creation of a product, over a set period of time. The key to determining surplus value is the calculation that the cost to sustain labour power must be less than the value of what individuals actually produce. This clearly places a ceiling on what can be paid as wages; conversely there is no floor short of nil.[5] That is, the logic of capitalism does not anticipate an average minimum wage; that is only established through the product of struggle between labour and capital.

Meanwhile, exchange value, or market pricing of commodities produced by labour, is held to be subjective: 'the exchangeable value of commodities', Marx explained, 'are only social functions of those things, and have nothing at all to do with their natural qualities'.[6] In other words the *use value* of exchangeable commodities is socially and culturally contingent something which is only achieved when labour is removed from reckoning the value of a commodity.[7] To derive a true price of any such commodity, the only thing common in these commodities is their labour. This important distinction is the basis for a claim that anything other than that created by

28 *Surplus value theory*

labour cannot be a commodity. Labour, for instance, is a not a commodity, or as Polanyi termed it, labour is a 'fictitious' commodity, partly because it does not behave like commodities. Labour is not itself created by the application of labour power *and consequent appropriation of any surplus value* by itself or capital.[8] Applying this to the idea of human capital and accumulated cultural capital, despite one's apparent 'self-investment' in training or skills development, individual human capital is not accumulated through the (self-)creation of value and self-appropriation of any surplus. There is no measurable surplus; Labour is not created as a commodity.

This does not mean labour is not *treated* like a commodity in a market – that it has socially variable use value identified through hire contracts. The (self) investment in skills as one of the possible 'necessities' that sustain labour, and so a factor in determining the subsistence or base price of labour, is part of Marx's formulation[9] But there is no 'transformation crisis' in the *price* of self-investment circulating back into the precise value given to one's proposed labour.

Moscato puts the whole issue of value more succinctly in her incisive book *The Value of Everything*.[10] If we accept that there is a moral question concerning value's creation and distribution then we must accept that value determines price; price does not determine value. Value's determination should not be 'in the eye of the beholder' but, rather, in the hands of the creator (labour). For, if the market is 'allowed' to set any price, as Moscato explains, prices and wages will be 'set by the powerful and paid by the weak'.[11]

Ethnic surplus value?

What does this mean for '*ethnic* surplus value'? If we accept that the very existence of surplus value is socially dependent, that its norms are established by and within a society, and over time, through say social stratification, geographies of disadvantage, reinforced through labour contracts[12] or less formal practices enforced by specific cultural values, then ranking ethnicity among the range of social norms that condition the extraction of surplus value is possible, both in its absolute and relative forms. Koffman and Raghuratnum have offered extensive argument and evidence concerning the variances attending social reproduction in relation to migration.[13] This 'polyversality' or intersectionality in the socially determined value of labour undergirds contemporary transnational production just as surely it has provided a rationale for labour migration since the emergence of 'free labour' under nascent 17th-century capitalism: capital seeks cheap labour (for greater surplus value) wherever it resides, while labour seeks better social conditions for its own subsistence.

Wage figures for Australian-born and migrants are provided below. It highlights a number of features: an epochal distinction where industrial

Surplus value theory 29

labour was organized and commanded high wages in the 1960s and 1970s; a modest upward trend in wages at the point where the migration shift towards skilled categories began. And it also shows a nuance in wages apparently based upon certain ethnocultural backgrounds: German migrants were far fewer in number but consistently earned more in Australia than Australian born, as did those categorised as Main English Speaking countries combined (UK, USA, Canada, New Zealand, etc.). That German and UK migrant cohorts, *inter alia*, occupied significantly more professional and managerial occupations – non-productive labour – is one explanation and is backed up by data. But so too is the fact that Australia had recreated the Colonial and prewar European hierarchies of value in who it selected and for which occupational forms in its post-war migrant intake. UK citizens were paid to migrate in order to maintain Anglo hegemony in the Colony. On the other hand, Many Italians, Yugoslavs and Greeks did not have their skills recognised or utilised, but were consistently undervalued and therefore underpaid in comparison with Australian-born.

Understood historically, as Collins's observations of refugees from Vietnam and Cambodia (formerly referred to as Indochina) in the 1980s serve to highlight, the devaluation of ethnic minority subsistence is systemically co-regulated outside the workplace:

> Finding accommodation is the first problem a refugee faces ... Many refugees 'double up' to share accommodation costs. One study of Vietnamese in Fairfield found that 44 per cent shared housing, with an average density of 6.7 persons per 2.5 bedrooms.[15]

Migration theory's contention that minorities concentrate for purposes of cultural maintenance, or to avail themselves of an ethnic social capital, belies some of its benefits. At the same time, ethnic minority labour is made vulnerable for devaluation. One only needs to review the volume of case work handled by the Australian Human Rights Commission to apprise themselves of the actually existing migrant social exclusion and discrimination persisting in contemporary Australia, for example.[16] Perceived or positioned to be less economically reliable or viable, minority migrants have tended to gain lesser access to quality housing, for example, often through overt discrimination.

It is worth noting here a statement found in a landmark report in 1988 to advise on Australia's immigration policy: '[b]ecause immigrants are under pressure to become established in a new environment they add drive and energy to the economy'.[17] This normative public statement might just as readily be interpreted as tacit acknowledgment that immigrants live under different circumstances and (sub)standards, and so present as cheap labour, hungry to earn. At the time of that report (late 1980s), the concept of 'ethnic ghettoes' had established itself in Australian debates about the

Surplus value theory

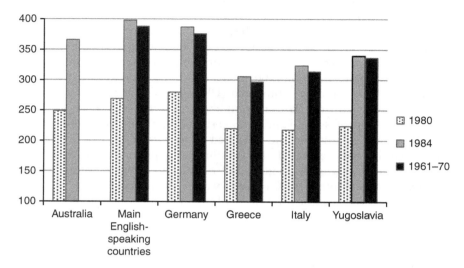

Figure 2.1 Comparative mean weekly earnings, Australian-born and selected migrant groups, 1961–70, 1980, 1984 ($A).[14]

sub-standard housing and neighbourhood conditions where migrants concentrated.[18] Yet, of the various interpretations of migrant living conditions, many concluded that choice was not an option, that economic circumstances dictated the need for immigrants to concentrate in certain locales to minimise cost; housing affordability ranked the single highest concern.[19]

From the discussion thus far it would seem that *'ethnic'* surplus value both isn't and is a dimension in a Marxist analysis of abstract labour, irrespective of any relationship to Productive Diversity.[20] Ethnicity *is not* a component of surplus value *insofar that it does not affect labour power*, the ability of workers to work 'harder' or 'smarter' simply because of their ethnicity; *it is*, on the other hand, insofar as ethnicity affects the normative base (replacement) value of that labour. And that – changing the norms around ethnicity and living standards – is achieved through social and particularly ideological means, through deliberate efforts to bifurcate, trifurcate, etc. labour into varied reproduction or replacement values. To increase any value from minority migrant productive labour, to make ethnicity 'yield' more surplus value, these social and ideological means must debase and degrade the social and economic conditions for such labour to replenish itself.

Recent attitudes expressed by industrial capitalists such as Gina Rinehart lauding the low cost of labour in Africa and calling for special economic zones to deploy such cheap labour in Australia, as sensational as they are, go to the core of this issue.[21] Reiterating her position in a mining periodical

Surplus value theory   31

in 2013, Rinehart explained: 'I know people hate me saying [it], but their [Africans] wage rates are so much lower over there and they're lower in lots of countries, like Indonesia, for instance, which is a coalmining country we're competing with'.[22]

Labour in Africa or Indonesia may generally be cheaper because of historical circumstances. Labour taken out of one historical material circumstance is reckoned by capital to retain its originally derived value (represented as its subsistence price) in another circumstance (Australia). A call some years ago by an Australian think tank, The Indonesia Institute, was for nannies or child carers to be imported from Indonesia for substandard pay of $200 per week. This was argued on the basis that it would be twice what such nannies might earn in Indonesia.[23] No reference was made to the cost of living in Australia. Another example from Australian retail capitalist Gerry Harvey struck a similar chord: 'Australia doesn't have cheap labour. Many overseas workers would be prepared to move here for a much better life and half the money Australians earn'.[24]

Harvey's point was that other advanced economies such as the US and Europe draw on diverse migrant labour because it is cheap; Australia should do the same. The examples that were suggested by Gerry Harvey (Mexicans, East Europeans respectively) and the historical facts of these matters also underscore that ethnic difference accompanies (all) such cheap migrant labour. Note that it is not their ready supply but migrants' material circumstances which are posited by contemporary capitalists as the justification for paying cheaper rates. The issue of a real market for labour is missing in this formulation.

Ethnicity (and not migrancy *per se*) could act like a dimension of relative surplus value where lower paid ethnic minority migrants are deployed by management alongside native-born labour as the norm in any given enterprise. If minority or ethnically devalued migrants were to replace other, presumably more costly native-born labour in a given enterprise, the relative dimension is then technically forfeited and becomes the norm. Migrant or 'ethnic' labour[25] is then subject to its own struggle with capital over the surplus labour extracted from it and it alone. Numerous studies in a range of countries have elaborated a dual-market for labour, which in effect inoculates native-born labour from rises in immigration, at the same time maintaining lower wage growth for immigrants.[26] A study of Australian migrant survey data demonstrated that the quality of jobs held, over time, does not support arguments that migrants do eventually climb out of lower tiers of paid work and can gain jobs much more readily. The study found that quality of available jobs declined for those notionally considered higher skilled. Ethnicity played a part in maintaining poorer outcomes.[27]

Ethnicity's value analysed within a sociological definition concerns patterns of social maltreatment through non-economic *exploitation* of migrants.[28] Labour outcomes, that is, available jobs, are a typical indicator of

32 *Surplus value theory*

such exploitation, with ethnic-minority migrants generally and historically faring worse in terms of job opportunities and conditions.[29] The concept of '3D jobs' – those deemed too dirty, dangerous or difficult, and therefore reserved or discarded as suitable only for the socially and economically excluded, including migrant workers – is now a historical and material feature of the migrant experience.[30] Piore's original arguments noted a distinction between jobs suitable only for migrants and non-migrants[31] and countered claims that migrants 'took jobs' from the native-born, a line of argument that persisted in Australia well into the 1980s. Whether migrants created jobs and stimulated demand became a site for ongoing and detailed examination by government and industry. But as this book explains, a qualitative shift emerged alongside Productive Diversity, with the idea that migrants were reframed as individual agents of change, representative of the new economic order of self-reliant progenitors of private wealth and market expansion: they were to create jobs directly by investment and business operation.

This was a complete upending of expectations that endured over postwar migrants to Australia recruited for unskilled and industrial 3D jobs, but as noted in Chapter 6, migrants who filled these jobs generally had higher skill levels than their Australia-born counterparts. Their supply was disconnected with the qualities of their labour power. Migrants' greater skill set should have given them some labour market advantage. It did not! Relatedly, and inversely, consider Bauder's point that 'International competition between top-level managers of multinational corporations has not depressed managerial outcomes.'[32] These elites continue to command high remuneration despite their ready supply.

Market-capitalist and neoclassical interpretations of human capital avoid the exploitation argument and its basis in generating surplus value via a lower available 'standard of life'. For such theorists[33] individual migrants make their own choices both before and after migrating and the entirely rational decision to pursue greater opportunity abroad represents a maximisation of their skills, their human capital, for maximum remuneration. A contradiction is apparent here: in a market rational choice analysis there is nothing rational for the individual migrant in helping to swell the supply of labour (productive or non-productive) in their destination country if an increase in supply is held to drive down the price of labour (through greater competition for available jobs). Migrants sometimes do make rational choices about relocating, but they serve the accumulation of capital in their decisions particularly in stratified or segmented labour markets.

Zimmerman presents a different, neoclassical approach, to the issue of migrant labour value: that despite pressures for assimilation of migrants over time, 'economic success requires the persistence of some differences between natives and immigrants'.[34] In other words, price differentials between labour, or its segmentation, based on difference has economic

Surplus value theory 33

outcomes beneficial to Capital. If difference is a factor in economic success of the combined polity as much as for the individual, assimilation is counterproductive in Zimmerman's ethnically segmented analysis.

Analyses of relativities in earnings capacity of migrants based on skill levels and country of origin status are not convincing of the central importance of human capital to migrant success. For example, earning or economic mobility across different earnings strata (given pay rates) are affected by any number of exogenous labour market factors. Duleep and Regets' longitudinal cohort study in the USA nevertheless claimed that:

> ...the highest annual-earnings growth rate was found for highly educated immigrants from less-developed countries; the lowest rate was found for highly educated immigrants from developed countries.[35]

The argument here is that unrecognised or immediately un-useful 'human capital' is still transferable, and possibly more so, proven by the higher wage growth generally experienced by those migrants from less-developed economies. To take the example of Duleep and Regets – that knowing how to use a hand saw (the imagined available technology of the less developed migrant source country) is a preliminary although not immediately transferable skill useful in learning to use a chainsaw (the technology of the migrant destination or host country) – presents a number of analytical problems: firstly, *relative wage growth* does not suggest latent or technologically irrelevant human capital (skill) is responsible. It may be just as likely that those migrants' motives or ability to move away from the low-end of the earning spectrum are a factor of the degree of value exploitation they typically encounter in low paid occupations. Comparisons with migrants from developed countries (the Global North) are also important but potentially misleading. In the Duleep and Regets study, 'highly educated migrants from *developed* countries' are thought to have transferred their human capital readily although their wage growth may not be as rapid as their developing country (Global South) counterparts. Questions remain unanswered as to how predisposed such migrants from the Global North are to entering a higher earnings bracket. This is in part because they may not be under the same economic compulsion to immigrate in the first instance, may transfer money capital that exchanges at more favourable rates (i.e., from developed country to developed country), and so, are more able to choose from available occupations and remuneration levels. With a presumption that the highly educated-developed country immigrants can enter *above the wage median* for a comparable occupation, logic would dictate that their wage growth *rate* must be slower, *ceteris paribis*.[36]

A separate material challenge to this example is that skill in using low or old technology (a hand saw) is not likely transferable to a job in finance, information technology, tourism or higher education, key growth

34 *Surplus value theory*

areas for post-industrial countries of immigration. To obtain a well-paid job in such fields would require not just latent or unrealised generic human capital (evidence of being able to learn, according to Duleep and Regets, as if this were restricted only to one cohort of migrants),[37] but more specific 'knowledge' or informational skills. If there is a more rapid growth in wages among those from 'less-developed countries', as contended, then this may speak as much to initial exclusion based upon social prejudices and policy restrictions, or the availability of local context-specific knowledge about job opportunities prior to settlement in the destination country – Borjas, for one, acknowledges this likelihood and posits that migrants' job market knowledge is expected to be imperfect for a certain period of time.[38] For human capital theorists such as Borjas, the measurable indicator is assimilation, akin to proximity to perfect knowledge of the labour market:

> The key prediction of human capital theory, therefore, is that the age/earnings profile of immigrants will be steeper than the age/earnings profile of natives. This 'catching-up' of earnings profiles reflects the 'assimilation' or adaptation of immigrants to the host country's labor [sic.] market.[39]

There is ample evidence that trenchant underutilisation of immigrant skills persists for reasons other than 'human' or for that matter 'cultural' capital. For example, the contemporary phenomenon of the immigrant taxi driver with tertiary qualifications is more than urban myth. A Canadian study of 2006 (published in 2012) suggested that 20% of immigrant taxi drivers had Bachelor's degrees or better, compared with only 5% of Canadian-born taxi drivers; those with doctorates outnumbered Canadian-born by 4 to 1.[40] Australia's taxi industry follows a similar pattern of ethnic concentrations although it relies upon migrants on student visas.[41]

In sum, the ongoing observable and well-documented exploitation of migrant labour highlights that human 'capital' (skills and capacities) does not guarantee access to an equal minimum wage, or equal access to socially defined 'necessities' to reproduce daily one's labour. Or, indeed, exploitation may be the restriction of opportunity only to the normative minimum. Meanwhile, cultural 'capital', typically viewed as access to opportunity through networks, in the case of Canadian taxi drivers presents as one of path dependency, not of emancipation or rapid wage growth for the highly skilled.

A separate analytical point is raised here: prevailing rational choice theories of neoclassical and neoliberal economics perversely might serve to entrench the notion that minority migrant labour *will* be exploited. Neoclassicism's normative 'deficit' logic is that migrants essentially emanate from inferior social and/or economic conditions; for why else would people migrate? Even business migrants targeted by Australian policy in the late 1980s were thought by government to be keen to migrate to escape regimes repressive of socioeconomic opportunity. Such thinking all too readily can feed a justification or indifference to migrants' exploitation in the receiving country by virtue of their apparent normative tolerance for inferior social and economic conditions. As we will come to see, this kind of thinking is apparent in Australian policy discourse concerning migration and diversity.

Conclusion

The analysis thus far, in many respects, is framed by classic historical materialist theory concerning productive labour and relevant to Australia at least until the retreat of Keynesian social protectionism and the underpinning industrial economy. That Keynesianism was routed in part by the stagflation crisis of the 1970s and advanced upon by neoliberal transnational market logic has broad agreement. The break-up of mass labour forms of production and the advance of market social relations in Australia, however, does not mean that historical materialist value theory has been invalidated. The obvious defence of this position is through an analysis of transnational labour relations or the international division of labour. Surplus value is readily extracted on mass scale in the Global South in conditions not far removed from the factories and mills of 19th-century European industry. Where Australia is placed in that transnational division of labour has had significant bearing on migration and diversity programming.

As noted in Chapter 1 and detailed in later chapters, Australian multicultural policy was premised on diversity as emancipatory for ethnic minority migrants. The early history of multicultural policy into practice in Australia did achieve significant social and economic advances in this respect. If this were then reasoned into the question of surplus value, ethnicity's greater acknowledgement and inclusion *should* lead to a *reduction in surplus value*: that is, if the socially useful labour required was more costly because the minimum standard of living was raised for migrants, the price capital has to pay for that labour is greater. If that is held to be true, it could not then be argued that Productive Diversity was a conspiracy of white elites or anyone to yield greater 'ethnic surplus value' from migrants. Ethnicity reified or turned into a marketable object through Productive Diversity became sought after. Any inclusion, nurturing and promotion of ethnoculture and within a society of diversity would surely reduce any surplus value prospects from ethnicity. Or, following simple labour market logic, employees with ethnocultural appeal and usefulness would command a higher wage price. Productive diversity as a variety of multiculturalism policy was at least on the surface a celebration and promotion of diversity, of ethnicities. Such social advancement in principle undermines the idea of increasing ethnic surplus value in

36 *Surplus value theory*

production achieved through the de-valuing of segments of labour. In this case, Hage's formulation needs re-thinking: ethnoculture does not valorise capital as though a factor in production, nor does it yield more value, but less, when ethnicity comes to be held in higher regard in its social conditions.

Notes

1 Marx, K. (1986 [1954]) *Capital*, Vol. 1, Moscow: Progress Publishers.
2 Hage, G. (2000), p. 128.
3 Marx, K. (1986 [1954]), p. 477.
4 David Ricardo had already identified value as derived from labour. See also Theocarakis, N.J. (2010) 'Metamorphoses: The Concept of Labour in the History of Political Economy', *Economic and Labour Relations Review*, Vol. 20, No. 2, July, pp. 7–37.
5 Marx, K. (1945) *Value, Price & Profit*, Adelaide: People's Bookshop, p. 40.
6 Ibid., p. 38.
7 NB: Use value here refers to the myriad possible uses for a thing and its fetishisation through exchange, not the idea that a use value is something created by labour for its immediate use.
8 Polanyi, K. (1944) *The Great Transformation*, New York: Farrar & Rinehart.
9 Marx, K. (1945); Marx, K. (1986 [1954]), pp. 51–2.
10 Mazzucato, M. (2018) *The Value of Everything: Making and Taking in the Global Economy*, London: Allen Lane.
11 Ibid., p. 13.
12 Peck, J. (1996) *Workplace: The Social Regulation of Labor Markets*, New York: Guilford Press. Marx (1986 [1954]) also explains this as the particular 'conditions under which … the class of free labourers has been formed' (p. 168).
13 Koffman, E. and Raghuratnum, P. (2017) *Gendered Migrations and Global Social Reproduction*, Basingstoke: Palgrave Macmillan.
14 ABS (1985) and ABS (1981) *Weekly Earnings of Employees (Distribution) Australia*, Cat. 6310, Canberra: Commonwealth of Australia.
15 Collins, J. (1991), p. 66.
16 Dozens of such cases of discrimination and hatred evidencing dominant social norms about race are handled annually. See https://www.humanrights.gov.au/complaints/conciliation-register/list?field_discrimination_type_value=discrimination_type_racial (accessed 23 February 2020).
17 Committee to Advise on Australia's Immigration Policies [Fitzgerald, S. chair] (1988) *Immigration: A Commitment to Australia – Committee to Advise on Australia's Immigration Policies*, Canberra: AGPS, p. 39. Hereafter, the Fitzgerald Report or CAAIP Report.
18 Blainey, G. (1984) *All for Australia*, Sydney: Methuen Haynes.
19 For an overview of these, see Zang, X. and Hassan, R. (1996) 'Residential Choices of Immigrants in Australia', *International Migration*, Vol. 34, No. 4, October, pp. 567–82.
20 Note, that in the Australian context, 'ethnic' and 'ethnics' are pejorative terms for migrants. Hence, Hage's concept of 'ethnic surplus value' applies only to migrants and not dominant (host or indigenous) ethnicities.
21 Ryan, P. (2012) 'Aussies Must Compete with $2 a Day Workers: Rinehart', *ABC News Online*, 5 September, http://www.abc.net.au/news/2012-09-05/rinehart-says-aussie-workers-overpaid-unproductive/4243866 (accessed 17 February 2020).

Surplus value theory 37

22 Heber, A. (2013) 'Gina Rinehart Reignites Foreign Worker Debate', *Australian Mining*, 26 February, http://www.miningaustralia.com.au/news/gina-rinehart-reignites-foreign-worker-debate (accessed 17 February 2020).
23 Wade, M. (2014) 'Call for Asian Nannies to Reduce Childcare Costs', *Sydney Morning Herald*, 29–30 March, p. 3.
24 Gerry Harvey, quoted in News.Com.Au (2007) 'Billionaire Plea for Cheap Labour', *The Sunday Telegraph*, 21 October, http://www.news.com.au/business/billionaire-plea-for-cheap-labour/story-e6frfm1i-1111114687834#ixzz2ad55wNIj (accessed 17 February 2020).
25 Ethnic-minority migrant labour is the historical norm. Most imported labour globally tends or is limited to selection based on ethnic difference from the native-born. Thus, the terms ethnicity and migrancy are used interchangeably in this section of the discussion, and not unintentionally conflated. Nevertheless, the case of UK labour migration to Australia throughout the postwar period of the 20th century provides a distinction to this assumption. There were, of course, different conditions afforded UK migrants in the migration and settlement process, beyond the scope of the argument here to detail, other than, for example, the funded or Assisted Passage available to UK migrants travelling to Australia.
26 Muller, T. (2003) 'Migration, Unemployment and Discrimination', *European Economic Review* 47, p. 426.
27 Junakar, P.N. and Mahuteau, S. (2005) 'Do Migrants Get Good Jobs? New Migrant Settlement in Australia', *The Economic Record*, Vol. 81, No. 255, August, pp. 834–46.
28 Cashmore. E. (ed.) (2004) 'Surplus Value', entry in *Encyclopaedia of Race and Ethnic Studies*, London: Routledge. See also Skeggs, B. (2004). See also this approach to commodification as social exploitation in Taksa, L. and Groutsis, D. (2010); Ho, C. and Alcorso, C. (2004).
29 Castles, S., De Haas, H. and Miller, M.J. (2014); Collins, J. (1991).
30 Castles, S., De Haas, H. and Miller, M.J. (2014).
31 Piore, M.J. (1979) *Birds of Passage: Migrant Labor and Industrial Societies*, New York: Cambridge University Press.
32 Bauder, H.'The Regulation of Labor Markets Through Migration', in Phillips, N. (2011) *Migration in the Global Political Economy*, Boulder, CO: Lynne Rienner Publishers, p. 44.
33 See, for example, Borjas, G.J. (1989) 'Economic Theory and International Migration', *International Migration Review*, Vol. 23, No. 3, pp. 457–85; Duleep, H.O. and Regets, M.C. (1999) 'Immigrants and Human Capital Investment', *The American Economic Review*, Papers and Proceedings of the One Hundred Eleventh Annual Meeting of the American Economic Association, Vol. 89, No. 2, May, pp. 186–91, http://www.jstor.org/stable/117104 (accessed 11 June 2013).
34 Zimmerman, K.F. (2007) 'The Economics of Migrant Ethnicity', *Journal of Population Economics*, Vol. 20, p. 488.
35 Duleep, H.O and Regets, M.C (1999), p. 188.
36 I acknowledge the fact that *ceteris paribis* in this example is entirely notional; that the reliability of comparison is problematic. It, or rather the Duleep and Regets findings, contains assumptions including comparability across and within wage brackets, for example. Nevertheless, wealth standards between so-called highly developed countries on average could be taken to be more consistent.
37 Ibid.
38 Borjas, G.J. (1989).

38 *Surplus value theory*

39 Ibid., p. 472.
40 Lu, X. (2012) *Who Drives a Taxi in Canada*, Research and Evaluation Section, Citizenship and Immigration Canada, http://www.cic.gc.ca/english/pdf/research-stats/taxi.pdf (accessed 17 February 2020).
41 KPMG/Salt, B. (2011) *Australian Taxi Industry Association – Demographic Analysis of the Australian Taxi Industry*, Melbourne: KPMG, http://www.victaxi.com.au/media/34361/kpmg%20analysis.pdf (accessed 11 August 2013).

3 Productive diversity, value and the question of cultural capital

Ethnoculture and symbolic capital

The terms *human, social* and *cultural* capital have different provenance but understanding what 'cultural capital' means in relation to Productive Diversity is important to theorising the place of entrepreneurial migrants in political economy. These 'capitals' explicitly referred to by Australian Immigration Ministers and ministerial bureaucrats throughout the 1980s and 1990s, and implicit in two major government reports on Australian migration and diversity and myriad other reports, and in specific collaborations between Government and an influential business think tank, the Committee for the Economic Development of Australia (CEDA). For example, the October 1992 national conference opened by Paul Keating, entitled *Productive Diversity: Profiting from Australia's Diverse Knowledge, Skills and Talents* and the May 1993 conference, *Productive Diversity: Gaining Export Advantage from Australia's Diverse Knowledge, Skills and Talent.*

The term 'social capital' strongly associated with theorising ethnic immigrant business networks has a longer and varied history. Marx, for one, spoke of it in reference to insurance or business liability, critiquing the idea of limiting such liability for the excesses of capitalists. Bourdieu stated, albeit in a footnote, to understand social capital was to understand the dynamics of a multiplied individual cultural capital 'in which different individuals obtain very unequal profits from virtually equivalent (economic or cultural) capital'.[1] There is a lack of clarity here as to how having the same economic capital can lead to unequal personal profits. For Bourdieu the moral question was central, as it was in classical political economy. Questioning the morality of an exclusionary, regulatory social order has not been a consistent theme in some applications of Bourdieu's concepts, while the confusion with economic epistemes has led to a de-facto acceptance of culture as an economic category.[2]

All capital is social in its relationship to economy, attested by material forms of production and consumption, accumulation and distribution of wealth.[3] Not all social or cultural relations need be economic, on the

40 *Productive diversity and cultural capital*

other hand. A materialist understanding of social and cultural forma-tions would view these as increasingly shaped one way or another by their economy. This is one of the key arguments that define neoliberalism as the encroachment or *dis-embedding* of the market from within society;[4] that neoliberalism transforms all relations into economic ones. Even the intangible can be accumulated and turned into propertied relationships: human knowledge and communications about social and cultural order are readily drafted into economic service. Cope and Kalantzis in their account of *Productive Diversity* theorised cultural knowledge and practice as a strength or generic asset but without a fuller critique of property relations.

Bourdieu's original conception of social and cultural capital partly mimics economics in analysing 'accumulation', but of the effect of tan-gible and intangible resources underpinning social and cultural norms and positioning. A strict economic analysis would dictate that non-market exchange of any 'capital' denies it an economic definition, including where it cannot be priced consistently, if at all.[5] Influential neoclassicist econo-mists such as Arrow, agreed that social capital was not 'akin to stock that can be accumulated', while others have argued that it is impossible to measure.[6] These arguments, of course, might be eschewed for being narrowly positivist. Marxist political economy holds that capital exists because of a certain set of social relations, principally between labour and propertied classes. Simply accumulating some *thing* and without reference to material relations of production is not capitalism! Culture is funda-mentally an accumulation, of knowledge and practises and related communicative forms. Acquiring cultural habits and ideas is sometimes enforced, sometimes given or received freely. It is the simplicity of the idea of accumulation that appears to have transposed an economic episteme onto the cultural or social.

Interpretations of cultural capital as inherently positive for its useful-ness is found in much migration-related research, such as Watts et al. (2004) and in Barker:[7] For these scholars, cultural capital is an 'endowment', an accumulation of heritage, of know-how, practices, ideas, etc. Using the concept 'capital' in terms of accumulation necessarily invites questions of the creation of any original value in this capital, and how the creation of any value is at all observable through equivalences of exchange, or how it is transferable and then consistently realised. Such readings are a major de-parture from the conferral and accumulation of an exclusive *privilege* in-tended by Bourdieu. In other words, can they be called cultural capital at all when they are not addressing the moral question behind Bourdieusian epistemology?

The other 'capital' that has shaped the political economy research on migration is the theory of human capital. Unlike cultural capital, human capital underpins attempts to price knowledge as it is embodied in in-dividuals. Theories of human capital, notably the ideas of Becker[8] and then

Productive diversity and cultural capital   41

Robbins[9] concerning the quality of labour, not coincidentally became influential in the wake of the economic crises of the 1970s and the shift away from mass industrial labour in the Global North. As with cultural capital, there is a central concern for the degree of agency or choice available to individuals.

Borjas's adaptation of human capital to construct a migration choice theory[10] suggests the interchangeability between human and cultural capital for the economics of migrants. Neoclassical migration theory assumes an end goal of better life chances despite structural disadvantages and the reality that migration and diversity policy and systems regulate such choices.[11] OMA and the Immigration Department were well aware of Borjas's analytical frame, including it to inform their own policy frame at one period in the mid-1990s.[12] The Australian migration points test as a measurement of skills and expertise, and overseas skills recognition system that evolved alongside refinements in the points system throughout the 1980s and 1990s remain as attempts to measure a formal base-line human capital. Former Research Director of the Committee for Economic Development of Australia (CEDA), Toni Fedderson, noted of the Australian Immigration bureaucracy's differential treatment of migrants skills: 'I think in many cases not all their [migrants'] qualifications were able to be recognised or were recognised and that was pretty tragic for some and a loss ... to them and the country'.[13]

While there is some interchangeability between human, cultural and social capital, such notions of symbolic capital have been interpreted differently and sometimes interchangeably including in policy rationales by government and business. Based upon the definitions given, international cultural business links, for example, could be forms of social or cultural capital, but not necessarily human capital. Such links may advance goods to market or create new markets; they may source cheap labour. The idea of trust networks has given social and cultural capital some purchase in research, for example on ethnic entrepreneurs. Rath argues a direct link between minority status as solidarity and business trust:

> 'Foreignness' may exist when a group is distinct from the rest of the society – or rather is considered to be distinct and becomes the object of prejudice... This type of situational solidarity constitutes an important source of social capital that can be used in the creation and consolidation of small enterprises.[14]

Importantly, all such concepts are considered here to be highly contingent and *not commodity forms as they have no identifiable surplus value invested in them*. By focusing on an embodied accumulation, on opportunity and privilege, as social, cultural and human capital do, surplus value as the fundamental dynamic which actually valorises capital is left out. That

42 *Productive diversity and cultural capital*

dynamic process whereby labour surrenders value absorbed by capital in production is a value then owned by certain others. Labour creates the conditions for greater material accumulation by others by transforming capital physically, but fundamentally labour transforms that capital into exchangeable commodities to create further capital because there is a new value added (by appropriation) to the original capital. And so on through a process of competitive circulation which continues to expand capital's value and concentrates its ownership.

Exchange and cultural capital

Bourdieu's position that cultural capital can claim the term 'capital' is part of an argument against macroeconomics which he strongly viewed as reductionist when applied to non-economic relations. Two contrasting claims are apparent:

> So it has to be posited simultaneously that economic capital is at the root of all the other types of capital and that these transformed, disguised forms of economic capital, never entirely reducible to that definition, produce their most specific effects only to the extent that they conceal (not least from their possessors) the fact that economic capital is at their root, in other words – but only in the last analysis – at the root of their effects.[15]

Cultural and social capital were formulated by Bourdieu to avoid both 'economism' or reductionist economic analysis of all phenomena, and what he called 'semiologism', or communicative relations. He noted further:

> the constitution of a science of mercantile relationships which, inasmuch as it takes for granted the very foundations of the order it claims to analyze – private property, profit, wage labor, etc. – is not even a science of the field of economic production, has prevented the constitution of a general science of the economy of practices, which would treat mercantile exchange as a particular case of exchange in all its forms.[16]

From Bourdieu's foundational treatise encapsulated in this excerpt, the idea of *exchange* is central to any claim for an economy. But to see economics as simply about exchanges is equally reductionist and misses a fundamental concern of political economy: that value or profit of commodities is created firstly in production, not through exchange. The kind of commodity fetishism that Marx alluded to, one that gave currency to things above their immediate use value was simply that: ephemeral, not

Productive diversity and cultural capital 43

able to be anticipated and in no way affective of surplus value, from which the source of profit typically originates. This is highly pertinent to the view of globalisation in Chapter 4; that value creation is so devalued, buried at the base of global value chains with the cheapest available labour in the Global South. Exchange value is more readily valorised or seen to be the source of value created through trade, profit shifting, and value adding at different stages.

Bourdieu emphasises context as a highly dependent variable, such that anticipating what is fetishised is contingent but possible within a certain set of (social or cultural) values. The problem with context is that this 'currency' (of time and place) then is not at all exchangeable when it comes to such contingency. Bourdieu's example of one being able to read among a 'world of illiterates'[17] only serves to highlight that in another context, or in relation to another practice, reading may be less valuable (but no less useful). Bourdieu's frame of *institutionalisation* does provide some fixity, such that professional credentials in one institution are transferable to others even across nation-states.

Bourdieu posits that cultural capital is symbolic

> [b]ecause the social conditions of its transmission and acquisition are more disguised than those of economic capital, [so] it is predisposed to function as symbolic capital, i.e., to be unrecognised as capital and recognised as legitimate competence, as authority exerting an effect of (mis)recognition.[18]

It is reasonable that things such as power and 'legitimate' competence can be symbolic of wealth or actual money capital. Such features pre-date *capitalism* as a unique form of economic exploitation and organisation of society. This presents a question of why individual and collective *behaviours* need be recognised epistemologically as *capital*. And why is it inadequate for these 'symbolic capitals' to be recognised as the *social effect* of wealth distributions, that is, class and its social reproduction? Such a definition of capital that divorces behaviours from capitalism in a causal relationship, but in totality supplants behaviours for capitalism as a social system is open for criticism.[19] It is also anthropologically and economically ahistorical; 'cultural capital' in the Bourdieusian sense, has existed far longer and more widely than competitive, growth-dependent *capital*ism. Cultural capital, as Bourdieu described it, could exist within feudalism, for instance.

Turning to the idea of exchange and so the salience of a market for embodied cultural capital, Bourdieu's idea of cultural capital is that it 'cannot be transmitted instantaneously'.[20] More telling of the mis-apprehension of a 'disciplined' definition of capital is found in the statement:

44   *Productive diversity and cultural capital*

any given cultural competence ... derives a scarcity value from its position in the distribution of cultural capital and yields *profits of distinction* to its owner. In other words, the share in profits which scarce cultural capital secures in class-divided societies is based, in the last analysis, on the fact that all agents do not have the economic and cultural means for prolonging their children's education beyond the minimum necessary for the reproduction of the labor-power least valorised at a given moment.[21]

A reading of this passage might see it almost as a tautology, that class divided societies are divided 'precisely' by social class! While the idea of 'profits of distinction' is a unique turn of phrase, it belies labour's appropriation and concomitant class conflict which contest profit in capitalist political economy. A 'scarcity value' derived from a 'distribution' of a cultural competence further complicates the epistemological strength of cultural capital. In the case of education it is reasonable to assume access can be restricted thus delivering social class differentials. But there is not explicit value to such a scarcity. Nor do we know if it is a commodity with an accumulation of value or in a natural state. In the case of capitalism, scarcity is a material condition. It is distinct from supply and demand in that scarcity is often derived from the fact that something scarce is so because it is too costly in terms of labour and capital to source and/or refashion into a useful commodity.

A further problem with the scarcity and accumulation feature of cultural capital is found in a footnote, whereby: 'In a relatively undifferentiated society, in which access to the means of appropriating the cultural heritage is very equally distributed, embodied culture does not function as cultural capital, i.e, as a means of acquiring exclusive advantages.'[22] According to this revelation, culture, or inclusion within a community identified by its practices, its tangible and intangible heritage can *negate* cultural capital, meaning that cultural capital is entirely concerned with privilege. It exists as a marker of privilege but it is not necessarily or simply in the acquisition or accumulation of cultural capital by one that others will miss out. It is neither 'Pareto efficient', nor inefficient in that sense, the implication being that culture does not contend with its own scarcity as (economic) capital does.[23] Revisiting Bourdieu's literate–illiterate example, a literate person cannot become less literate the more others become literate. Yet, economically, the capitalist can expect to incur a loss the more labour demands in wages. Nor is the literate person deriving their literacy from those illiterate. It is not as a capital–labour dichotomy. Her or his 'profits of distinction' may ultimately lose their supposed value when others learn to read, as Bourdieu's footnote admits. On the other hand, the 'distinction' might be enhanced by more people becoming literate, expanding and enriching that cultural community at the same time homogenising it. Bourdieu's

Productive diversity and cultural capital 45

example suggests there is a *material* gain in being the sole literate person in a community of illiterate or less literate – access to knowledge on how to invest funds, where to buy or sell something, gaining a better job, etc. being some applied examples. This is not 'capital' but currently exclusive knowledge or privilege that might be put to use in a contested exchange for goods or services, etc.

Another example is illustrative here: better communication in ethnically diverse workplaces made sense where information was a vital ingredient in given production. Diverse language abilities in a given workplace, however, could be viewed as both facilitating or improving production in one circumstance, and hindering it in another (through miscommunication). Moreover, there is a distinct difference in valuing better communication in production for its efficiency and valuing language diversity as a competitive advantage. As it applied to Australia's economic planning, from the government's viewpoint, language and cultural competence provided opportunity for international market access. Valuing diversity simply as a feature of efficiency is a more contingent proposition. Ethnocultural knowledge residing in workers might provide answers to firm- or sector-specific production problems, just not at all times or in all cases. This raises a peculiar division of labour question: communicative competence as it was viewed within the diversity management field concerns labour process and the maximisation of surplus value; language interoperability, or multilingualism, also applies to non-labour processes in the maximisation of exchange value, largely through market opportunity, investment in productive capital, etc.

On networks and association

The idea that networks are important to ethnic migrant business success, from the small shop to the global corporation, is an established theme. In some instances this is suggested as a form of solidarity. Bourdieu's distinction between cultural and social capital is clear: the latter concerned with networks between associations of people, notably the inherited form of familial social capital, and with the institutionalisation of ritual that constitutes associations. Note the simple epistemic claim, however, that:

> The volume of the social capital possessed by a given agent thus depends on the size of the network of connections he [*sic*] can effectively mobilize and on the volume of capital (economic, cultural or symbolic) possessed in his own right by each of those to whom he is connected.[24]

A further and unsubstantiated claim is that network social capital is never reducible to an individual 'because it exerts a multiplier effect on

46 Productive diversity and cultural capital

the capital he possesses in his own right'. Whatever this multiplier is remains incalculable. As Chapter 7 in this book discusses, the economics of migrant business networks rest in the relative advantage in contested exchange.

Of additional concern is the reference to *solidarity* as the result of the 'profits which accrue from membership in a group'. Other philosophical, sociological and historical materialist formulations of solidarity are etched more firmly in experience, regardless of or often in spite of individual cultural status, and not in personal reward or individual benefit derived, and not merely by association.[25] To that end solidarity can be viewed as a form of distributive justice 'according to need'.[26] Solidarity has been understood differently throughout Western philosophical and material 'modernity', is distinct from the universalism of *fraternity*, and is more recently conflicted by an increased emphasis on the rights of individuals and the role of the neoliberalising state to protect this.[27] This *faux* solidarity is sometimes referred to as 'agency', a point discussed elsewhere in the book. Bourdieu's social capital argument appears subtly critical of solidarity as a hollow concept, where unconscious self interest in association derives some personal 'profit'. The main discussion here, however, is to understand whether or not social networks (whether based upon Bourdieusian cultural capital or other social capital claims) are constitutive of solidarity.

Applying to migrant minority political economy, the particular would present different prospects for solidarity even if that were the substance to be found in cultural capital. The ability for a migrant to trade back to their country of origin, drawing upon certain social networks, can not be said to be constitutive of solidarity although it may derive a personal 'profit of membership', in material terms a market knowledge advantage. In real terms, such an example is also that of the self-interested individual entrepreneur drawing upon whatever resources are available to effect a transaction, and not to reproduce nor reconstitute a social network in the first instance. There may also be a *quid pro quo* or reciprocal payment for any exchange that is facilitated, which would suggest not an experiential solidarity and not one beneficial to a group,[28] but a mutually agreed economic outcome between individual agents, likely to be undermining of any social or cultural worth for either party unless there are other immediate social bonds such as family in play. Arguably, the use of money (or a material payment) in any exchange involving a network would suggest that capital's monetary substitute is the *quintessential* feature, not forms of social or cultural relationships. Studies of entrepreneurial migrant networks for their productive capacity suggest the importance of cultural affinity, while the idea of solidarity features more in relation to supportive networks for migrant labour in marginal work or enterprise. Nevertheless, studies of ethnic minority entrepreneurs and business people generally do not account for the actual costs or payments, the material reciprocity that may be required in continuing a network. A study of migrant remittances, on the other hand, might yield a different analytical argument.

It is possible to consider the Australian government's migration program as an accumulation of people to create and accumulate real capital to expand the national economy, its GDP, terms of trade; ultimately its share of global wealth. Whether that was for a Keynesian economy or a neo-liberal market economy is moot. The fact that these different eras of productive relations required different skills and knowledge of labour and sought more non-labour types to effect global production chains does not make it human or cultural capital. Labour in many parts of the global economy was required, non-productive labour to support and direct it and to ensure the circulation of capital. Australian Governments sought neither human, cultural nor social 'capital' first. Rather, they sought non-productive and market expanding occupations increasingly to position the economy globally. The main concern with the definitions above is how a national accumulation of such capital is epistemologically consistent and actually possible in practice.

Conclusion

Ultimately, cultural capital as Bourdieu meant it has metaphorical purchase in understanding the individuation of economic responsibility, and salience for the marketisation of society. Marx's value theory, meanwhile, does not formulate values of specific *qualities* of labour, its relative value according to skill, for instance. There is a distinct difference between the variable cultural or social 'value' in pursuing skills and the basic economic value of receiving more wages supposedly for greater or more useful productivity. There is however, to give scholarly Postmodernism its due, some resonance in the *disciplining* feature of pursuing skills and qualifications in economic, social and cultural spheres. Foucault is the obvious reference point here.

Human capital is about choice and self-improvement; cultural capital as Bourdieu theorised it[29] was essentially a critique of privilege embodied in individual knowledge and practices. Nevertheless, Bourdieu's appropriation and transposition of value theory terms such as 'profit', 'accumulation' and selective distribution on to what he called 'symbolic capital' have left his ideas open to subsequent criticism for their epistemological confusion.

It is this appropriation of value as a measure of culture that has also led to an alternative interpretation of cultural capital as something which can be empowering and of use to migrants in the market. There is evidence of migrant entrepreneur theory in particular adopting a bastardised reading of

48 *Productive diversity and cultural capital*

social and cultural capital that has largely missed the moral dimension within Bourdieu's analysis.

Cultural capital has become not just an intangible good but a good that purports to measure efficacy in market exchange. By extension this suggests minority migrants' welfare is enhanced by drawing upon or deploying cultural capital. As noted in Chapter 2, social theories have already critiqued the essentialising and hegemonic nature of culture. Yet, in the case of migrant networks for business, ethnocultural affinity is viewed for its relative usefulness in material gain. The idea of privilege intended by Bourdieu is conspicuously absent in such abstractions. The idea that cultural capital, one's ethnoculture as a unique variable or advantage has a value, is however conspicuously present.

At this point, a notion of cultural capital would appear unhelpful as an economic concept or factor. Such 'non-economic capital' is to some extent exchangeable with the human capital concept, particularly in understandings of migrant entrepreneurialism. And despite this, as a prevailing orthodoxy for international skilled labour and entrepreneur recruitment, governments of countries such as Australia pursued migrants' ethnocultural knowledge with vigour through policies such as Productive Diversity. Considering Australia's position *vis-à-vis* Asia Pacific and global economic growth as subsequent chapters detail, the kind of cultural knowledge envisaged through Productive Diversity appears to have little tangible or special relationship to the measurement of GDP or the capital account. Productive Diversity as a feature of Australia's migrant selection, however, served as a transformative function of the social relations of production as it relied on accumulating entrepreneurial talent globally and fostering individual responsibility to profit generation in the workplace. In breaking down collective forms of labour, but based on a division of labour, a specific form of accumulation was occurring.

Australia did seek to accumulate more capital. In doing so it recruited more people with certain skills and knowledge, but also with money capital to effect that goal. But the instruments of selection were so blunt and blind and the nature of the competitive global market so unpredictable that any form of embodied or symbolic capital could not be an accurate predictor of usefulness.

Notes

1 Bourdieu, P. (1986), footnote 11.
2 Fine, B. (2010a).
3 Fine, B. (2007) 'Eleven Hypotheses on the Conceptual History of Social Capital": A Response to James Farr', *Political Theory*, Vol. 35, No. 1, pp. 47–53; Marx, K. (1986 [1959]).

Productive diversity and cultural capital   49

4 Konings, M. 'Neoliberalism and the State', in Cahill, D., Edwards L. and Frank Stilwell (eds) (2012). Konings's point is that there must exist a market logic exogenous to society for the need to control it to exist.

5 Ibid. NB: I don't mean the price of a thing need be consistent; rather what factors are drawn upon to derive a value need consistency.

6 Woodbury, cited in Throsby, D. (1993) 'Cultural Capital', *Journal of Cultural Economics*, Vol. 23, p. 5.

7 Watts, N., White, C. and Trilin, A. (2004) *The Cultural Capital Contribution of Immigrants in New Zealand*, Palmerston North: Massey University; Barker, cited in ibid., p. 1.

8 Becker, G. (1975).

9 Robbins, S.P. (1991) *Organizational Behaviour: Concepts, Controversies and Applications*, Upper Saddle River, NJ: Prentice Hall.

10 Borjas, G.T. (1989).

11 Castles, S., De Haas, D. and Miller, M. (2014); Borjas, G.T. (1989).

12 See Jupp (2007), p. 154 for claim about Borjas's influence on Australian immigration department following the Keating government. Correspondingly, New Growth Theory focused attention on the value of SMEs to economic growth in postindustrial economies. Because labour productivity was held to be one of the key inputs attributed to growth, New Growth Theory focused on individual motivation and social organisation.

13 Toni Fedderson, Interview, 24 January 2012, Melbourne, Australia. NB: Toni Fedderson was previously known as Toni Steinbrecher.

14 Rath, J., 'Introduction: Immigrant Businesses and Their Economic, Politico-Institutional and Social Environment', in Rath, J. (ed.) (2000) *Immigrant Business: The Economic, Political and Social Environment*, Basingstoke and New York: Palgrave Macmillan, pp. 15–16.

15 Bourdieu, P. (1986). NB: Online reproduction – no page number.

16 Ibid.

17 Ibid.

18 Ibid.

19 Fine, B. (2010a), (2008).

20 Bourdieu, P. (1986).

21 Ibid. (my emphasis).

22 Ibid., footnote 6.

23 I am not suggesting that a culture cannot become scarce. An economistic argument could be advanced that Indigenous languages the world over, for example, have become scarce by the 'allocation' (read colonial imposition) of other languages. But learning an Indigenous language does not make it scarcer for others. The Pareto efficiency concept is used here to merely illustrate another way that 'cultural capital' does not meet numerous macroeconomic analytical concepts.

24 Bourdieu, P. (1986) 'The Forms of Capital', in Richardson, J. (ed.) *Handbook of Theory and Research for the Sociology of Education*, Westport, CT: Greenwood, p. 241.

25 Durkheim, E. (1997) *The Division of Labor in Society*, trans. L.A. Coser, New York: Free Press; Rorty, R. (2002) 'Solidarity or Objectivity', in Wray, K.B. (ed.) *Knowledge and Inquiry: Readings in Epistemology*, Peterborough, ON and New York: Broadview Press. Seccombe, W. and Livingstone. D.W. (2000) *Down to Earth People: Beyond Class Reductionism and Postmodernism*. Aurora, ON: Garamond Press. Durkheim's separate concept of 'mechanical solidarity' was as much concerned with *retributive* as *distributive* justice.

50 *Productive diversity and cultural capital*

26 Millar, D. (2009) *Principles of Social Justice*, Cambridge, MA: Harvard University Press, p. 27.
27 Baeyertz, K. (1999) 'Four Uses of Solidarity', in Baeyertz, K. (ed.) *Solidarity*, Dordrecht: Kluwer, pp. 4–6.
28 Ibid.
29 Bourdieu, P. (1986).

4 Framing the global political economy since the 1970s

Transnational production, value chains and the emergence of a market economy

> All this means that Australia is now the safe, secure and adaptable economy in which to launch trade and investment in the Asia-Pacific region. And many overseas businesses seeking market opportunities in the region have already realised this, and made the move here. In fact, over 430 multi-national companies use Australia as a location for their Asia-Pacific management and/or service functions.[1]

Establishing globalisation

Population diversity as an emergent social and economic phenomenon is largely linked to late 20th-century globality. From the post-Second World War period, greater and better industrial production is strongly implicated in a phase of material development marked by increased spatial and temporal connectedness among people but also in the systems of production and accumulation of capital. The patterns of mobility of people are inextricably linked with the patterns of mobility of capital (including finance capital) and both facilitated by industrial-technological changes. These are significant processes demarcating modern globalisation.

The postwar period also marked the de-structuring of centuries of European colonial empire building, corresponding with counter hegemonic uprisings, coups, revolutions and wars of independence throughout many former colonies of Africa, Asia and Latin America. Beneath this was a re-systematisation or restructuring of an international economy that preserved the accumulated capital of much of the late colonial or imperialist world order, but with the USA as the principal heir. Capitalism survived the colonial and imperial eras of high 'primitive accumulation', even if its European champions were all but economically exhausted after the Second World War.

There are, of course, many nuanced interpretations of globalisation and its origins. The intention here is not to engage heavily in that debate. It is possible to accommodate a complementarity of views, as they relate in some way to unfettered capitalism as a problematic force. For some, globalisation is controlling and organised as though states can 'own' capitalism; the

52 *Global political economy since the 1970s*

World Systems approach is influential here, after Wallerstein.[2] For others, globalism is somewhat chaotic: capitalism ultimately is not subject to any 'ownership' and survives on 'fixes' by governments or groups of individuals[3] Studies on postindustrial world order based upon informational capital, following Castells,[4] are also highly pertinent: that is, *Informationalism* as both an analysis of a systems approach and at the same time recognising the fluidity of capital's formations, ushering in new cultural forms of work. Sassen's spatial or geographic frame for an elite global culture is another defining form of measuring globalisation – the increase in global elite spaces and services highlighting at least a shift in capitalism as conspicuously transnational.[5]

Some of the most pertinent theorisations for an analysis of Productive Diversity policy concern marketisation and financialisation as self-sustaining political forces, whether under a prevailing hegemonic world power system, or atomised relations between individual agents. Here the rationality of capital is demarcated in the contemporary period by government emphases on monetarism, or money supply, and/or financialisation of relations between people and social forms, neutralising those social institutional forms for their apparent market distorting effects.[6,7] Fine makes a strong argument for considering interest-bearing capital distinct from merchant and industrial capital, and suggests that despite an expansion of credit or the separateness of shareholder wealth interest-bearing capital ultimately remains dependent upon any surplus value created. Production is not negated in financialised accumulation.[8] Bryan argues that globality is marked by difference, upheld by the vagaries nation-states, for example. Such difference remains vital to ensuring competitive accumulation but Bryan argues that 'it is through the operation of globally integrated financial markets ... driven almost entirely by capital's need for mechanisms that will bridge differences.'[9]

The special role of elites has relatedly become a feature of the neoliberal power relations that typify global capital. Robinson and Carroll, among others, focus on corporate interactions and highlight the social reproduction of elite power relations, also integral to processes of financialisation.[10] Bauman's analysis of global capital spaces and the elites that organise and inhabit them suggests it is the lack of fixity ('liquidity') in economic production and organisation that is definitive of global neoliberal relations.[11] A theme throughout this is the (lack of) agency of individuals no longer able to be represented by social forms and institutions, and instead dependent directly upon the market for services. Harvey's notion of 'accumulation by dispossession' is another approach detailing the narrow role for the state to de-socialise or hollow out all extant relations, allowing capital to be ever more fluid but also unable to be challenged by organised resistance. Castells' claim is of a 'placeless logic of an internationalized economy' subverting the 'traditional structures of social and political control over development, work and distribution'.[12]

Global political economy since the 1970s   53

The global market economy is by no means certain. What then, are we to make of government attempts to build and sustain an order of migration of entrepreneurs, business and market professionals?

Transnational production – structure

One assumption that governments understood all too well of 20th-century globalisation is the core–periphery dichotomy, typified by the differential value of commodities produced and accumulated in the global North and South. In very general terms, transnational corporations 'off-shore' low-value production to the periphery, and retain and develop high-value and 'value-added' production in the core.[13] Ultimately, this is because of differentially lower cost of labour, based as it is on lower subsistence or living costs maintained between the Global North and South.

Production and accumulation processes within a global bifurcation of core–periphery is not a matter of simple binaries but more complex and variegated associations or networks. Global Value Chains (GVCs) can be viewed as a telling contemporary feature of globalisation reinforcing North–South relations. The OECD's major review (OECD et al., 2013) of GVCs as a system lauds the production side of value chains for their efficiency and yet simultaneously fails to address the fundamental point of the unequal accumulation of value. That report notes:

> This international fragmentation of production is a powerful source of increased efficiency and firm competitiveness. Today, more than half of world manufactured imports are intermediate goods (primary goods, parts and components, and semi-finished products), and more than 70% of world services imports are intermediate services.

The OECD et al. report provides detailed evidence of 'increasing international fragmentation of production'.[14] Since then, UNCTAD has reported on measures of global value chain economics beyond simple FDI flows and drawing upon international Trade in Value Added datasets (e.g. OECD TiVA) produced only in the last decade to measure more consistently GVCs as a global systems phenomenon. When we come to consider migration and the agents of capital later in the book, understanding this distinction between value-added and FDI is important.

Growth in commodity or value chain production is noted not as uniquely new to capitalist production but for its scale, and is therefore arguably a key component marking post-1970s globalisation. There is also a qualitative dimension differentiating governance over trade according to OECD et al.: 'the mercantilist approach that views exports as good and imports as bad, and that views market access as a concession to be granted in exchange for access to a partner's market'[15] is outmoded. Globalisation in this view is purposefully about a material *flow*.

54 *Global political economy since the 1970s*

The intent of this section of the chapter is to establish the rise of global value chain production as a basis and background to then explain the efforts of successive Australian governments somewhat obsessed with managing the quality and origin of skilled and professional productive and non-productive labour. The two decades coterminous with the millennium are the focal point here. While GVCs were only beginning to be theorised in the 1990s[16] – the time when the Labor Governments in Australia were restructuring that country's economy towards the logic of the global trade in value-added – by the end of the first decade of the 21st century, the GVC form of production and accumulation (and its measurement) had grown exponentially; unsurprisingly, the global financial crisis of the mid-2000s was indeed global!

The following chart illustrates this periodised account of global value chain growth and includes a gross account of the growth in labour through foreign-affiliate companies. These are just two of a range of measures corroborating the argument about the period of growth of GVCs. It is clear that on both measures, the 15 years from 1990 show the most rapid growth. The most recent decade since the mid-2000s has shown remarkably less growth on these key indicators. This may be attributable to governance over trade and investment since the financial crisis. It might also indicate a saturation point, within dispersion cycles of technology and innovation.

Focusing on GVC participation rates at a country level, data from 1995 to the end of the 2000s shows a general increase with country-specific effects, and are shown in the following table data reproduced from OECD et al.:

Almost all countries represented in the figure increased total participation in GVCs. For Australia, the increase is from approximately 35% to approximately 41%, over the period.[19]

The figure also explains the flow of goods used in processing for further export. From the figure, Australia's total exports of intermediate goods and services (i.e. part-processed for further 'handling' in the next country in a chain) for 2009 was approximately 41%. Imports of inputs for transforming these 41% intermediates into further export for 2009 were approximately 12%. In other words, Australia transformed less than half its exports, but around 30% of that transformation process relied on additional foreign goods or services.[20] This means around two-thirds of export value adding of intermediates in Australia were through domestic goods and services. This is comparable with Brazil, Indonesia and Japan. China, Korea, Germany and France tend to import more per related intermediate export. Only through industry sector analysis can the reasons for these differences be understood. For example, the USA might be considered as a prime case for producing and accumulating final added value because of its high technology use and patent ownership. Comparatively, the US exports less intermediate goods for further export than Australia, but of these the US relies slightly more on other foreign inputs.

Global political economy since the 1970s 55

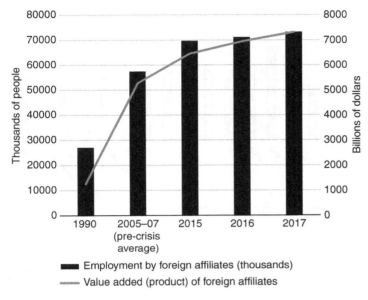

Figure 4.1 GVC growth period: 1990–2017.[17]

What the OECD et al. report also highlights is that domestic content includes services, and that this has been on the rise as a share of value-added content in the G20 since 1995. OECD member countries averaged 42% of domestic content of gross exports as services as of 2009. Australia experienced a slight decline in services value adding to gross exports between 1995 and 2009; as did Indonesia, Russia, Mexico and Turkey. Services can range in use value but the implication to be discussed later is that certain types of value adding from services are concerned purely with circulation of subjective market value rather than creating commodities in production. For example, marketing is typically a service 'value adding' that aims to increase consumption and market share, and is central to reinforcing competitive exchange relations. It may have effects on what commodities are produced but like all non-productive occupations has a blurred boundary as to the extent it is labour surrendering its own value or capital deriving its material position from the cumulative stock of surplus labour value. Services such as these are questionable therefore whether they are 'value adding' at all in the strict labour sense of value given their emphasis on exchange in the market.

Consistent with much of the of globalisation research, countries such as Australia, the UK, USA and Japan are theorised as being further up the value chain in general terms, more so by the degree of value that is added and/or appropriated. Among the G20, between 1995 and 2009, their share

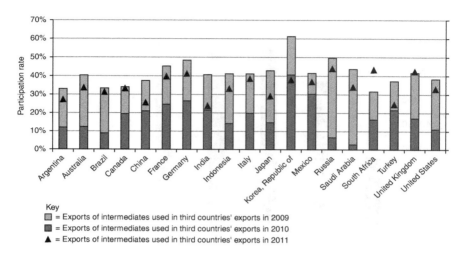

Figure 4.2 GVC participation, 1995 and 2009.[18]
Key: ☐ = Exports of intermediates used in third countries' exports in 2009. ■ = Imported inputs used in these exports in 2009. ▲ = Total participation in 1995.

of income from exports of final value-added products rose annually in real terms by an average 7.6%, while the remainder of Africa and Latin America 'still account for a limited share of world GVC income'.[21]

The overwhelming majority of the 34 OECD countries are advanced economies (excluding Mexico, Turkey, Chile and some eastern EU states). It is clear from Figure 4.2 that the wealthier fraction of nation-states represented by the OECD have maintained the lion's share final value added exports between 1995 and 2009. The trend decline for the OECD is notable, while a corresponding rise for 'emerging economies', especially the G20 Emerging group is largely accounted for by China, Brazil and India. There is still a sizeable periphery from these figures that does not participate in 'downstream' where greater value notionally accumulates.

Saad-Filho observes a related trend (from earlier OECD data): that in 1990, trade within the Global North was nearly 60% of all global trade, while trade within the Global South was 'barely reaching 8%'. By 2008, intra Global North trade declined sizeably to 40% with intra Global South trade up to 20%.[22] Saad-Fihlo's point is that this is more symbolic than real of any redistribution of wealth over time, especially if the emphasis is placed upon the vertical relationship between global North and South and the concentration of value in the final product for export market. Consequently, GDP of any country should not be mistaken for comparative increased trade volumes where the value of products is in various stages of circulation.

Global political economy since the 1970s 57

A UN Industrial Development Organization (UNIDO) report similarly concluded in 2011 that the total global trade in manufactured intermediate goods had grown significantly between the 1990s and early 2000s, but that more detailed analysis at the product level indicated that with international trade comes 'requirements for higher levels of specification and explicit coordination than in the past, creating cross-border interdependence'.[23] Knowledge and control of processes is therefore hierarchical. The UNIDO report concluded that this interdependence presents 'learning opportunities for suppliers in developing countries'.[24]

The idea that there is open sharing and learning through participation in GVCs comes with a caveat about proprietary relations. Knowledge created for production (whether in GVCs or not) typically is private property. Intellectual property (IP) in the form of patents and trademarks on goods, services, designs and processes is guarded and contested. It also forms a key part of the 'value adding' that occurs in GVC production. During the period under close consideration – the 1990s and 2000s – high-income countries held more than one-third of original design trademarks, with the bulk of these in what the World Intellectual Property Organization terms upper-middle income. It is clear that developing nations are largely excluded from owning knowledge of production, markets and inventions despite increases in recent years in numbers of filings. So, by 2012, there were approximately 8.66 million patents worldwide, with high-income countries holding a majority of patents and approximately 47% of multi-class trademarks (covering the application of knowledge for different purposes and sectors).[25] Multi-class trademarks are often anticipatory of future downstream use and so the implication is that the 'knowledge industry' provides as yet unrealised returns.

Reaffirming its historical position as the leading advanced capitalist economy, USA still holds the largest share of operational patents, but like China, has close to half of the items are owned by foreign interests. Japan is notable for its fairly exclusive control of IP in Japan which also matches another point observable of Japanese GVCs – of the 93% of that country's exports in 2010 achieved through value chains, only 8% were by foreign affiliates based in Japan.[27] Japan has a stronger degree of control over commercial design and production than its high income competitor countries which only serves to emphasise that globalisation is not equally porous

Table 4.1 Majority share of world patents in force by 2012 – top countries[26]

	% share of world patents	Of which resident %	Of which non-resident %
USA	26	52	48
Japan	20	86	14
China	10	54	46

58 *Global political economy since the 1970s*

or permeable – nation-states can serve their own interests above global ones.

Beyond the period in question, and a note on the present, China is the main growth country in recent years for IP rights held by lower income countries. As WIPO notes: 'China surpassed the EPO (EU) and the Republic of Korea in 2005, Japan in 2010 and the U.S. in 2011' for total patent filings, such that in 2018 it accounted 46% of total patent filings. Nevertheless, the US still holds some 3.1 million *patents in force*, followed by China with 2.4 million.[28] Globalisation of knowledge ownership continues with a concentration among only a few players.

The summary intellectual property information drawn upon here merely indicates that GVCs are not benevolent societies as the UNIDO report might suggest. Corporations develop and protect their knowledge and markets through legal instruments. IP licensing becomes one part of a profit maximising strategy for firms and GVCs. The large number and continuing growth of patent applications[29] is evidence that IP is major global concern in production. Such corporate apparatus' and instruments rely on a range of legal specialists, representing another example of a non-productive labour/professional service segment growing proportionately with greater global fragmented production. This non-productive segment, like marketing, can be disassociated from labour in production but essential to the circulation of capital and contestation over global market share, over accumulation now and into the future.

Production and share of value within chains

UNCTAD notes the structural bias or inequity that is a feature of the advanced–developing or core–periphery world dynamic:

> The value-added contribution of GVCs can be relatively small where imported contents of exports are high and where GVC participation is limited to lower-value parts of the chain. Also, a large part of GVC value added in developing economies is generated by affiliates of TNCs, which can lead to relatively low 'value capture', e.g. as a result of transfer pricing or income repatriation.[30]

Gereffi et al.'s germinal studies of global *commodity* chains exposed supply-demand dynamics within chains, focused on SME export opportunities and TNCs gross developmental effects, Labour or value appropriation was not directly a feature of this analysis.[31] Since then, research has burgeoned. More recently, Gereffi and colleagues have identified a process of 'upgrading', showing how low-wage, limited-elaboration manufactures and work can be a springboard for breaking out or advancing along the chain, thereby bringing higher wages. Upgrading is dependent upon skilled supply fundamentally, and stratifies both local and global workforces. Nevertheless, it has also focused attention on the

Global political economy since the 1970s 59

vagaries of poor working conditions leading to rights-based advances in some sectors and units of GVC work houses and factories.[32]

The idea of identifying where and why value creation and appropriation occurs within and throughout a chain marks a more critical understanding of the competitive circulation and accumulation of capital.[33] Following the earlier chapter in this book on surplus value, labour is still the fundamental condition for creating value. As Mulholland and Stewart note of an earlier study by Taylor:

> reducing the process of production to a technical function where the dominant firm distributes labour tasks ... 'misses the prior issue of the character of production within firms including how value is produced before its subsequent distribution among networked firms'.[34]

Consistent with the idea of the historically contested, socially determined price of labour, it is unsurprising that 'cheap' labour in abundance found in developing economies is the source of much initial or simple transformation of goods for downstream adding. Mulholland and Stewart document the relationship between value's appropriation and value chain hierarchy through a study of the food distribution sector.[35] They show how the exploitation of supply structure including labour is entrenched and acted upon by capitalist interests at the top of the chain. One way to theorise value chain hierarchy is the 'proximity' to gross surplus accumulation and point of final demand, where inputs must always be lower cost upstream (backwards) than downstream (forwards to market). This assumes a single linear process although GVCs may appear more pluralistic in terms of input–output stages. Regardless, and despite global fragmentation of processes, for decades most GVC trade has been intra-firm but is shifting.[36] Cost can be more readily shifted or absorbed within a company through transfer pricing mechanisms to the locus of owning interest. In reality, proximity to the value chain hierarchy is a metaphor for a historical and actually existing trend of advanced capitalist economies operating from a position of prior accumulated wealth.

Returning to the period in question and with Australia as the reference, a comparison between advanced economies and then with a selection of developing economies from the Asia Pacific is offered below (Figure 4.5, Figure 4.6) to further the point. By looking at *final demand*, that is, the furthest point downstream before consumption, and drawing upon Figure 4.2 in terms of overall participation in GVCs, a sense of a country's position within the overall scheme of value chain hierarchy – and greatest proportional share of gross income – can begin to be better constructed. To add complexity to this comparison, the size of a country's workforce and relative wage cost must be brought into the frame, for both immediate understanding of any given sets of output and the fact that capital in competition will source the cheapest available labour. Figure 4.4 shows that the USA has by far the largest workforce in the advanced economy group.

60 *Global political economy since the 1970s*

Australia is diminutive by comparison, with approximately 7% the size of the USA workforce. And, while Australia's workforce grew at 14%, the US workforce grew 11% between 1995 and 2005. The ILO notes for the Asia Pacific region as a whole, there has been greater GDP growth than workforce growth at least since 1999.[37] This suggests a factor production multiplier effect such as quality of employees – their relative surplus value – and/or, technology, etc., all the while presumably in response to a given demand.

Moving to Figure 4.4 below, concerning leading advanced economies, in all cases there is an absolute upward trend over the 15 years in domestic final value added of intermediate goods and therefore 'proximity' to gross profit or surplus. Compared to the leading economies of the world, Australia is a small value-adding economy of intermediate goods in monetary terms for products at their final stage of transformation before consumption (final demand). However, the size of the available workforce, its relative growth and cost of labour, as well as industry sector specifics impacts any analysis. Australia's workforce is significantly smaller than all other advanced countries. And while Australia generates significant wealth from raw materials such as from mining, these invariably are not considered products for *final* consumption – they may be part-processed (e.g. storage, haulage, handling) inputs for further downstream activity and so should not be considered necessarily as dominant of Australia's performance in *final value adding*, as per Figures 4.4 and 4.5. These commodities would need certain degrees of processing to qualify in the OECD TiVA data sets.

On a workforce per capita basis (Figure 4.4), between 1995 and 2005, Australia slightly outperforms Korea in terms of final value adding in GVC production (Figure 4.5), though Australia lags behind all larger advanced economies in simple volume terms. Australia's domestic value added for final demand proportionally in comparison to US value added growth grew 25% in the decade to 2005. In other words, Australia produced more in relative terms as it entered and took root in the emergent global market. This might be partly attributed to the greater labour force growth for Australia over the same period (Australia, 14%, USA 11% growth), but not entirely.

Figure 4.5 below compares Australia to the developing and industrialising economies of the Asian region, where much of Australia's trade burgeoned in the 1990s.

Australia is clearly a dominant supplier of final product value adding, more so given its available workforce is smaller in numbers than Indonesia, Malaysia, the Philippines, Thailand and Vietnam. Importantly, while Australia's final-process value adding in dollar terms doubled between 1995 and 2005, its available workforce did not grow anywhere near as fast. Total labour force (persons) increased 14% between 1995 and 2005 in Australia.[41] Australia's total hours worked increased steadily over time between 1995 and 2005, also rising 14%.[42] Greater workforce productivity may have contributed to Australia's final export value adding over time and relative to its

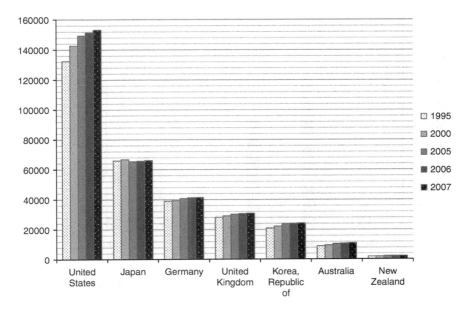

Figure 4.3 Gross labour force international comparison – major advanced economies, Australia and New Zealand, 1995–2007, millions of people.[38]

neighbours. The ILO estimates that since 1999 'average labour productivity has increased more than twice as much as average wages in developed economies'.[43] Australia's wage rates are the highest of all those countries, but its workforce is the nearest the median of nine sample countries (fourth-smallest after New Zealand, Cambodia and Singapore).[44] Overlaying wages in a key globally integrated sector, manufacturing, the picture of value share is grim: between 2002 and 2012, for example, Australian wages almost trebled, while those in the Philippines doubled. The 'sting' in this tale is that Australian wages moved from $17.42/hour to almost $48/hour; for Filipino workers wages grew from a paltry $1.00 to a meagre $2:10![45] The ILO report meanwhile noted that for a major developing economy, China, despite real wage growth in that country since the mid-2000s, the share of income distributed to labour since at least 1992 has been in trend decline. Real wage growth does occur in developed and developing countries as a result of trade in value added goods and services, but the related dynamic of accumulation, profit share, is being consistently eroded and this is a trend more recently and increasingly affecting developed economies.[46]

The greater (relative) increase in amount of final value-added growth suggests technology and innovation advances no doubt are a factor. A relative decline in cost of inputs another possible factor for increased returns for advanced countries such as Australia – imports could be made cheaper by

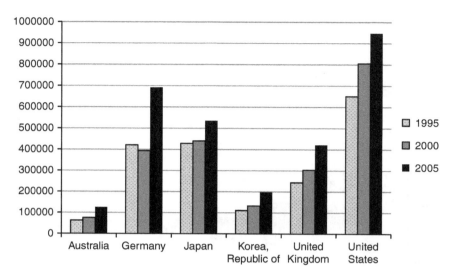

Figure 4.4 Domestic value added embodied in final foreign demand – 1995, 2000, 2005 (USD millions) – advanced economies.[39]

exploiting labour and production conditions upstream. Most of the countries in Figure 4.4 and Figure 4.5 record a significant growth between 2000 and 2005, suggesting greater integration, technology advancements, relative labour gains, etc. or combinations of relative surplus value extraction in both upstream and downstream value chains. Of related importance is that employment growth in Australia since the 1960s has been in services, despite its primary and heavy industry export industries providing significant export income. From the early 1970s to 2012, services is the only industry sector in Australia to have grown in employment terms, from almost 60% share of employment to almost 80%. Employment in manufacturing as the only other sizeable sector declined from around 25% to less than 10% over the same period.[47]

The two main points that can be gleaned from the above sets of figures are, first, that advanced economies have been more involved in final value adding activities, which might involve expert and professional information-rich services, financial planning, market analysis and design, contract resolution, quality assurance and human resources within the GVC supply chain, software programming, etc. In other words, a greater specialised workforce including more non-productive labour and notably personnel engaged in market expanding activities. Concomitantly, and arguably as a consequence, advanced economies experience a greater share of total income from GVCs. Second, labour overall is still exploited in terms of increased hours worked and wages returned relative to productivity gains made. Mulholland and Stewart's research on 'backward-driven demand'

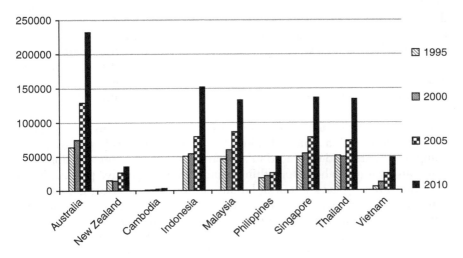

Figure 4.5 Domestic value added for final foreign demand – 1995, 2000, 2005 (USD millions) – Asian developing economies.[40]

retail supply explains that 'price competitiveness via the average socially necessary labour time' to produce goods for retail supermarket is critical to controlling and conditioning labour's cost.[48] Barnes's extensive research into auto supply chains in India exposes a uniquely orchestrated tier-system of supplier price competition has deliberately left workers in the most precarious of conditions.[49] Labour and its control remain central to determining value in GVCs. Fragmentation of production has been implicated as a key to enforcing this control. While the value of labour is connected with given social conditions, the value it renders for profit can be obscured in value chains.

Value's production in Global Value Chains is sometimes measured by the type of product, but this should be taken as a proxy for relative social labour costs. As one news report attempted to explain:

> U.S. factory workers do have one critical advantage over others: They're really productive. In fact, U.S. factory workers produce $73.45 per hour in output, one-third more than German factory workers and twice as much as workers in Taiwan, according to the BLS. That's in part because U.S. workers still tend to *build more expensive products* than someone in Taiwan, such as airplanes instead of shoes.[50]

This example contains assumptions about usefulness as value that demand further discussion. According to this account the global division of labour has material cause and effect: it divides by exchange-value the type of

64 *Global political economy since the 1970s*

product in stages of production. This sits uneasily against Marx's principle definition in Capital: use value as a 'property of commodities ... is independent of the amount of labour required to appropriate its useful qualities'.[51] While, the value surrendered by labour does not accumulate as products are exchanged and possibly repurposed or used in *further value creation*; it does, notionally, if we consider value chains as an extended assembly line where goods or services go through different stages of *value adding*.

Another way to understand *value* in Global *Value* Chains is this: shoes might be produced in a limited value chain, an aircraft has huge varieties of component parts and produced in all manner of places of production. This is not an argument about something being a more expensive product by its usefulness, but by the amount of labour and productive effort globally and generally that sum the parts. Fragmenting production allows for all manners of socially necessary labour to be summed differently.

It is here we must return to Castells' study of informationalism. An implication in Castells' argument about an informational mode of capital is that the global division of labour has been facilitated and possibly created by type or usefulness of commodities produced – but also by the 'raw' materials: *information*. Where the availability of certain raw materials might have previously influenced or dictated the place of production, secondary and tertiary goods production, informational goods, mass consumer goods, etc. as much as automobiles and 'airplanes', can be designed and produced anywhere.

A spatial dichotomy in reality does not exist – globalisation as it is expressed in corporate relationships is everywhere. The literature only touched upon here shows through the scattered organisation of production through 'value chains' (local and global) this original value created by labour is usurped at different stages of a given production. Milberg highlights a key passage from Arndt and Kerzkowski on the calculated compartmentalisation of production, and partially reproduced here:

> Spatial dispersion of production allows factor intensity of each component, rather than the average factor intensity of the end product, to determine the location of its production. The international division of labour now matches factor intensities of components with factor abundance locations.[52]

This raises a number of issues about the global sourcing of labour and other resources. In particular, it explains an economic rationale for increasingly separated and spatialised segments of production and related market and distribution. Contemporary examples of this are discussed in Chapter 2 concerning labour value theory, precariousness and the international division of labour. Illustrating the complexity of global and local in terms of production and value chains, Harris cites a 2007 study on Chinese transnational capital by Rosen and Houser, whereby:

Global political economy since the 1970s 65

the majority of oil bought by Chinese TNCs never reaches China, but is sold in international markets. No energy from Canada, Syria, Venezuela or Azerbaijan is used inside China, and 'only a fraction' from Ecuador, Algeria and Colombia is used ... China is not tying up resources for its own use, but is involved in joint projects producing mutually shared global profits ... When Nigerian oil powers the assembly lines at Honda and Volkswagen, or Iranian energy lights up FoxConn so computers for Dell and HP can flow off the assembly line, just who is benefiting? This is part of the vast transnational value chain; it doesn't simply serve the Chinese national economy.[53]

Such examples highlight complexity in international trade; and this should not be mistaken for fair trade. Despite this apparent interconnected web of production, as UNCTAD notes, countries such as the USA and Japan are 'global service and technology leaders' and consequently they 'capture a large part of trade-generated value added domestically'; their share of foreign value added for some years has been relatively lower than other developed economies such as Germany partly because they own and produce more of the information-dependent goods and services themselves,[54] but precisely because the information used in production comes with patent or IP rights as explained earlier. It is not a free (*gratis*) flow of information. It is proprietary!

Another feature transnational corporations have at their disposal is profit maximisation through transfer (mis)pricing. This allows for the exchange of a good or service within a TNC or GVC for an unrealistic price, or using a tax haven to avoid tax on the transaction.[55] As a 2011 study noted, the world's top ten TNCs 'controlled over 6,000 subsidiaries, a third of which were incorporated in secrecy jurisdictions'.[56] Even unitary and national-based firms may buy or sell to tax havens. But the kinds of intra-firm dealings that can occur where a TNC uses tax loopholes and inconsistencies in different countries to pass on value, either *gratis* or over or under a normative price, are tangibly beneficial either to one TNC over another firm, or as has been documented, to parent companies located in the global North.

The thinking on accumulation and globalisation has evolved steadily. Compare the above with the claim of Landau, who, as early as 2001, suggested globalisation was once about trade volumes, but is best represented by Foreign Direct Investment (FDI). Landau also compares the period since the Bretton Woods collapse, drawing on UNCTAD data:

> Over the period 1945–1973, there was an increase of trade, but since the 1980s trade has not been the most important element of globalization. Trade has been eclipsed by the growth of FDI, which is the driving force of globalization. The global FDI stock increased twenty-five fold during the last quarter-century ... Between 1982 and 1994, FDI doubled as a percentage of world gross domestic product to 9 per cent. In 1996 the global FDI stock was valued $3.2 trillion, rising from

66 *Global political economy since the 1970s*

$1 trillion in 1987 and $2 trillion in 1993. It increased at an average annual rate of 34 per cent compared with an annual rate of 9 per cent for global merchandise trade.[57]

UNCTAD has reported global FDI flow peaked and troughed over the last four years to 2018, approximately between $1.4 and $1.9 trillion. FDI stock has increased far more since the 1990s. Between 2000 and 2017, inward and outward stock have each grown more than fourfold from $7 trillion to approximately $31 trillion. World GDP, meanwhile, roughly trebled over three decades from 1990.[58]

FDI as a 'measure' of actual global financial activity helps point to the increasing web of corporate interest. It also highlights the expanding role of investment and interest-bearing capital in growth. Castells had sometime earlier focused attention on global FDI, and already claimed that this was the 'driving force of globalisation'. Castells linked this directly with growth in multinational firms and associated networks, and perhaps for good reason: at the time he wrote his *informationalism* trilogy 'The number of multinational firms increased from 7,000 in 1970 to 37,000 in 1993, with 150,000 affiliates around the world, and to 53,000 with 415,000 affiliates in 1998'.[59] Milberg, astutely contributed to the dimension of financialisation with the growth in transnational or Global Value Chains. His analysis of Fortune 100 companies in the US highlights some astounding production dispersal, but with greater dividends to shareholders from companies with highly fragmented production. 'Dell, the PC assembler that revolutionized mass customization in the PC market, purchases 4500 different parts from 300 suppliers'.[60] This is separate to the branding and design work that are 'added value' typically sourced in the global north.

Financialisation

The overview thus far provides a way of highlighting the concentration or accumulation of wealth in advanced capitalist countries through GVCs as a contemporary means of capitalist production. This ironically is achieved through a process of production dispersal. Consideration of production and distribution through Global Value Chains and networks provides a more nuanced understanding of a complex web to maximise value and organise economies throughout a geopolitical economic order.[61] The GVC relationship brings together industrial, merchant and interest-bearing capitals within the one organisational logic for transnational corporate and shareholder interest.[62] Fine and separately Milberg point to the efforts of non-finance companies to make profit in finance sector activities, investing not in their immediate productive capacities, but in other stocks and shares. This, they argue, is the essence of financialisation and a uniquely influential form of global capital.[63] Neoclassical economics also theorised this within a stages of growth paradigm, from which 'new growth theory emerged.[64] An

Global political economy since the 1970s 67

ILO study on capital share reported that the finance sector experienced the fastest growth in share gain relative to non-finance corporations or industries. It also noted that for advanced economies, those also commanding the most value from GVCs: 'profits of *non-financial* corporations have increasingly been allocated to pay dividends, which accounted for 35 per cent of profits in 2007', which led to 'increased pressure on companies to reduce the share of value added going to labour compensation'.[65]

Peters presents further measurements of actual financialisation but to argue this qualitative phase of capital's global power over labour value and not just reach.[66] Trends on company acquisitions and mergers are placed to show both job losses and fragmentation of companies and thereby de-organising of labour. Hence, capital necessarily and actively sought to break labour's gains. Or as Farazmand puts it bluntly: 'People do not downsize themselves; elites do. Common people do not privatize government functions. Public organizational elites do'.[67]

For countries such as Australia, which in the 1980s suffered from an apparent lack of finance and investment capital to fulfil Government growth goals, FDI was highly sought after. Notable however is that most FDI reported by Australia's Foreign Investment Review Board in the late 1980s to mid-1990s concerned acquisitions, not new capital investment.[68] Australia's domestic value-added exports not necessarily reflecting the final resting place of net profit is underscored here by the extent of foreign interest in Australia capital.

Also notable was that much growth in Australia's FDI came from a few Asian countries. As subsequent chapters in this book detail, the Australian Government took extensive steps to attract investment as it 'globalised' its economy. Importantly, the Australian Government also constructed its (inward) migration programme as an integral part of this process.

Taking a mid-point between the 1995–2005 GVC data analysed above, foreign-owned businesses in Australia in mid-2001 were only around 1% of total registered business. This 1% did however employ 12% of Australia's workforce and possessed a quarter of Australia's total fixed capital formation.[69] This suggests they were comparatively larger businesses, while business domestic ownership had a greater proportional share of smaller enterprises. In mid-2001, the lion's share of Australia's foreign owned businesses was with the USA. Measured by their gross fixed capital formation, the US had four times as much of the capital in Australia as Japan or Germany, with the UK second-largest capital owner. Foreign business dominated IT components (development and supply) for both wholesale services sector and manufacturing sector at this time.[70] The importance of IT as information infrastructure for production and circulation of capital is noted in numerous globalisation studies. These figures are offered here as proxies; without specific analysis of each industry, the value of capital does not provide deep understandings. It could be generalised however that FDI income in GVC flows out of Australia

68 Global political economy since the 1970s

were returning to the Global North at this time. Indeed, two-thirds of FDI incomes globally in 2012 are reported to have been repatriated or invested elsewhere.[71] Nevertheless, UNCTAD's observation of overall FDI dynamics was that 'even where exports are driven by TNCs, the value-added contribution of local firms in GVCs is often very significant. And re-investment of earnings by foreign affiliates is, on average, almost as significant as repatriation'.[72]

Fragmentation or New Growth – a note on small and medium business

The large transnational corporation is the typical image of global value chain production and FDI. Corporate colonisation of the periphery as portrayed in the critical globalisation literature inevitably focuses on the powerful large corporations. However, these corporations are agglomerations of smaller material units of production. If post-1970s globalisation has been marked by deindustrialisation and downsizing in the advanced economies of the Global North as the literature presents, some detail on small and medium enterprises (SMEs) is important to understand both the structures and attendant social relationships. The strongest exploitation of labour may be concentrated in the mass sweatshops of the Global South. Meanwhile, the accumulation of value-added returns for the global North integrates resident SMEs and foreign affiliate firms. As will be discussed in Chapter 5, one way of understanding the relationship between SMEs and global production is through migration occupation categories countries such as recruited by Australian governments.

The Australian Bureau of Statistics estimated that between 1983 and 2001, the small business sector grew annually by 3.5%, such that by 2001 they represented 97% of all private sector business.[73] Larger business on the other hand accounted for the bulk of income. Focusing on export businesses, in 1997–98, to take an example, there were some 21,800 exporting businesses in Australia and, of these, 77% were considered small enterprises by size of their workforce. The bulk of all exports were in goods (82%) rather than services (18%).[74] Combined with Figure 4.1 data, a picture of Australia in the mid- to late 1990s could be one of significant GVC activity, but largely in a milieu of smaller firms. Further analysis is required to understand this fully, but a prevalence of smaller business in exporting would fit with the idea of GVC production relying on fragmented, deindustrialised social relations.

During the 1990s Australian export businesses were a small fraction of total registered businesses, but growth in this area is the more remarkable feature. Between 1994 and 1998, the number of export businesses in Australia grew 8% annually. Actual income from export revenue tailed behind somewhat at 3% annually for the same period. This corresponds with the arguments about Australian restructuring towards export oriented

Global political economy since the 1970s 69

small business. Finally, the industry sectors involved in export by quantity and export revenue are dominated by manufacturing (32%), then wholesale (28% approx.); property and business services generates little revenue but represents 22% of total export firms. Conversely, mining is significantly small in terms of numbers of exporting business but produces far more export income for the size of the sector.[75]

Conclusion

Late 20th-century globality has entrenched interconnected production markets, finance and investment in ways that colonialism never could. Nevertheless, an overarching schema of free market capitalism has continued a historical pattern of accumulation in the global north at the expense of the periphery. This is not necessarily a geographically sparse phenomenon in one sense: The North American Free Trade Agreement (NAFTA) for example, is coterminous between USA (Global North) and Mexico (Global South). On the other hand, the emphasis on Global Value Chains or transnational production spreads and intersperses the core and periphery globally. Technology has expedited this situation at a general level and also revolutionised social relations of production within companies and industries. Finance and investment are equally relevant to these changes and gaining in importance as an indicator of a global market economy. Market relations are materially manifest in the borderless circulation of intermediate goods and services and complicated webs of production and control. Labour is de-organised through the mobility and fragmentation of capital in production. The Australian case confirms that country's integration into the global systems of production and exchange thus allowing a different lens to be applied to how migration selection policy might be understood in that country.

Notes

1 Mark Vaille (former Australian Government Minister for Trade, 'Australia as a Trading Nation', *Speech to Business Club of Australia*, Sydney, 15 September 2000, http://www.trademinister.gov.au/speeches/2000/000915_trading_nation. html (accessed 12 March 2014).
2 Wallerstein, I. (1989) *The Modern World- System III: The Second Era of Great Expansion of the Capitalist World-Economy, 1730–1840*. New York: Academic Press; Hadrt, M. and Negri, A. (2000) *Empire,* Cambridge, MA: London: Harvard University Press; Arrighi, G. (2009) *Adam Smith in Beijing: Lineages of the Twenty-First Century,* London: Verso; Chomsky, N. (2004) *Hegemony or Survival: America's Quest for Global Dominance,* Crow's Nest, NSW: Allen and Unwin.
3 Harvey, D. (2003) *The New Imperialism,* Oxford: Oxford University Press.
4 Castells, M. (2000a) *The Information Age: Economy, Society and Culture – Vol I: The Rise of the Network Society,* 2nd edn, Malden, MA and Carlton, VIC: Blackwell.

70 Global political economy since the 1970s

5 Sassen, S. (2001) (*The Global City; New York, London, Tokyo*, 2nd edn, Princeton, NJ: Princeton University Press.

6 See also Westra, R. and Zuege, A. (eds) (2003) *Value and the World Economy Today: Production, Finance and Globalization*, Basingstoke and New York: Palgrave Macmillan; Bryan, D. (2010) 'The Duality of Labour and the Financial Crisis' *Economic and Labour Relations Review*, Vol. 20, No. 2, July, http://elr.sagepub.com/content/20/2/49.full.pdf+html (accessed 26 October 2012), DOI:10.1177/103530461002000204.

7 French, S., Leyshon, A. and Wainwright, T. (2011) 'Financializing Space, Spacing Financialization', *Progress in Human Geography*, Vol. 35, No. 6, p. 799.

8 Fine, B. (2010b) 'Locating Financialization', *Historical Materialism*, Vol. 18, No. 2, pp. 97–116.

9 Bryan, D., 'Bridging Differences: Value Theory, International Finance and the Construction of Global Capital', in Westra, R., and Zuege, A. (2003), p. 62.

10 Carroll, W. 'Capital Relations and Directorate Interlocking: The Global Network in 2007', in Murray, G. and Scott, J. (eds) (2012) *Financial Elites and Transnational Business: Who Rules the World?* Northampton, MA: Elgar; Robinson, W.I. (2009) 'Global Capitalism Theory and the Emergence of Transnational Elites', Working Paper 2010/02, Finland: UNU World Institute for Development Economics Research (UNU-WIDER), http://www.soc.ucsb.edu/faculty/robinson/Assets/pdf/WIDER.pdf (accessed 26 July 2013).

11 Bauman, Z. (2002) *Society Under Siege*, Cambridge: Polity Press; Bauman, Z. (2000) *Liquid Modernity*, Cambridge: Polity Press.

12 Castells, M. (1990) *The Informational City: The Informational City: Information Technology, Economic Restructuring, and the Urban Regional Process*, Oxford, UK and Cambridge, MA: Blackwell, p. 348.

13 Milberg, W. (2008) 'Shifting Sources and Uses of Profits: Sustaining US Financialization With Global Value Chains', *Economy and Society*, Vol. 37, No. 3, August, pp. 420–51.

14 *Implications of Global Value Chains for Trade, Investment, Development and Jobs, Prepared for the G-20 Leaders' Summit, St. Petersburg* (Russian Federation) September 2013, npp: OECD, WTO, UNCTAD, 6 August, pp. 12–13.

15 Ibid., p. 19.

16 Notably Gereffi, G., Korzeniewicz, M. and Korzeniewicz, R. (eds) (1994) *Commodity Chains and Global Capitalism*, Westport, CT: Praeger.

17 UNCTAD (2018) *World Investment Report: Investment and New Industrial Policies,* New York and Geneva: United Nations. Table constructed from figures on p. 20.

18 Figure updated and revised from OECD, WTO and UNCTAD (2013), Figure 1, p. 10. Data for the figure drawn from the OECD TiVA (Trade in Value Added) database, 2014 release. TiVA is a public searchable database: http://stats.oecd.org/Index.aspx?DataSetCode=TIVA_OECD_WTO (accessed 17 February 2020).

19 That is, from the tip of the triangle to the top of the bar. Figure 4.2 does not include actual value but only volume.

20 That is, 12/41*100.

21 Ibid., p. 14, from Figure 8.

22 Saad-Fihlo, A. (2014) 'The "Rise of the South": Global Convergence at Last?' *New Political Economy*, Vol. 19, No. 4, p. 587.

23 Sturgeon, T.J. and Memedovic, O. (2011) 'Mapping Global Value Chains: Intermediate Goods Trade and Structural Change in the World Economy', *Development Policy and Strategic Research Branch Working Paper* 05/2010, Vienna: UNIDO, p. 18.

Global political economy since the 1970s 71

24 Ibid.
25 WIPO (2013) *World Intellectual Property Indicators – 2013* Geneva: WIPO, pp. 6–7, http://www.wipo.int/ipstats/en/wipi (accessed 29 July 2014).
26 Ibid. Figures tabulated from summary data, p. 7.
27 UNCTAD (2013) *World Investment Report: Global Value Chains: Investment and Trade for Development*, New York and Geneva: UNCTAD, p. 136.
28 WIPO (2019) *World Intellectual Property Indicators 2019*. Geneva: World Intellectual Property Organization, http://www.wipo.int/ipstats/en/wipi (accessed 18 February 2020), pp. 14, 19.
29 WIPO (2019), WIPO (2013).
30 UNCTAD (2013), p. xxiii.
31 Gereffi, G. (2019) 'Global Value Chains and International Development Policy: Bringing Firms, Networks and Policy-Engaged Scholarship Back in', *Journal of International Business Policy*, Vol. 2, No. 3, September, pp. 195–210; Gereffi, G., Korzeniewicz, M. and Korzeniewicz, R. (1994) 'Introduction: Global Commodity Chains', in Gereffi, G. and Korzeniewicz, M. (eds), pp. 1–14.
32 Gereffi, G. and Lee, J. (2016) 'Economic and Social Upgrading in Global Value Chains and Industrial Clusters: Why Governance Matters', *Journal of Business Ethics*, Vol. 133, No. 1, pp. 25–38.
33 Smith, A., Rainnie, A., Dunford, M., Hardy, J., Hudson, R. and Sadler, D. (2002) 'Networks of Value, Commodities and Regions: Reworking Divisions of Labour in Macro-Regional Economies', *Progress in Human Geography*, Vol. 26, No. 1, pp. 41–63.
34 Mulholland, K. and Stewart, P. (2014) 'Workers in Food Distribution: Global Commodity Chains and Lean Logistics', *New Political Economy*, Vol. 19, No. 4, p. 540.
35 Ibid.
36 OECD et al. (2013), p. 136; Saad-Fihlo, A. (2014).
37 ILO (2013) *Global Wages Report 2012/13*, Geneva: ILO, pp. 19–23.
38 U.S. Department of Labor, Bureau of Labor Statistics: *International Comparisons of Annual Labor Force* Statistics, Table 3–1 1972–2012, compiled 7 June 2013, http://www.bls.gov/fls (accessed 31 March 2020).
39 OECD Stat.Extracts: OECD-WTO Trade in Value Added (TiVA) Database – June 2015 release; http://stats.oecd.org/Index.aspx?DataSetCode=TIVA_OECD_WTO# (accessed 31 March 2020). Korea in 1995 was not considered an advanced economy by a number of indicators. Its position has changed somewhat over the decade to 2005, and is included here for comparative discussion.
40 Ibid.
41 Confirming figures from Figure 4.3, see ABS (2006) *6202.0 Labour Force, Australia,* Table 03. Labour force status by Sex. Column A163161K. The US Bureau of Labor figures from Figure 4.3 round up to 15% for the same period, a slight deviation that does not affect the argument. The overall population increase in Australia was approximately 2 million between 1995 and 2005.
42 ABS (2006) *6202.0 Labour Force, Australia* Table 21. Quarter measure of aggregate monthly hours worked by Industry Sector – Seasonally adjusted.
43 ILO (2013), p. 45.
44 ILO (2013) *Global Wage Report 2013/13: Wages and Equitable Growth*, Geneva: International Labour Office. Original source: *US Bureau of Labor Statistics*
45 U.S. Department of Labor, Bureau of Labor Statistics BLS: *International Comparisons of Annual Labor Force Statistics*, selected data: 'Hourly Compensation, Manufacturing HR Compensation, USD, 2002 to 2012 Data';

72   Global political economy since the 1970s

compiled November 2019, http://www.bls.gov/fls/data.htm (figures in US dollars) (accessed 31 March 2020).

46 UNCTAD (2018).

47 Lowe, P. (2012) 'The Changing Structure of the Australian Economy and Monetary Policy', *Address to the Australian Industry Group 12th Annual Economic Forum*, Sydney, 7 March. Figures derived from Graph 1. Reserve Bank of Australia, http://www.rba.gov.au/speeches/2012/sp-dg-070312.html (accessed 27 January 2014).

48 Mulholland, K. and Stewart, P. (2014).

49 Barnes, T. (2018).

50 Kavoussi, B. (2012) 'Average Cost of a Factory Worker in the U.S., China and Germany', *The Huffington Post*, 19 March, http://www.huffingtonpost.com/2012/03/08/average-cost-factory-worker_n_1327413.html (accessed 11 February 2014) (my emphasis). Assumptions about the cost of such goods being more expensive but not calculated on the relative cost of labour's reproduction only serve to highlight how contingent is *use value* or the quality of things. It is impossible to compare shoes and aircraft.

51 Marx, K. (1986 [1959]), p. 44.

52 Milberg, A. (2008), p. 429.

53 Harris, J. (2012) 'Outward Bound: Transnational Capitalism in China', *Race & Class*, Vol. 54, No. 1, pp. 13–32.

54 UNCTAD (2018), p. 23.

55 Ronen, P. (2006) *The Offshore World: Sovereign Markets, Virtual Places, and Nomad Millionaires*, Ithaca, NY: Cornell University Press; Van Fossen, A. 'The Transnational Capitalist Class and Tax Havens', in Murray, G. and Scott, J. (eds) (2012), pp. 76–99; Chang, H.-J. (2007) *Bad Samaritans: Rich Nations, Poor Policies and the Threat to the Developing World*, London: Random House.

56 Gillespie, P. (2012) Tax Troubles: How TNCs Enhance Profits by Avoiding Taxes', *Third World Resurgence*, No. 268, December, pp 14–17, http://www.twnside.org.sg/title2/resurgence/2012/268/cover01.htm (accessed 1 January 2013).

57 Landau, A. (2001) *Redrawing the Global Economy: Elements of Integration and Fragmentation*, Basingstoke and New York: Palgrave, p. 109.

58 UNCTAD (2018), p. 188.

59 Castells, M. (2000a), p. 251.

60 Milberg, W. (2008), pp. 438–39.

61 See Devinney, T. and Kirchner, S. (1997) 'Perspectives on Growth: Implications for Asia, Australia and New Zealand', *Agenda*, Vol. 4, No. 4, pp. 407–18, highlighting neoclassical economic theory of Porter on value chains, factor input theory and competitive advantage.

62 Fine, B (2010b); Milberg, A. (2008). Both Fine and Milberg point to the efforts of non-finance companies to make profit in finance sector activities, investing not in their immediate productive capacities, but in other stocks and shares. This, they argue, is the essence of financialisation.

63 Ibid. Fine dismisses domestic financialisation as the key determinant, something critiques of neoliberalism and analysts of the 2007–08 Global Financial Crisis are concerned with. See, for example, Bryan, D. (2010). In Chapter 5 I note in passing the emergence of limited liability laws in England in the mid-1800s. Drawing upon Robert Bryer's 1997 article on Mercantile Laws, Jeffreys' claim is noted that financialisation and a *rentier* class had already an 'appetite' for generating profit simply from financial cross-investment.

64 See Devinney, T. and Kirchner, S. (1997); Landstrom, H. (2008) 'Entrepreneurship Research: A Missing Link in Our Understanding of the Knowledge Economy',

Journal of Intellectual Capital, Vol. 9, No. 2, http://www.emeraldinsight.com/1469-1930.htm (accessed 26 October 2012).

65 ILO (2013), p. 44.

66 Peters, J. (2011) 'The Rise of Finance and the Decline of Organised Labour in the Advanced Capitalist Countries', *New Political Economy*, Vol. 16, No. 1. DOI: 10.1080/13563461003789746.

67 Farazmand, A. (1999) 'The Elite Question: Toward a Normative Elite Theory of Organisation', *Administration and Society*, Vol. 31, No. 3, p. 322.

68 The majority of acquisitions being for developed real estate, including commercial. See FIRB (various dates) *Annual Report*, Canberra: AGPS, e.g. 1987–88, p. 4, 1990–91, p. 2.

69 ABS (2004) *Economic Activity of Foreign Owned Businesses in Australia, 2000–01*, Cat.5494.0. Canberra: Commonwealth of Australia, p. 6.

70 Ibid., p. 4.

71 UNCTAD (2013), p. xvi.

72 Ibid., p. xxiii.

73 ABS (2002) *Small Business in Australia 2001*, cat.1321.0, Canberra: Commonwealth of Australia.

74 Pink, B. and Jamieson, C. (2000) *A Portrait of Australian Exporters: A Report Based on the Business Longitudinal Survey*, Canberra: Commonwealth of Australia, p. 1.

75 Ibid., p. 5.

5 Global capital and its agents

A merchant, it has been said very properly, is not necessarily a citizen of any particular country.[1]

Transnational production and agency

Globality is not only about inward and outward flows of capital. As a feature of capitalist production it concerns the control over surplus value creation and accumulation. This requires a theory of economic agency attending the structure. While the use of the term 'agency' suggests self-direction and control over the structural dynamics of contemporary globalisation, different classes and categories of occupations are assumed to operate largely within the basic process of capitalism to create, circulate and accumulate value. The explicit control of one class over another is not the main point of discussion about agency here. Rather it is the extent to which the constituents of one class operates in accordance with the fundaments of capitalism, and how this is anticipated to play out in the evolving global context as described.

States, governments, social organisations and corporations all play a part. The overview of globalisation literature in Chapter 4 acknowledged the role of nation and state in relation to a globalised economy. A view with some substance is that global capital's interests undermine sovereignty and the very existence of national borders, with political ramifications for the degree popular control over economies and societies. The fact is that this has only been partially realised. After some thirty years towards multilateral and regional trade agreements (e.g. GATT, EU, NAFTA, the BRICS, APEC, etc.),[2] mobile transnational production and concomitant mobility of people to move between nation-state borders is contested. Elements within governments and populations, multilateral agencies and localised social organisations continue to exercise varying degrees of agency and control, but this can be understood relative to the degree or extent of neoliberal market relations.

Agency should not be interpreted here as another term for cultural or human capital as the basis of individual action but rather the relationship of occupations to productiveness, or the creation or circulation and accumulation

Global capital and its agents 75

of value. For labour, 'agency' is evident in its collective contest over profit. For other, non-productive occupational strata engaged in a capitalist market economy, agency can be thought of as the contest over exchange value, or market transactions, as much as contest with labour; In any case, over profit and market share.

Capitalism may be a self-replicating and yet self-destructing system, but it is daily made of and by (but arguably not for) people. Recall the argument of Farazmand cited in Chapter 4 '[p]eople do not downsize themselves; elites do. Common people do not privatize government functions. Public organizational elites do'.[3] If so, it is to transnational corporate elites who orchestrate and manage the flow and accumulation of capital that global value theory necessarily addresses. Smith et al. undertake detailed analysis of governance structures to validate a claim by others about 'how production, distribution and consumption are situated in networks of relational power rather than in linear chains'.[4] More pertinent to this analysis of Productive Diversity, these same authors highlight the importance of analysing how value actually flows and by whom it is created, facilitated and directed:

> Rather than just enabling us to map and analyse the form that economic networks take across space, the focus upon flows of value and the differential power and position of economic actors in the governance of these flows potentially allows for an understanding of *which actors* and *which places* benefit from or lose out from such flows.[5]

Corporate globalising elites have attracted significant scholarly attention, but the idea and contention of a transnational capitalist class predates much of the work on globalisation. Indeed, the year before the Nixon Shock of 1973, the *coup de grâce* of Bretton Woods accord on US domination of a world trade pricing mechanism, Canadian economist Stephen Hymer is credited by Carroll with exposing:

> 'the great pull' of the multinational corporate system 'toward international class consciousness on the part of capital', facilitated by the corporate form of business which enabled 'the 1 percent of the population that owns the vast majority of corporate stock' to maintain control of key investments of increasingly international scope while delegating operational power to hired managers.[6]

Carroll draws further on Hymer's original claims, reproduced here again to highlight the period in which this was claimed:

> Due to the internationalization of capital, competition between national capitalists is becoming less and less a source of rivalry between

76 *Global capital and its agents*

nations. Using the instrument of direct investment, large corporations are able to penetrate foreign markets and detach their interests from their home markets. Given these tendencies an international capitalist class is emerging whose interests lie in the world economy as a whole and a system of international private property which allows free movement of capital between countries.[7]

However, the reality of a class acting as one is more complex. Within this line of inquiry, the relevance of national allegiance for members of the growing transnational capitalist class challenges the 'new imperialism' thesis championed by David Harvey. That idea suggested a deliberate nationalist approach by (US) capitalists and elites. Robinson argues the transnational capitalist class largely does not have a national identity. 'There is', he claims 'conflict between national and transnational fractions of capital'.[8] This is in part due to their global investments that such elites are considered not aligned to developing any particular national interest. Carroll is sceptical of a singular transnational class, pointing to historical alliances between the USA and Europe replicated in regional rather than truly global capital formations.[9] However, there is, at least since the Global Financial Crisis of 2007 an observable concentration in ownership of transnational production due to finance capital: 'Neither people nor industrial corporations appeared as major multinational shareholders, underlining the importance of financial institutions as central organizations in the allocation and control of corporate capital.'[10] That a unified or coherent transnational capitalist class, one that acts with consciousness or agency, would seem to be (im)pending and being brought into existence by high finance or interest-bearing capital. The importance of finance capital to global production is discussed in the following section.

Within a general acknowledgement of the dynamic of capital, there are conflicts between transnational capitals, between rival TNCs and the elites who control and advise them. This has real and unintended effects at localised levels. Ley's analysis of wealthy migrants from East Asia to Canada highlights a more complex picture.[11] Those that attempt to settle or maintain transnational lives do not always fare well. Business failure, familial dislocation and the problems of recreating social class, poorly informed investment choices and neighbourhood dynamics all play a part in upsetting the 'cosmo-mobility' thesis concerning elites. In the case of business migrants settling Vancouver, Canada, where the state provided the initial opportunity for migration and investment, local community dynamics proved to be more complex between wealthy migrant and those communities 'receiving' them. In this scenario 'nation' rather than state apparently presents a divide or barrier for the globally mobile.[12] This by no means challenges the central idea of the mobility of global elites of the calibre that Sassen, Robinson, Carroll and others refer to. It does,

Global capital and its agents 77

however, raise issues about the politics of diversity in local contexts, such as established neighbourhoods, rather than in international hotel chains among high-density global cities – the geographic habitat of the mobile elite.

Global elites then are characterised by a certain sameness of culture related to their sameness of purpose. Farazmand highlights the point that there are strategic corporate elites and actual company elites, the former more like Hymer's view of elites as having a political leadership function over the economy, basically an eye on broader basis or rationale for systemic corporate profit.[13] There are also those who may be neither the 'captains' of an industry, but nevertheless influential in their circles of global finance and production. One example here serves to illustrate a profile of these 'lesser' elites and their agency. In discussion of growth in Asia Pacific economies, and whether there would be a peak in the 'boom' from that region's economies, a media report of the 1990s identifies one 'K.C. Lee, a fund manager at Fidelity Investments (Hong Kong) and one of the least gung ho' about the prospects of the economy. Lee, apparently identified for his relative influence and connection with global market dynamics reportedly speculates: 'I find it very difficult to argue against investment in these markets. Economic growth will still be higher than most markets and corporate earning's growth will be better'.[14] Whatever Lee's opinion, his position and occupation are the concern here. To provide a more relevant indicator, data sourced by Birrell et al. in 2004[15] gives detailed Australian migration figures for finance professionals. Between 2000 and 2003, for example, Australia extended skilled and business visas to 1,172 permanent or long-term-stay migrants classified as 'Financial Dealers and Brokers'. A further 722 arrived as business visitors (up to three months). Notably, there were also 1,410 residents departing from Australia under this occupational classification – highlighting a circulation of such professionals. Similarly, there were 557 'Financial Investment Advisers' arriving as permanent or long-term-stay migrants, and another 325 such business visitors. Inversely, 475 resident Financial Investment Advisers left Australia in this period.[16] In fact, there was as much circulation of such professionals by this time as there was their contribution as migrants to Australian production, finance and investment.

These figures on finance personnel exemplify growth in importance of a few specific occupations in Australia to the post-1970s global market economy milieu as described in Chapter 4. It is suggestive of an observed global trend of increases in professional occupations in former advanced industrial economies. According to IMF data, between 1980 and 2005 unskilled work declined by 15% in both Japan and the United States, and by 10% in Europe. This was matched by an absolute increase in skilled workers 'educated to tertiary level and above' in the order of 7% for the USA, 2% for Japan and 8% for Europe.[17]

78 *Global capital and its agents*

Migration and the agents of capital

The example of migrant financial advisers introduces the role of migration as part of the circulation and accumulation of capital globally. Where global corporate elites are considered to be able to move wherever and whenever they so choose, states, regions and even cities exert relative degrees of influence over the mobility of stratified agents of capital. For many corporate functionaries and smaller scale entrepreneurial advisers who are often located where required within affiliate branches of a transnational corporation, migration, residency and citizenship laws and policies have evolved to regulate their flow, and in some cases even contest their 'ownership' or national fealty. Mobility policies concerning economic productivity and market expansion can have very specific characteristics depending on geospatial and broad and historical economic position of a country within the global North-South bifurcation described in Chapter 4. In Australia, a specific and relatively unrestricted visa class solely for migrant corporate executives, for example, has existed at least since the 1980s. Productive Diversity, as will be shown later, was more significant as an ideological as well as practical intervention supporting the flow and attempted accumulation global market capitalism in Australia.

At the intersection of structure and agency, globalisation concerns the relative power of states and capital, working both together and separately at a systemic or macro level. The concept of the embeddedness of capital, noted in Chapter 4 explains the tension between the dynamic nature of capitalist accumulation and its conflictual relationship with extant social control. Harvey's analysis of neoliberalism as a feature of globality holds that governments work *for* corporate interests by accepting the rationality of the market. For the many entrepreneurs, market economy professionals and independently wealthy migrants and transnationals, arguably their degree of agency, and their degree of being 'owned' or accumulated by the states that attract or 'visa' them, is in some proportion to the extent of their economic or corporate integration and also their volume of personal and/or business capital. By this is meant that the wealthier elites are constructed or assumed to be more influential, have greater agency, greater fluidity and mobility. Bauder summarises this position but specifically in relation to migrant entrepreneurs:

> Immigrant groups that possess financial capital and credit worthiness may find entrepreneurship more attractive than less affluent groups. In this case, the entrepreneurial spirit displayed by some immigrant groups may be a response to local opportunity structures and other contextual and structural circumstances, rather than pre-migration habitus.[18]

It is not the intention of this book to test whether there is an exact or real ratio between wealth, employment sector and identity and agency of

Global capital and its agents 79

migrant entrepreneurs and skilled professionals. The intention of government policies and relationships with such types of occupations is the critical point of analysis. Migration and related population diversity patterns and policies are one useful approach to this, whereas simply referring to 'circulation' of occupational populations implies a complete absence of embeddedness, of contestation.

At this point, the immediate focus remains to explain the movement of certain occupations as a feature of contemporary global value chain processes and transnational production. The next section provides some compelling indicators of the circulation of migrant capitalists and market economy professionals in Australia, focusing on the last full two decades, 1990s-2000s. Later chapters will explain and contextualise policy developments in Australia in relation to a changing migrant occupational and demographic profile.

To put the figures noted above about finance professionals in Australia within a broader frame, the trend in migrant occupational categories entering Australia from the mid-1990s shows a definite bias towards professionals and business operatives – towards the 'non-productive' and market expanding occupational categories. Figure 5.1, drawn from a study by

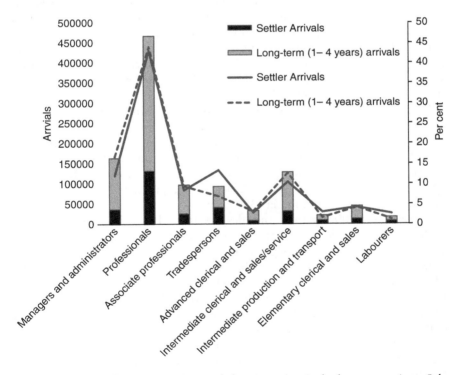

Figure 5.1 Australian permanent and long-term arrivals by occupation, July 1997–June 2004.[21]

80   Global capital and its agents

Hugo et al. and sourced from Australian immigration department data,[19] highlights the dominance of such non-productive labour, of managers and professionals; an average of around 60% in these classifications constituted permanent and long-term arrivals combined. Labourers and tradespersons combined represented only 16% of permanent and less than 10% of long-stay entrants under this scheme. Note, though,that clerical and service admin was significant but not as much as the professional categories.[20] *Productive labour* was clearly not as inwardly mobile or wanted by the Australian government. As later chapters detail, this was a significant turnaround in Australia's traditional migrant intake pattern towards unskilled labour.

Within the Managers and Administrators nomenclature, Generalist Managers, according to the Australia Standard Classification of Occupations definition include chief executive, directors-general, managing editor, medical superintendent (and even a trade union secretary); for example, in 2001–02, some 3,500 'computing professionals' and 1,000 accountants were visaed from on-shore.[22] These may fall into either labour or non-productive occupations. However, the broad nomenclature 'Managers' also included Importers, Exporters and Wholesalers, Construction and Manufacturing Managers, and Sales, Financial and Marketing Managers. A more detailed analysis affirming these assumptions about the Managers and Administrators and the Professionals categories can be found in Brownlee.[23]

In 1999–2000, midpoint of the table data, and four years after new business visitor migration classifications had been introduced, 35,006 long-stay business visas (visa 457) were granted. The strata of occupations for this cohort was as in Figure 5.2.

Hugo et al. identify the 'top five specific occupations' for this particular cohort: computing professionals (12.6%), self-employed (10.4%), general managers (8.3%), accountants (5.1%) and chefs (4.4%).[25] Highlighting a global dimension, nonetheless concentrated in the Anglophone Global North, the highest percentage of countries of origin are were UK (23%), USA (10%), India (8%), South Africa (7%), Japan (6%), China (4%), Canada, Ireland and Indonesia (3% each).

Beyond the 2005 period and despite the Global Financial Crisis of 2006–08, the prevalence of managers and professionals in the *long-stay* visa categories has continued to grow. In 2009–10, this group accounted for almost 91% of entrants to Australia; in 2010–11 they accounted for 80% of entrants. Across the period 2009–11, the sectors of employment for these managers and professionals were roughly equally dominated by Health Care and Social Assistance, the ambiguously titled 'Other Services', construction, and then Information, Media and Telecommunications.[26]

It should be noted that *short* (one week to three months) and long-stay visas, or 'business visitor' and 'business resident' categories under the temporary migration schemes Australia introduced in 1996 drew from wider areas than a separate *permanent* entrepreneur/business migration

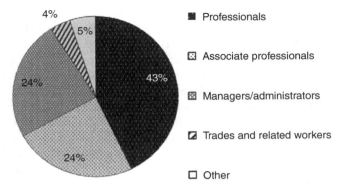

Figure 5.2 Long-stay business migrants 1999–2000, occupational strata %.[24]

programme in operation since the late 1970s. In 1999–2000, a total of 236,085 short-stay 'business visitor' visas were granted. Hugo et al.[27] used Labour Force Survey data of temporary business entrants to also note that by 2004 some 23% were in 'property and business services', concluding that this reflected the high number of managers and professionals recruited, The main countries of origin for these were: combined Asia, 35%, South Africa 19%, UK 14%, US 3%, and Germany, 3%.[28] Discussion on the salience of the Asian figures and the permanent business migrant programme ensues in later chapters.

This snapshot of figures gives an example of the circulation (not permanent relocation) of skilled professional and business migrants, acceding a key feature of globality: the mobility of capitalists and their 'lieutenants', supporting the main forms of transnational production especially global value chains. This is backed up by UNCTAD analysis of foreign affiliate offices of GVCs, the staffing of which is populated by a growing mobile elite. The UNCTAD report states that the 'presence of foreign affiliates is clearly an important factor influencing both imported contents in exports and participation in international production networks'.[29] These 'GVC outposts' through their personnel in 2012, for example, 'generated sales worth $26 trillion (of which $7.5 trillion were for exports), increasing by 7.4 per cent from 2011 and five times the sales figure of 1990'.[30] Foreign affiliate 'work' is implicated strongly in domestic and further international market expansion vital to the downstream flow and ultimate accumulation of profit for parent companies. A separate and abstract statistical regression study by Javorcik et al. found that the degrees of presence of migrant professional cohorts (college educated or above) in the US had a positive correlation with the magnitude of outward FDI to those migrants' home countries.[31] The suggestion was that networks of knowledge were the likely explanation for the correlation. If true, it would be logical to assume a

82 *Global capital and its agents*

certain number of those same migrant professionals in some way would be involved in facilitating the FDI outflow. That is, they are not simply stimulating circular consumer demand passively by their presence in the US.

Governments and other actors within certain limits and path dependencies can affect the economic and social terrain. Competition in a market economy can turn on specific knowledge and decisions or unpredictable events. Central to following chapters is the extent to which the state attempted and was able to accumulate such economic actors described in this chapter, mainly through migration and citizenship options. The economic value such migrants both brought in assets and were anticipated to create through knowledge of the global market by virtue of their ethnocultural heritage is at the centre of the tension between structure and agency. As will be argued, despite the façade of a claim to agency, Australian government business migration policies reinforced the global market structures notably the international division of labour and non-productive labour.

Migrant entrepreneurs and 'commodification'

The discussion thus far identifies the importance of 'professionals', of significant capitalist interests and their lieutenants commanding value through complex global chains. Toward the other end of the spectrum are independent professionals and small and medium enterprise (SME) entrepreneurs who migrated in numbers from various parts of the 'periphery' to countries such as Australia, Canada, the USA and New Zealand from the mid-1980s onwards.[32] The previous chapter noted that almost all business in Australia by 2001 were in the small category. The agency of small business owners and operators and their relationship to structure are characterised completely differently in the literature and in policy. The SME business people and entrepreneurs as a migrant group, tend to be ascribed a highly personalised agency. Interpretations are based largely upon constituent ethnicities as 'cultural capital' and their *predispositions* for 'hard work', or self-productivity and self-reliance as migrant minorities – a key point which will be elaborated in subsequent chapters. This is significant in Australia's case also for the fact that most of its business and entrepreneurial migrants were actively sought from a number of countries within Asia for a considerable period of time.

Australian government and business sector experiences seem to bear out theory constructions concerning elite migrant business-entrepreneurs and professionals as globally mobile and not able to be 'accumulated' in this era of transnational production. This applied equally to the Australian-born leaving Australia, highlighting circulation of these occupational groups as much as their settlement. Over the 7 years 1994 to 2000, for example, approximately 64% of the Australian-born total workforce for the period which migrated *permanently or long-term* to the USA and 50% who did the

Global capital and its agents 83

same to the UK, were managers and professionals. The actual numbers of managers and professionals who left for these two countries averaged 10,000 per annum.[33] The proportions of managers and professionals are even higher for the same category emigrating from Australia to Asian countries. Roughly three quarters Australian born emigrants were managers and administrators or professionals. States or governments may nonetheless try to 'own' their capitalist class.

Gilding points to a different line of thinking in his early analysis of wealthy migrant entrepreneurs in Australia as a form of 'new money' tilting at the establishment 'British money'.[34] Gilding's work conveys a sense that these migrant elites have some fealty to Australia, although this is not the point: rather, the Australian economy counts these migrant elites and entrepreneurs, as did the Australian *Business Review Monthly* (Gilding's key source of data for the study), by virtue of their citizenship, not necessarily by their sense of being wealthy national developers. Knowledge of where they pay their corporate tax and invest their capital is needed to understand 'fealty'. And as the previous chapter has shown, capital investment is increasingly global, dependent principally upon the rate of return not identity or belonging. Government bureaucracy planning and monitoring of permanent and then temporary business migration is discussed with this in mind in later chapters.

In the case of the SME migrant group (*i.e.* other than capitalist elites and global corporate professionals), issues of national allegiances of capital are largely silent in the literature.[35] The assumption tends to be that migrants in the small business sector aim to integrate into the host society, save for historically racialised economic barriers to equal participation that might prevail. Castells' understandings of growth in professional outsourced service industries, new models of management with small and spin off companies, and Sassen's concept of the professional services that spring up to serve global corporations and their elites argue this represents a fluidness and de-territorialisation.[36] This is not necessarily an advancement of agency for these economic groups.

At local levels, or at the SME level the relationship between agency, capital assets and influence is less certain. 'Ethnic entrepreneurs' are construed in the literature and policy as hard-working and self-reliant but more dependent upon or affected by micro policies and practices of the nation and state. They both have agency and are path dependent, conceptualised in their ability to enact 'ethnic breakout' or moving away from supply of goods and services for their own mostly migrant communities.[37] In fact, many such SME entrepreneurs historically are forced in to self-reliance and ultimately self-exploitation because of labour market barriers. Rath and Kloosterman found that migrant enterprises are typically (in the Global North) at the bottom of the market structure, in part due to having lower finance capital and local market opportunity knowledge.[38] Other literature identifies policy-related barriers faced by the small business entrepreneur-immigrant servicing

84 *Global capital and its agents*

the global city dynamic,[39] and; the small business mixed embeddedness argument of Kloosterman et al., which identifies 'the intricate interplay between socioeconomic and ethnosocial characteristics of the group in question and the opportunity structure – which in itself is primarily a function of the state of technology, the costs of production factors ... and the institutional framework'.[40] The idea of mixed embeddedness is an enduring one: ever since Waldinger et al., 1990, which presented a similar dichotomy of structure and agency in relation to migrant entrepreneurship much scholarship continues to explain the barriers facing migrant entrepreneurs mainly in localised contexts.[41]

Cognitive approaches to migrant entrepreneurs' motivation as a form of agency are a distinct line of inquiry not covered in detail here. It is worth noting that measuring behaviour and its connection to specific ethno-cultural traits is contested in the literature.[42] Such research is criticised for its essentialist view of cultural and psycho-social factors as derived from ethnicity. 'Human' and 'cultural' capitals are some of the most difficult concepts to specify from this line of inquiry.

Indications of SME growth in the 1980s, particularly from the USA, showed that migrant and minority business activity was emerging as a viable jobs and growth generator.[43] Self employment among ethnic minorities assumed greater significance worldwide in both policy and research circles from the 1980s,[44] as post-1970s restructuring of the national and the global economy began to take shape, alongside increasing numbers of migrants and refugees worldwide.[45] Castles and Collins observed much the same for the EU and Australia.[46] Strahan and Williams claimed that ethnic minorities were a significant part of SME growth in Australia in the 1980s for reasons of industrial restructuring, which affected the non-migrant and typically Anglo-Celtic population differently.[47]

Prior to changes in Australia's postwar industrial economy in concordance with the features of globalisation outlined in Chapter 4, SME entrepreneurial activity by migrants in countries such as Australia was limited by market opportunity as much as the relative abundance of unskilled industrial and manual labour work. Another argument suggests the pursuit of international trade (whether importing or exporting) in the 1970s was in relative terms considered costly business in Australia, bound as it was by limited business-level infrastructure to overcome distance and time, and tariff arrangements.[48] However, the lack of impetus for bulk trade in anything other than a few primary goods and the historical trade dependencies upon the UK were the more salient factors in Australia's narrow breadth of SME goods and services export trade. Establishing ethnic-oriented businesses likewise provided limited market opportunity within a regime that was dominated largely by Anglo-Celtic cultural parameters.[49] What is evident in the broader discourse concerning Australia detailed in later chapters is a conflation or blurring of boundaries between labour and small and medium enterprise: ownership is a substitute for operating;

Global capital and its agents 85

self-employment in other words. And so, ideas of productivity that are ascribed to all skilled and SME migrants under the Australian government's policy rubric of Productive Diversity can mean many things.

Taksa and Groutsis focus on skilled migrants' contributions to business activity but still as 'employees', and argue that Australian government policy took a very narrow view of skilled migrant agency just as it had migrant labourers:

> In this regard we refer to the rhetoric used to describe migrants who came to Australia in the decades after World War Two as 'factory fodder' and the more recent rhetoric associated with Diversity Management (DM), which construes those migrant employees who possess cultural knowledge and multilingual skills as 'business assets'. Both representations, we argue, treat migrants as commodities. By foregrounding their labour power or knowledge or skills, both render invisible the bearers of these attributes and in doing so also deny their agency.[50]

The argument above might be interpreted that migrant minority labour (skilled or unskilled) is a commodity, but non-migrant labour is not. That presumably is not the intention of the authors. To apply the argument of Taksa and Groutsis that the significant numbers of 'ethnic' business migrants and market economy professionals entering Australia are 'commodities' poses problems for their agency as a social concern *because* it poses a problem in consistency in a theory of value. Commodification is, after all, part of a Marxist conceptualisation of value creation. Insofar as specific (embodied) skills might be considered *commodities*, they must be made of some labour and have an anticipated market to be exchangeable for something. If such 'human' or 'cultural' capital is not itself made of appropriated labour the question arises as to how an exchange value is derived; therefore, how their valorisation as commodities can be reliable or predictable.[51] The measure of valorisation highlights the fundamental determinant of labour's value as in its cost of daily reproduction; ultimately that it is time and effort (labouring), not skill which is appropriated for actual value.[52] Skill and education are important features in reckoning the contest between capital and labour over the share of value – the social processes of education in themselves conditioning the capacity and expectations of highly educated labour to envisage their material needs commensurably with their overlords.

An argument consistent with this chapter would view business migrants and entrepreneurs, highly skilled salaried and market economy professionals within or rather on one side of a transnational division between (productive) labour and non-productive occupations: *non-productive labour* being far more useful in expanding capital by sourcing and putting productive labour to task for maximum value, especially in the global

86 *Global capital and its agents*

'periphery' where it continually resides in abundance, and; by pursuing the various value-expanding and value appropriation strategies mostly from within the 'core', aiding interest bearing capital, foreign direct investment, intellectual property creation and control, etc.

If the role of entrepreneurs and market professionals supporting or advancing the interests of corporate transnational production and financialisation is essentially about replicating competitive market relations, and certainly not about their role as labour, their social agency is predetermined fundamentally in other ways: they are 'economic citizens' of a global market so long as they help construct the social milieu in the economic terms. Whether they act as a 'class' is a moot point as capital is driven by competition between such actors.

The distinction regarding commodification that needs to be emphasised here is that between labour and non-productive labour and the boundaries of economic life. By this is inferred that productive labour has boundaries and limits on its daily use, contested as these boundaries are. For migrant and ethnoculturally diverse populations, the contest can be partly over the extent to which ethnoculture is separated between economic and social and cultural spheres (although racism as a main challenge may be experienced equally in all aspects of life). This serves a proxy for the competitive dynamic of capitalism – that is, human activity for the expansion of capital can be constant where all social relations are marketised. This is the essence of Hayekian neoliberalism. For those engaged in business and market-expanding activities, this might appear more problematic where competition over market share and accumulation of wealth is not organised or delimited as labour traditionally has been. Capital does not seek to rest! Its circulation is vital to its expansion. The porous borders of the global market economy facilities constant exchange over time and space. This however draws on the argument presented earlier about the extent of embeddedness of capital for both labour and for non-productive and market expanding occupations.

Conclusion

The discussion in this chapter reinforces an assumption that a corresponding rise in the importance of non-productive occupations are vital to the accumulation of wealth in a global market economy characterised particularly by global value chains. There are differing components or strata of occupational forms, and these individuals act as agents of global capital within their spheres of operation and that this frames their agency.

Discussion of global capital typically focuses upon elites for the relative political and economic influence of their decision-making roles. However, as the chapter explains, there are sub-strata of global market agents and global value chain functionaries (in small scale industries and large) who

Global capital and its agents 87

have grown in number in certain countries and at the expense of labour – a point demonstrated by occupation trends in migrant intakes in Australia. This, however, only reinforces arguments of previous chapters that labour is further marginalised and co-located with mass production where it is least cost, typically in the periphery. The growth or dominance in migration patterns of managers and administrators, and the specific occupations of financial advisers, are telling of Australia's efforts to engage a certain global production hierarchy. Defining post-1970s deindustrialisation in advanced economies is helped by considering the growth phenomenon of non-productive, global market economy-oriented occupations. The relative share of capital in wages they gain over labour as reported in Chapter 4 is salient here too as it positions corporate 'lieutenants', market operatives and entrepreneurs as more desirable for governments and nation-states tending their workforces. The relative growth in numbers of this set of occupations in advanced postindustrial economies, including Australia, is often overlooked as a deliberate strategy; as revealed later in this book, on the eve of globalisation those representing capital had lamented and cautioned Government that Australia lacked globally effective entrepreneurs and CEOs.

For smaller business migrant types, and for many corporate functionaries who follow the mobility of global capital, government policy and other locational and situational factors intersect or have more impact. Migration policies of nation-states are specific instruments of control in this respect. The phenomenon of small business 'ethnic' entrepreneurs highlighted their opportunity as subject to a range of constraints because they are migrants, economically and socially vulnerable. It is their sense of agency typically (mis)understood as ethnocultural capital as discussed in detail in Chapter 3, which is the point where governments and policies have come to operate to facilitate or restrict ethnic SME entrepreneurs.

This however raises the point about agency and governments *vis-à-vis* migration policy. In all cases, the analysis of agency is that it is conditional and challenged by path dependent opportunities. Local policy contexts affect migrants involved in business but they are still subject to the over-arching demands of global competitive accumulation. It is apparent from the discussion that the global market economy dominated by global value chain systems has both generic, and at the country level, unique social relations of production. For Australia, successive governments aspired to participate in this economy as a higher value adding country. Non-productive labour migration, entrepreneurs and business migrants were important to this goal.

Policies supporting the migration of non-productive labour, business and entrepreneurial occupations as a feature of post-1970s global change are now positioned for deeper analysis. The rationale is that migration supporting global value chains and small and medium enterprise (SME), was viewed by government and capitalist interests as part of a wider strategy of

88 *Global capital and its agents*

postindustrial growth open to advanced economies of the Global North. As a concern of political economy, the broad field of transnational production and global value chains encompasses both the distribution of wealth and a consideration of the allocation of resources, in this case, skilled professional and entrepreneurial migrants as features in the international division of labour. Australia provides a case for understanding the political economy of migration as it changed in line with global economic developments post-1970s. This is the subject of the remainder of the book.

Notes

1 Adam Smith, *Wealth of Nations*, cited in Robinson, W.I. (2004) *A Theory of Global Capitalism: Production, Class, and State in a Transnational World*, Baltimore, MD: Johns Hopkins University Press, p. 33.
2 The General Agreement on Tariffs and Trade; North American Free Trade Agreement, Brazil, Russian Federation, India, China and South Africa bloc, Asia Pacific Economic Cooperation.
3 Farazmand, A. (1999), p. 322.
4 Smith et al. (2002), p. 54.
5 Ibid. (italics in original).
6 Stephen Hymer, quoted and paraphrased in Carroll, W., 'Whither the transnational capitalist class?' in Panitch, L., Albo, G. and Chibber, V. (eds) (2014) *Socialist Register 2014: Registering Class*, Vol. 50, p. 164.
7 Ibid.
8 Robinson, W.I. (2010) 'Beyond the Theory of Imperialism: Global Capitalism and the Transnational State', in Anievas, A. (ed.) *Marxism and World Politics: Contesting Global Capitalism*, Abingdon, Oxon and New York: Routledge, p. 63, http://www.soc.ucsb.edu/faculty/robinson/Assets/pdf/Beyond.pdf (accessed 28 July 2013).
9 Carroll, W. (2014).
10 Ibid., p. 178.
11 Ley, D. (2010) *Millionaire Migrants: Trans-Pacific Life Lines*, Malden, MA: Wiley-Blackwell.
12 I accept Robinson's critique on the reification of categories. To this point the concepts of nation and state, and nation-state, are used here as proxies for the classes and actors that contribute to their conflicted existence. Nation and state are not *a priori* categories but a historical site of class relations. It is migration that has challenged this binary of nation-state just as has the free flow of capital investment and the emergence of transnational corporations. I make a further point in agreement on the aspect of agency below.
13 Farazmand, A. (1999), esp. p. 326.
14 Bruce, R. (1993) 'The Asian Boom: Too Much Optimism?' *International Herald Tribune, MONEY REPORT*, 29 May. Copy downloaded via University of Sydney Library 'factiva' portal. Syndicated and also available online at New York Times, http://www.nytimes.com/1993/05/29/your-money/29iht-mrea.html (accessed 17 February 2014).
15 Birrell, B., Rapson, V., Dobson, I.R. and Smith, T.F. (2004) *Skilled Movement in the New Century: Outcomes for Australia*, Canberra: Department of Immigration, Multicultural and Indigenous Affairs (DIMIA). Consistent Australian migration statistics broken down to actual occupation are difficult to obtain. This report provides a detailed appendix with DIMIA data generally not

available publically. Most migrant occupational data are aggregated at level of 'professional', 'managers and administrators' and the like, but with more detailed descriptors for each classification.

16 Ibid., see pp. 91–92. DIMIA classifications equate these occupations' professional level with 'Associate Professor', in terms of expertise. It does not refer to academics. Nevertheless, business visas do include academics.

17 ILO (2013), p. 43.

18 Bauder, H. (2008) 'Explaining Attitudes Towards Self-employment Among Immigrants: A Canadian Case Study', *International Migration*, Vol. 46, No. 2, p. 112.

19 Hugo, G. (2006) 'Temporary Migration and the Labour Market in Australia', *Australian Geographer*, Vol. 37, No. 2, p. 219, Table 4. See also Hugo, G., Rudd, D. Harris, K. (2001) *Emigration from Australia: Economic Implications*, Melbourne: CEDA.

20 Service industries span both productive and non-productive labour but largely grew within the market economy context. Castells suggests it was because of the technological reorganisation of work (networked information flows), and not the market *per se* that services have grown so rapidly since the 1970s.

21 Adapted from figures provided in Hugo, G. (2006), p. 219, Table 4.

22 Birrell, B. et al. (2004); see Table 3, p. 6. The authors note that there were very few skilled occupational categories allowable as 'on-shore' applicants. The figures are thus included here as a gross indicator, not for comparative purposes.

23 Brownlee, P. (2016).

24 Adapted from figures in Hugo, G. et al. (2001), p. 51.

25 Ibid., pp. 51–52.

26 DIAC (2012) *Subclass 457 State/Territory summary report: 2010–11 to 30 June 2011*, n.p Canberra: Commonwealth of Australia, p. 7.

27 Hugo, G. (2006), p. 220.

28 Hugo, G., et al. (2001), p. 52. The South Africa figures ebb into further into the first decade of the 2000s, reflecting 'capital flight' by non-Blacks from post-apartheid South Africa. See also Hugo, G. (2006).

29 UNCTAD (2013), p. xv.

30 Ibid., p. xvi, see Table 2. NB: All figures are in current prices.

31 Javorcik, B., Ozden, C., Spatareanu, M. and Neagu, C. (2011) 'Migrant Networks and Foreign Direct Investment', *Journal of Development Economics*, Vol. 94, pp. 231–41.

32 I use the abbreviated term SME as a generic one to capture a range, but without a specific industry form. Australian government records drawn upon throughout the book variously consider SME to be anywhere from 1–20 to 50 employees, but also gradients of annual financial turnover, e.g. < $1million; $1–5 million, etc. See Trewin, D. and Australian Bureau of Statistics (2001) *Small Business in Australia, ABS Catalogue No. 1321.0*, Canberra: Commonwealth of Australia.

33 Hugo, G. et al. (2001), p. 48.

34 Gilding, M. (1999) 'Superwealth in Australia: Entrepreneurs, Accumulation and the Capitalist Class', *Journal of Sociology*, Vol. 35, No. 2, August, pp. 169–82. See also Murray, G. 'Australia's Ruling Class: A Local Elite, a Transnational Capitalist Class or Bits of Both?' in Murray, G. and Scott, J. (eds) (2012), for more recent discussion of local and global Australian capitalist elites.

35 Other than say the issue of remittances which might suggest issues of fealty, but also of assisting further migration.

36 Castells, M. (2000a); Hardt, M. and Negri, A. (2000).

37 Lassalle, P. and Scott, J.M. (2018).

38 Kloosterman, R., Van Der Lun, J. and Rath, J., (1998) 'Across the Border:

90 *Global capital and its agents*

Immigrants' Economic Opportunities, Social Capital and Informal Business Activities', *Journal of Ethnic and Migration Studies*, Vol. 24, No. 2, pp. 249–68.

39 Collins, J. (2003a) 'Cultural Diversity and Entrepreneurship: Policy Responses to Immigrant Entrepreneurs in Australia', *Entrepreneurship and Regional Development*, Vol. 15, No. 2, April–June, pp. 137–49.

40 Kloosterman, R., Van Der Lun, J. and Rath, J. (1999) 'Mixed Embeddedness: (In)formal Economic Activities and Immigrant Businesses in the Netherlands', *International Journal of Urban & Regional Research* Vol. 23, No. 2, p. 253. For more on immigrant entrepreneurship following the mixed embeddedness framework, see also Rath, J. 'Introduction: Immigrant Businesses and Their Economic, Politico-Institutional and Social Environment', in Rath, J. (ed.) (2000) *Immigrant Businesses: The Economic, Political and Social Environment*, Basingstoke and New York: Palgrave.

41 Ram, M., Jones, T. and Villares-Varela (2016) 'Migrant Entrepreneurship: Reflections on Research Practice', *International Small Business Journal: Researching Entrepreneurship*; Vol. 35, No. 1, pp. 3–18. DOI:10.1177/ 0266242616678051. Also Waldinger, R., Aldrich, H. and Ward, R. (eds) (1990) *Ethnic Entrepreneurs: Immigrant Business in Industrial Societies*, London: Newbury Park.

42 Wennekers, S. and Thurik, R. (1999) 'Linking Entrepreneurship and Economic Growth', *Small Business Economics* Vol. 13, p. 47; see also Rath, J. in Rath, J. (ed.) (2000).

43 Pages, E.R., Freedman, D. and Von Bargan, P. 'Entrepreneurship as a State and Local economic Development Strategy', in Hart, D.M. (2003) (ed.) *The Emergence of Entrepreneurship Policy*, Cambridge: Cambridge University Press.

44 Ibrahim, G. and Galt, G. (2003) 'Ethnic Business Development: Towards a Theoretical Synthesis and Policy Framework', *Journal of Economic Issues*, Vol. 37, No. 4, December. pp.1107–19.

45 UN figures of an aggregate increase from 75 million people migrations in 1960 to 200 million by 200, as cited by Docquier, F. and Lodigiani, E. (2010) 'Skilled Migration and Business Networks', *Open Economic Review*, No. 21, see p. 566; see also Castles, S., De Haas, D. and Miller, M.J. (2014).

46 Castles, S. and Collins, J., 'Restructuring, Migrant Labour markets and Small Business', in Cope, B. (ed.) (1992) *Policy into Practice: Essays on Multiculturalism and Cultural Diversity in Australia*, Paper No. 20, Wollongong: Centre for Multicultural Studies, University of Wollongong.

47 Strahan, K. and Williams, A. (1988) *Immigrant Entrepreneurs in Australia*, Canberra: Office of Multicultural Affairs. Department of the Prime Minister and Cabinet.

48 Adams, M., Brown, N. and Wickes, R. (2014) *Trading Nation: Advancing Australia's Interests in World Markets*, Sydney: NewSouth Books.

49 Collins, J. et al. (1995).

50 Taksa, L. and Groutsis, D. (2010), p. 78. This interpretation is close to one argument in this book but with an important distinction about business and entrepreneurial activity and its relationship to value.

51 Klaus Offe (c.1976) is credited for a related argument about the impossibility of calculating a true market price for labour because production is so complex and incomparable at the margins. A copy of this work is unavailable and thus citation not supplied.

52 Marx, K. (1986 [1959]).

6 The nation on the eve of globalisation

Australia's general Keynesian policy worldview up to the 1970s had identified migrants as good for the industrious postwar nation-building project. In 1966, Government Senator John Marriott, speaking about dual citizenship proposed in a Bill before Parliament, reflected unequivocally: 'Where would our Snowy Mountains scheme, the Tasmanian hydro-electric schemes, the rail standardisation work, and our bridge and road construction work be if it had not been for the work that the migrants have done?'[1]

Estimates of labour demand suggest that more than 50% of all *jobs* in the postwar decades were unskilled, with migrants destined to meet this demand.[2] Postwar migrants were expected and for a period originally indentured to take up those jobs not favoured by the 'non-migrant' population.[3] Although by the early 1960s, the Conservative Liberal government claimed 'while every facility is given to migrants to assist them in finding suitable employment, no migrant is "directed" to employment'.[4] In other words, migrants supposedly had choice in their employment options where 'particular occupation[s] in which they are seeking employment, their occupational skills and experience, their knowledge of English, their mobility and the availability of accommodation in relation to the size of their families' were considerations.[5] The occupational profile of the industrial labour force belied this portrayal of hiring processes; migrants consistently ended up in the lower segment of the workforce.

Postwar demand for migrants was fundamentally based on an issue of labour quantity over quality. However, it would be erroneous to see migrants as *only* a 'reserve army' or in their entirety as an expendable, supplementary unskilled labour force.[6] The Prime Minister, in 1963, made clear the interest in seeking skills from among the migrant intake, and that Australia's economy in the early 1960s clearly was not training enough of its own native-born:

> As a result of the talks that I had with the Maltese Minister about the quality of the Maltese migrants who are available and especially the possibilities of our being able to obtain more skilled workers from Malta – we badly need skilled workers in this country – I was able to

92 *The nation on the eve of globalisation*

arrange with him for an extra 1,000 assisted Maltese migrants to come to Australia in this financial year.[7]

Scholars have explained that migrants traditionally were viewed as a supplementary labour force, largely because their skills were poorly recognised and their vulnerability meant they would follow available job prospects that Australians rejected or deemed inferior.[8] Exploited they were! However, postwar migrants were recruited as frontline industrial workers essential to rapid industrial growth. They were not a reserve, nor did their numbers create one among non-migrants. The skill quality of their work may have been deemed a subordinate concern but low unemployment figures over the first 15 years after the Second World War suggest labour demand not an oversupply. The fact that permanent residency and eventually citizenship were bestowed on willing migrants suggests not a contradiction in logic[9] but an acknowledgement that migrants were not *labour* supplements, despite the fact that their skills were typically not recognised. Only in the period of Australia's second major economic transformation towards a 'postindustrial' market-based economy from the mid- to late 1980s did productive *labour* (migrant or otherwise) become increasingly supplementary.

Figures for the postwar period do suggest there was a typically stratified set of occupations that migrants might have expected to be employed in. What is very clear is the ethnic and racial divide. The figures for the year prior, 1962, highlight that despite the overwhelming majority of migrants coming from the UK and Eire – more than four times any other country – there were more labourers coming from Italy (2,776) than the UK (1,249), more farmers coming from Greece (1,184) than the UK (1,107), and more protective services (including military), sports and recreation skilled migrants from both Greece (4,387) and Italy (2,780) than from the UK (2,366).[10] Where the UK contributed more workers overwhelmingly were in professional, technical, clerical, management and sales occupations.

Australia's Assisted Passage Scheme, or subsidy paid by the Australian government to attract migrants, only reinforces these figures. Assisted passage only very rarely helped Italian or Greeks arrive in any of these white-collar occupations. Conversely, well over one-third of all UK and Eire clerical arrivals were recruited in the year 1962; and one quarter of all UK and Eire professional, technical and related arrivals were recruited.[12] While not all migrants worked in their preferred occupation, the assisted passage scheme clearly sought skill to meet perceived demand. Overall, there were clear ethnocultural preferences for job segments among those approved for entry to Australia, and arguments that a path dependency prevailed[13] would seem sustainable. These ethnocultural patterns would turn upside down in the postindustrial period.

Following recessions in the 1970s and early 1980s, parcelled with the growing relocation of manufacturing and industrial output from high- to low-wage economies (i.e the New International Division of Labour), Australia, like its counterpart Western capitalist economies of the UK,

Germany, France, the USA and Canada, re-tooled its migration programme, scrutinising and demanding certain skills and productive qualities from an increasing proportion of their annual migrant intake. For instance, where in 1980–83, permanent arrivals of (skilled) Metal Trades workers averaged 4,300 per annum, between 1983 and 1986, it averaged 1,000; migrant electrical and buildings trades workers saw a similar rapid decline.[14]

Data on migrant skill levels from the mid-1980s to the end of the Keating Labor Government, meanwhile, suggests that skill was also the focus of recruitment across *non-skilled* visa streams. In other words, family reunion and family related migration also required of migrants a skill level. An eventual rise in skilled immigrants, from around 46% in 1988 to a peak of almost 75% by 1992, is telling. Notably, it was far above the skill levels of the Australian-born, consistent throughout the Labor Government period at around 45%.[15]

Australia's Numerical Multi-factor Assessment System (NUMAS), a points-based assessment of migrant capability introduced as early as 1979, included occupational skills and language ability as weighted criteria for gaining a visa.[16] This is not to say that *only* skilled migrants were henceforth selected, or that unskilled work disappeared from postindustrial economies. Low-skilled, undesirable or otherwise difficult and repetitive labour did not disappear or relocate *in toto* with the New International Division of Labour; industrially developed countries were just as likely to continue to employ vulnerable migrants in services and remaining manufacturing industries.[17] Labourers and related workers in 1991–92, for example, still made up 5.2% of permanent workforce arrivals, and 3.5 % of long-term workforce arrivals; sales and 'personal service workers' 7% and 7.8% respectively.[18] By 1995, the category 'Labourers' and related workers were down slightly to 4.9 %.[19]

By and large, labourers were mostly males. While gendered divisions of labour and productivity are not the focus of this analysis, an addendum to the statistics here highlights a significant increase in female migrants as workers: Between 1980 and mid-1986, the percentage of women workers was 32% of total workforce permanent arrivals. By the biennium 1994–96, women were 47% of the total workforce permanent intake.[20] The gender profile also changed for non-productive occupations: the first half of the 1980s saw only 16% of women in 'business and commerce'; a figure that changed significantly by the mid-1980s.[21] Further research on women and globally oriented professionals and entrepreneurs' migration to Australia is needed.

While this data indicates a trend in Australian postindustrial restructuring, there is also significance for understanding a relationship between occupational forms and ethnoculture relative to Australia's productive forces. The source countries for the growth in white-collar skilled and professional occupations and business people are significantly different between the pre- and post-1970s periods (cf. Table 6.1). In terms of ethnocultural segmentation, the UK dries up as the wellspring of managers and financial brokers and

94 *The nation on the eve of globalisation*

Table 6.1 Percentage proportion of professional, management and administration (white collar) migrant arrivals by key source countries – 1962[11]

	UK	US	Italy	Greece	Germany	Netherlands
Professional, technical & related	88.8	5.3	0.9	1.0	1.8	2.3
Administrative, executive & managerial	79.9	8.2	1.8	4.8	2.5	2.8
Clerical	91.8	1.5	0.8	1.1	2.7	2.0
Sales	86.1	86.1	0.9	1.7	3.1	3.2

marketers as it had been in the early 1960s. New migrations particularly from Asia in the 1980s, and described in later chapters, however, were not seamlessly woven into the prevailing national mythology of postwar nation building because of concurrent deindustrialisation in line with the emerging globalised economy. Sizeable layoffs at steel mills and coal mines, an emphasis on new labour-saving technologies, small and medium enterprise growth including outsourcing, etc. all bear upon diversity policy making.[24] For a brief period from the early 1970s to the early 1980s, the twilight of industrial labour migration from Europe, Australia's diverse population does come to be celebrated for their contribution to Australian economic development.

Multiculturalism: recognition of migrant Australia

Many observers have cited the August 1973 speech by the then Labor Party Minister for Ethnic Affairs, Al Grassby, as the birth of multiculturalism in Australia, when he declared 'each ethnic group desiring it, is permitted to create its own communal life and preserve its own cultural heritage indefinitely, while taking part in the general life of the nation'.[25] This was a major statement although in reality Grassby was speaking to his 'family of the nation'[26] – essentially to those who had settled, assimilated or were, as Stratton argues, morally similar 'marginal whites'.[27] Multiculturalism at this time was largely – and for good reason – an ideology of anti-racism and group welfare rights, emanating from the work of key activists engaged in progressive social movements in the late 1960s and Labor Party politics into the 1970s.[28] Exploitation of migrant labour in particular was being challenged at a structural level, notably with significant trade union support.[29]

Immigration departmental policy on immigrant selection was still largely racist and kept the bar higher for the small number of migrants coming from less 'familiar' origins such as Asia. The Labor Party (itself), prior to its election in December 1972 made public contradictory statements itself on matters of race and immigration.[30] For instance, from official records of J. H. Paddick, then Immigration Attaché to Africa in 1972, Neuman explains in a footnote one cause for Australia's failure to accept Indians about

Table 6.2 Labourers as of total workforce intake – permanent arrivals, 1980–96[22]

	1980–83[23]	1983–86	1990–91	1991–92	1992–93	1993–94	1994–95	1995–96
Labourers/ unskilled	21630	12880	3192	2336	1974	1801	2081	2094
Total workforce	135420	98250	50119	44706	33319	29857	37925	42585
Labourers %	**16.0**	**13.1**	**6.4**	**5.2**	**5.9**	**6.0**	**5.5**	**4.9**

to be expelled from Uganda: 'Most of those discouraged from applying [for a visa to Australia] probably never got past Paddick's typist, who was his "door-keeper" and "screener" in the High Commission in Nairobi and accompanied him to Kampala'.[31] Grassby was aware of resistance within the Ethnic Affairs bureaucracy and their sense of propriety over immigrant selection policy based upon assimilationist ideals.[32] What is acutely evident is that the ability to select was still very much the preserve of the bureaucracy, and that Australia was under no compunction to source anything from Asian migrants except in-demand specialist skills.[33] As George Papadopoulos, a Greek community leader during the Fraser years, recounted some time later:

> Whitlam himself and Grassby created that environment of the legitimacy of ethnic affairs in the governmental area. That was resisted by the bureaucracy to a greater extent than what people realised.[34]

Grassby set about to change the racist practices of the immigration bureau, and in fact Immigration was abolished as a separate ministry. Nevertheless, as Lopez points out the 1975 Racial Discrimination Act was in effect the first legislation that properly reflected or related to multiculturalism as a form of equal rights.[35] Grassby had lost his position in Government by this time. Grassby's 'multiculturalism speech' in 1973 was not a policy speech introducing legislation, it was an invited address at a function, and was written independently by his Departmental staff in consultation with at least one migrant welfare activist. The point is that cultural diversity in Australia in 1973 was still highly 'protected' and regulated, not unlike the country's economy. The market-oriented economic shifts beginning to develop at this time would also rapidly move multiculturalism beyond ameliorative social justice within Anglo-Celtic group hegemony. Nascent developments in multicultural policy included mother-tongue language maintenance support,[36] through community grants and media broadcasting, for example. This was an important acknowledgement in recognising intrinsic features of ethnicity. However, language diversity that materialised with structural economic change in the next decade also came to serve a policy direction toward the 'preferred economic characteristics of migrants' as Inglis[37] terms it.

96 *The nation on the eve of globalisation*

Despite a growing interest in migrant welfare, the abolition in 1972 of the racially selective White Australia Policy (officially, the Immigration Act of 1901), and the afterglow of the broader civil rights campaigns, the *nation* was not suffering an identity crisis of 'whiteness'[38] in 1973. The *state* on the other hand was about to be buffeted by the trade winds of global change. Prime Minister Whitlam had been moving towards a more global concept of foreign relations, or at least independence from the UK, advocating an anti-protectionism line within the Labor party well before his election in December 1972.[39] However, the Labor Party didn't go to the polls with such a message, with some of Whitlam's pre-election statements in Parliament confirming that the Labor Party wasn't quite ready to embrace the free market globalisation it would facilitate around a decade later. Arguing against the growth in foreign capital finance, particularly for infrastructure development, Whitlam warned in a lengthy speech that 'Australia is a colony no longer, but more than ever before in her history she has become a tributary state'.[40]

The significance of Whitlam's economic policy for Australia's nation-hood is in the acknowledgement that the country was not able to compete with the emerging manufacturing capacities in other countries, while its traditional dependence upon the UK had been shaken by the Oil Crisis of October 1973 and ensuing global recession among other things, pointing to the need for Australia to develop greater self-reliance in its ability to export from its manufacturing base and fund its own infrastructure. Note that Australian merchandise exports as a percentage of GDP managed to account for 9.5% of GDP in 1973, having grown less than 2% since 1950.[41] In spite of a period of major postwar industrialisation the Australian economy relied only a narrow base of commodities for export income. Australia's large primary industry sector was declining also in its returns – in 1958–59, wool accounted for a massive 40% of Australia's export dollars; in 1966–67 it was 27%. Compounding dependence on this single industry were less reliable commodity prices, with 1970–71 a particularly bad year, as the price for wool dropped dramatically.[42] According to a NSW Department of Decentralisation and Development report at the time, 'competition from man-made fibres' but from especially overseas production was a chief cause.[43] In other words, imports of manufactured clothing was assuming greater market share, but as has been stated, Australia's manufacturing was heavily protected leading to inflated prices and a sector that was not competitively export-oriented. One example highlights how overseas capital also took advantage of Australia's protection system: 'Fairchild and National Semi-Conductor, two of the "Silicon Valley" giants, both set up small facilities in Victoria for making components in the 1960s; both were closed after the 25% tariff cuts of 1973'.[44] Chapter 2 noted how transnational capital seeks low-cost labour; the example here also demonstrates the imperative of transnational capital to seek economic advantage in whatever form available. Barry Jones, a Labor Party Senator, delivered a speech on the importance of the challenge of technological change to a Party meeting in 1981. Jones reflected on a number of examples where Australia had failed to capitalise on its initial manufacturing successes, surrendering ownership or investment in major manufacturing areas such as car manufacturing and computer research and development.[45]

Meanwhile, base commodities such as ores and metals were only as stable as the international economy – by the time of the second global oil crisis of 1978–79, reliance on raw commodities highlighted major vulnerabilities for Australia as a second recession affected the whole ASEAN (South East Asian) region.[46] Given its small population base, the essence of Australia's economic growth challenge in the mid-1970s was in its ability to carve a niche for itself as global production and trade started to become more mobile (transport being a significant sector), the recession effects of the Oil Crisis and the New International Division of Labour (NIDL), changing geopolitics with America's defeat in Vietnam, the emergence of the European Economic Community and Britain's economic realignment away from its former colony, all impacted. Amid this tectonic realignment of the global economic and political mantle, Asia's observable growth in manufactures was compelling Australia to re-orient its export, investment and consumption patterns. David and Wheelwright compared the share of manufacturing in GDP across the countries of region: Between 1965 and 1985, while Australia experienced a decline of 39% on this measure, Japan's decline was only 6%, while Korea, Taiwan, Singapore, Malaysia and Indonesia, among others, all saw *increases* in manufacturing as a share of their GDP of between 47% and 111%[47] (additional growth figures are discussed later in this chapter). US and UK businesses continued to invest strongly in Australia but the example of Japanese investment in 1972 in the heavy industry sector was portentous. A a major contract for a gas pipeline from South Australia to NSW was awarded to a Japanese company in that year, which in turn prompted Whitlam (as Labor Opposition leader and campaigning for the Prime Ministership) to call for the development of an Australian Industry Development Commission.[48]

What this period foreshadows is the macroeconomic challenge globalisation was to pose for successive Australian governments of forging and sustaining economic independence and competitiveness within a globalising capitalism. Regulation on foreign ownership of productive capacity and resources was still within the legal and political means of the Australian government. The Japanese pipeline example exposed Australia's limited ability to independently fund productive infrastructure and services; such was the country's savings and productive base. Concerns about Australia's productive base and comparative regional growth became more enveloped by market globalisation, a *force majeure* that, via de-territorialisation of the means of production and neoliberal means privileging private (productive) property rights, independence from state or government, and the replacement of the postwar social contract with an individual citizen contract[49] would decouple nation from its postwar economic and cultural

98 *The nation on the eve of globalisation*

collaboration with state. As discussed in Chapter 4, and framing the argument herein about the political economy of cultural diversity, the idea that the state would disappear with globalisation was only partly plausible. It was more that the *nation-state* relationship was being disassembled.

Following this general argument about the necessity for global economic change as the precursor to a fundamental change in national identity politics, a more striking source point foreshadowing the emergence of multiculturalism and the importance of diversity is not Grassby's multiculturalism address, but 18 July 1973, when Prime Minister Whitlam announced without warning that he was to reduce Australia's longstanding protectionism by cutting all trade tariffs by 25%, a decision which Whitlam subsequently claimed marks the beginning of the 'internationalisation of the Australian economy'.[50] For a Labor government this was a major ideological fault line as blue-collar manufacturing workers stood to bear the brunt of the drop in trade protections and competition from cheaper imports. Some trade unions opposed cutting tariffs for this reason. The then head of the Australian Council of Trade Unions, Bob Hawke, was also the president of the Labor Party at this time, and straddled what was a significant fault line in workers' politics. Bob Hawke would also preside over more tariff reductions during his Prime Ministership in the 1980s. An impetus for how Australian multiculturalism was to evolve from a conventional model of anti-racism and hegemonic group welfare can be found in the cut in protectionism in pursuit of an idealised global competitiveness, which for Australia was chiefly a challenge in the rapid growth region of Asia. This point problematises the notion that multiculturalism was a natural evolution from 'integrationism' after a period of social agitation and change. Only by analysing the material conditions is there a clearer basis for this being able to occur when and where it did.

Conventional historical signposts explain multiculturalism's political development beginning with Grassby's speech, then the first Ethnic Communities Councils and the 1975 Anti-Discrimination Act under Labor governments, to the landmark 1978 *Galbally Report* on 'Post Arrival Services', and the establishment of Australian Institute of Multicultural Affairs (AIMA), the Federation of Ethnic Communities Councils (FECCA) and SBS Television under the conservative Liberal–National Coalition government of Malcolm Fraser and Doug Anthony. It is tempting to read this early and significant history as simply an epiphany of prior neglect by Labor and then Liberal–National governments. As Gough Whitlam declared in July 1975: 'The migrant communities in Australia are not small, isolated, separate, divided, but they are part of the living pulse of this city, this state, this country.'[51] At this time, however, 70% of immigration was still from the UK and 'Western' Europe; by the time of the Galbally Report of 1978 this figure had dropped substantially to under 40%.[52] These changes in immigration were in a sense a barometer for Australia of emergent globalisation and the mid-seventies shake up of the world

The nation on the eve of globalisation 99

economy and political order. The Galbally Report was after all, a review of 'Post Arrival Services'. That it was ostensibly concerned with those who had arrived in the postwar European migration waves of the late 1940s to late 1960s would be a naïve reading. Its heavy emphasis on English-language access foreshadowed the need make new migrants increasingly from the non-Anglophone, non-European world (including South American and Vietnamese refugees and migrants from the Middle East), into productive workers, just as much as it was concerned about cultural maintenance for those who had settled in the 1950s and 1960s. Alan Matheson, then ACTU ethnic liaison officer (with an important lobbying role), also noted the lack of political equality that came with limited access to English education, although his concern reflected a more radical workers' rights agenda:

> English language has always been a dominant systematic continuing part of every agenda discussing multiculturalism and migrant workers. And so right through the seventies the debate for the union movement was all about how do we get English language for workers.[53]

The specific situation of the many Vietnamese refugees who fled to Australia following the Vietnam War adds further to the distinction between the multiculturalism experienced during and after Whitlam. What could not be avoided was the need – somewhat after Australia's 'long boom' – to provide socioeconomic opportunity for a sizeable group of dispossessed people from a diametrically 'different' social and cultural milieu. The sheer fact that as of the 1976 Census, there were only 2,427 Vietnamese people recorded as part of the Australian population (resident or citizen), compared with 41,097 recorded in the following Census five years later,[54] highlights the greater pressure during the Fraser years to develop a model for migrant inclusion initiated by the Whitlam government that did not revert to the quaint assimilationist patronage of the *Good Neighbour Councils* or anglophile *Big Brother Movement*.[55] The Good Neighbour Council programme began in 1949 essentially to coordinate a civic volunteer approach to migrant settlement support. Federal government funding assisted some level of coordination, but relied on the community to enforce its assimilationist approach to migrant settlement. In 1968, Federal government funding increased substantially to bolster the Councils' role.[56] Jupp suggests that the Government eventually realised that the trade union movement for one was providing a more progressive support structure for migrant services, thus Government efforts such as in 1968 were an attempt to reclaim the conservative approach to assimilation services.[57] That the *Galbally Report* of 1978 recommended a transfer from hegemonic control of migrant services from the assimilationist Good Neighbour Councils approach to ethnospecific self-advocacy represents a significant shift in government thinking.

100 *The nation on the eve of globalisation*

The *Galbally Report* is also significant because of its conception of affirmative action, access and equity and emphasis on consultation with ethnic NGOs on their needs. Nevertheless, ongoing services were conceived of as 'whole of community'[58] although this did not dismantle the patronage system that often dogs cultural maintenance approaches to multiculturalism. It reflected a minority rights approach[59] and was considered a defining moment for Australian multiculturalism. Devolving welfare responsibility in cooperation with ethnic group associations that were themselves essentialised ethnic forms is problematic. Their purpose beyond an immediate counter-hegemonic lobbying role challenges normative assumptions about the stasis or material detachment of multicultural societies.

Conservative to neoliberal

If anything, the *Galbally Report* was a social contract for ethnic minorities befitting a Mashallite conception of nation and Keynesian conception of state.[60] Notable, then, is that the *Galbally Report* was commissioned by the conservative Fraser government (1975–83), not the progressive, previous Whitlam government. The point here is that the familiar political affiliation – demarcated between conservative and progressive-liberal – was being challenged by a third force in neoliberalism. Nascent neoliberal ideas were gaining acceptance following the 1970s stagflation period, permeating conservative thinking about an entirely different social contract, based upon a reading of the world order in terms of free markets and individual productiveness. Indeed, neoliberal icon Friedrich Hayek had visited Australia in 1976, giving a lecture entitled 'Whither Democracy' at right-wing think tank the Institute for Public Affairs, and met directly with the then Prime Minster, Malcolm Fraser, reportedly advising him to 'float' the Australian currency.[61] The Fraser government was split between its neoliberal acolytes and those comfortable with the conservatism that flourished under familiar models of Keynesian economic growth, the stagflation crisis notwithstanding. Former Australian Senator Fred Chaney, a member of the Fraser Liberal government recollected that 'here was the government … at the cusp between the new and the old economic policy, and that was largely fought out within our party with the [economic] "dries".'[62] Chaney was drawing upon British Prime Minister Margaret Thatcher's depiction of conservative politicians as either 'dry', or of conviction in their economic rationalism, or 'wet': those conservatives who 'leaked' controversial policies and ideas for public scrutiny or feared social backlash.[63] How the neoliberal political worldview took hold in Australia – traversing conservative and Labor landscapes – has its own unique history. Chapters 7–10 provide evidence readily interpreted as neoliberal, although the purpose overall is not principally an argument about the neoliberal condition. Nevertheless, its relevance in influencing a nascent multiculturalism is as a question of economic value, bound up in the politics of Australia's transnational economic relationship with the *tigers, dragons*

The nation on the eve of globalisation 101

and other animations of Asian economic growth. Chapter 7 details that growth.

Notes

1 Marriott, Sen. J., in 'Nationality and Citizenship Bill 1966 Second Reading Speech' *Hansard*, 28 April 1966. Source ID: hansard80/hansards80/1966-04-28/0054.
2 Castles, S. and Collins, J., in Cope, B. (ed.) (1992), p. 88. NB: The source implies that 50% of jobs were filled by unskilled migrants – the intent, based on the statistics, is that half the postwar migrant cohort was skilled; just as half the *jobs filled* were unskilled.
3 Collins, J. (1991), pp. 21–23.
4 Downer, A., in 'Answers to Questions: Unemployed Immigrants', *Hansard* (House of Reps), 17 October 1961. Source ID: hansard80/hansardr80/1961-10-17/0183.
5 Ibid.
6 See in particular, Jamrozik, A. et al. (1995); Collins (1992).
7 Holt, H. in 'House of Representatives Question Immigration Speech', *Hansard* (House of Reps), 16 October 1963. Source ID: hansard80/hansardr80/1963-10-16/0011 (my emphasis).
8 Jamrozik et al. (1995).
9 The point raised in Jamrozik et al. (1995) being that it would surely be illogical to offer recognition and incorporation via citizenship to a migrant reserve army of labour, for they would be a legally distinct reserve, no more.
10 Figures compiled from Commonwealth Statistician report tabled by MP Alexander Downer (Senior) to Parliament: Downer, A. in 'Answers to Questions Immigration. (Question No. 92)', *Hansard* (House of Reps), 30 October 1963, Source ID: hansard80/hansardr80/1963-10-30/02.
11 Ibid.
12 Ibid.
13 Jamrozik, A. et al. (1995).
14 DILGEA (1986) *Australian Immigration Consolidated Statistics, No. 14*, Canberra: AGPS, pp. 42–43, Table C.7.
15 Brooks, C. (1996) *Understanding the Labour Market*, Canberra: Bureau of Immigration, Multicultural and Population Research, p. 9.
16 Collins, J. 'Asian Small Business in Australia', in Brownlee, P. and Mitchell, C. (eds) (1998) 'Migration Research in the Asia Pacific: Australian Perspectives', *APMRN Working Paper No.4*. Papers presented at a workshop sponsored by the Academy of the Social Sciences of Australia, Wollongong University April, Wollongong: Institute of Social Change and Critical Inquiry, p. 56.
17 Castles, S. et al. (2014).
18 BIPR (1993) *Australian Immigration – Consolidated Statistics No. 17*, Canberra: AGPS, p. 18, Figures 6 and 7.
19 BIMPR (1996) *Immigration Update, Dec Qtr*, April, Canberra: AGPS, p. 15, Table 1.8; BIMPR (1995) *Consolidated Statistics, No.18*, January, Canberra: AGPS, p.12 Table 2.5.
20 DIMA (1997) *Australian Immigration – Consolidated Statistics No.19, 1995–96*, May. Canberra: Commonwealth of Australia, p. 12, Table 2.5.
21 DILGEA (1986), p. 42, Table C.7. This refers to business and commerce as profession.
22 Table derived from BIPR (1993); BIMPR (1996); DILGEA (1986), pp. 42–43,

102 *The nation on the eve of globalisation*

Table C.7 All statistics exclude unemployed and not in workforce categories, which includes children and pensioners.

23 NB: The nomenclature for the periods 1980–83 and 1983–86 was 'Unskilled' where 'Labourers' is used in the later BIPR/BIMPR/DIEA statistics. All other occupational nomenclature between the different publications are essentially consistent meaning Labourers has been substituted for Unskilled. Note also that the figures from mid-1983 show effects of a recession, as do figures for 1992–93. If the period 1980–82 were segregated, the percentage intake of unskilled/labourers would be significantly higher again.

24 Apart from the statistics provided in BIPR (1993), BIMPR (1996), DILGEA (1986, see also Castles, S. and Collins, J., in Cope, B. (ed.) (1992).

25 Al Grassby, cited in Jupp, J., 'Immigration and National Identity', in Stokes, G. (ed.) (2007) *The Politics of Identity*, Cambridge: Cambridge University Press, p. 143. Further research reveals that Prime Minister John Gorton said approvingly in an interview, quoted in *The Australian* on 26 January 1971, 'I think that if we build up gradually inside Australia a proportion of people without white skins, then there will be a complete lack of consciousness that it is being built up and that we will arrive at a state where we have a *multicultural* country'. The concept had emerged some time before Grassby's efforts.

26 Lopez, M. (2000a); Lopez, M. (2000b) 'The Politics of the Origins of Multiculturalism: Lobbying and the Power of Influence', Paper delivered at the *10th Biennial Conference of the Australian Population Association* 'Population and Globalisation: Australia in the 21st Century', Melbourne 28 November to 1 December 2000, Melbourne, Australia, http://www.apa.org.au/upload/2000-5A_Lopez.pdf (accessed 1 July 2009).

27 Stratton, J., 'Multiculturalism and the Whitening Machine, or How Australians Become White', in Hage, G. and Couch, R. (eds) (1999) *The Future of Australian Multiculturalism: Reflections on the Twentieth Anniversary of Jean Martin's The Migrant Presence*, Sydney: Research Institute for Humanities and Social Sciences, University of Sydney, p. 180.

28 Lopez, M. (2000a), (2000b).

29 Ibid; Hage, G. (2000); Castles, S. et al. (1992).

30 Neuman, K. (2006) 'Our Own Interests Must Come First – Australia's Response to the Expulsion of Asians from Uganda', *History Australia*, Vol. 3, No. 1, June, http://publications.epress.monash.edu/doi/abs/10.2104/ha060010 (accessed 21 July 2009).

31 Ibid., see p. 14, footnote 22.

32 Ibid., p. 10.

33 Neuman, K. (2006); Freeman, G. and Jupp, J. (eds) (1992) *Nations of Immigrants: Australia, the United States, and International Migration*, Melbourne: Oxford University Press, pp. 25–26.

34 George Papadopoulos interview for Making Multicultural Australia (MAA), 1994 in Jakubowicz/MAA (2002), http://www.multiculturalaustralia.edu.au/library/media/Audio/id/397 (accessed 1 July 2009).

35 Lopez, M. (2000a), (2000b).

36 Jupp, J. (2002).

37 Inglis, C. 'Australia: Educational Changes and Challenges in Response to Multiculturalism, Globalization, and Transnationalism', in Luchtenberg, S. (ed.) (2004) *Migration, Education and Change*, London and New York: Routledge, p. 189.

38 Hage, G. (2000).

39 Leigh, A. (2002) 'Trade Liberalisation and the Australian Labor Party' *Australian Journal of Political History*, Vol. 48, No. 4, pp. 487–508.

The nation on the eve of globalisation 103

40 Gough Whitlam in 'Question: Foreign Investment and Associated Matters', *Hansard*, 26 September 1972, p. 1925. System ID: hansard80/hansardr80/1972-09-26/0156.

41 Leigh, A. (2002). This small growth is more telling when considered against the larger growth happening in parts of the Asian region. However, as argued in Chapter 1, this measure is only partially effective in understanding the nature and extent of a globalised economy. Market share and growth in services, among other indicators, are crucial to understanding globalisation. These elements feature in subsequent labour government policy of Hawke and Keating.

42 Wilkinson, J. (2000) *Changing Nature of the NSW Economy – Background Paper No 1*. Sydney: NSW Parliamentary Library Research Service. The wool price did recover but fluctuated substantially from the surety of its decades supplying the Empire.

43 NSW Department of Decentralisation and Development (1970) *Economic Projections to 1980*, p. 41, cited in Wilkinson, ibid., p. 9.

44 Jones, B. (1981) *Technological Change Seminar*, Carnarvon, WA, 2 August. Keynote speech delivered to Geraldton-Gascoyne A.L.P. Electorate Council, p. 4. Jones was then Shadow Minister for Science and Technology, M.H.R. for Lalor, http://parlinfo.aph.gov.au/parlInfo/search/search.w3p (accessed via *Hansard* 3 March 2014).

45 Ibid.

46 Lim, H. (2009) 'Regional Trade Agreements and Conflict: the case of Southeast Asia', in Rafi, S. (ed.) *Regional Trade Integration and Conflict Resolution*, Abingdon, Oxon and New York: Routledge, in association with the International Development Research Centre, Ottawa, http://www.idrc.ca/openebooks/414-7 (accessed 3 October 2009).

47 David, A. and Wheelwright T. (1989) *The Third Wave: Australia and Asian Capitalism*, Sutherland, NSW: The Left Book Club Co-Op, p. 7.

48 See 'Question: Foreign Investment and Associated Matters', *Hansard*, 26 September 1972, p. 1925. System ID: hansard80/hansardr80/1972-09-26/0156.

49 See, for examples and supporting arguments, David and Wheelwright (1989); Wiseman, J. (1998).

50 From Whitlam, E.G., 'A Tribute to a Modest Member', Address to the Centre for Independent Studies, Burt Kelly Lecture Series, 1997, cited in Wiseman, J. (1998), p. 42.

51 Whitlam, G., 'Speech at the Inaugural Meeting of the Ethnic Communities' Council of NSW, Sydney, 27 July 1975.

52 Galbally, F. (1978) *Review of Post Arrival Programs and Services for Migrants* (The Galbally Report) Migrant Services and Programs, Canberra: AGPS, p. 3.

53 Alan Matheson – Interview for *Making Multicultural Australia*, 1994, in Jakubowicz, A./MAA (2002), http://www.multiculturalaustralia.edu.au/library/media/Audio/id/394.Ethnic-Rights (accessed 1 July 2009).

54 Census of Population and Housing, 30 June 1981, *Summary Characteristics of Persons and Dwellings*. Table 8. p. 8. NB: Table 8 includes countries of the Middle East, which for the purposes of this analysis are inappropriate in the general understanding for Australia of the term 'Asia'. Countries excluded from figures presented here include Cyprus, Iran, Iraq, Israel, Saudia Arabia, etc.

55 The *Big Brother Movement* was originally a 'Melbourne establishment' sponsored support group assisting the passage and settlement of young UK migrant boys to Australia, set up in the 1920s. Sherrington, G. (2002) 'The Big Brother Movement and Citizenship of Empire', *Australian Historical Studies*, Vol. 120, pp. 267–85.

104 *The nation on the eve of globalisation*

56 See Jakubowicz/MAA 'Achievements of the Good Neighbour Movement 1949–72', *Making Multicultural Australia*, http://www.multiculturalaustralia. edu.au/doc/deptimm_3.pdf (accessed 3 August 2009).
57 Jupp, J. (1992), see pp. 132–33.
58 Galbally, F. (1978), p. 4. See summary recommendation 1.14; Jupp, J. (2007) 'Immigration and National Identity', in Stokes, G. (ed.).
59 Akin to Kymlicka's conceptualisation of welfare support as noted in Chapter 1.
60 Cf. Carter, A. (2001) *The Political Theory of Global Citizenship*, New York: Routledge; see also Barbalet, J. (1988) for an extended account of Marshall's conceptualisation of civil society. In essence, this involved recognition of social and political institutions in relationship that, while conflicted, were nonetheless interdependent within industrial capitalism.
61 See Commonwealth of Australia (1977) Procedural text – 'The House of Review', *Hansard*, 24 February, http://www.parliinfo.aph.gov.au (accessed 2 April 2020). System ID: hansard80/hansards80/1977-02-24/0207; see also, Australian Broadcasting Commission (2007) 'An Attitude of Mind and Faith – Liberalism in Australian Political History', *Hindsight*, 4 April. Radio broadcast, https://abcmedia. akamaized.net/rn/podcast/2007/04/hht_20070401.mp3 (accessed 23 February 2020). Fraser of course did not do this – it was later done by the Labor Government of Bob Hawke.
62 Fred Chaney, quoted in Australian Broadcasting Commission (2007) Hansard.
63 Ibid.

7 Terms of engagement I
Australia and the Asian Region

Australia and Asian regional growth

Australia's global positioning relative to Asia, economically, geo-graphically, geopolitically and, with increased migration, culturally dominates the political economy of the decade and a half following the 1978 *Galbally Report*. While intense lobbying by established ethnic communities was occurring in the lead-up to *Galbally*, a form of foreign relations lobbying specifically relating to Asia concurrently gathered momentum. The formation and work of the Asian Studies Association of Australia (ASSA) was telling of what was to become a strong theme of economic engagement with Asia – 'Asia literacy'. The idea of being 'culturally literate' about 'Asia' can assume many forms and inter-pretations, not least because Asia is not a homogeneous entity. Cultural literacy becomes a main theme of Productive Diversity in relation to market knowledge as will later be discussed. The initial idea of Asia literacy promoted in the late 1970s was marked by a major conference of the ASAA in 1978 led by Stephen Fitzgerald, former diplomat to China and later author of numerous influential reports and works on China and Asia more generally.[1] The *Sydney Morning Herald* newspaper headline announced '600 academics' converging to debate the matter, arguably brining the kind of media attention that few such academic conferences have gained since.[2]

More to the point was how knowledge of Asian societies and cultures would later become an influential concept in policy terms. In its early years (mid-1970s), the ASAA provided an influential think-tank type presence to de-mythologise Asia in the public sphere, in education and for policy makers in Canberra.[3] Fitzgerald's influence continued strongly throughout the following decade of Labor rule, crowned by Prime Minister Hawke in 1990 as head of a new Asia-Australia Institute based at the University of New South Wales, with its stated mission to create 'an Asian community in North and Southeast Asia and Australasia'.[4] Fitzgerald also chaired the controversial 1988 government report of the Committee to Advise on Australia's Immigration Program (CAAIP), an issue discussed later in this chapter.

106   *Terms of engagement I*

Asia literacy, founded upon genuine political and cultural engagement with the diversity of the region, by the early 1980s was still an idea more than practised reality. Nevertheless, there have been numerous arguments advanced about the inevitability of this over many decades and for different reasons. Kivisto[5] cites London (1970) in claiming that Australia's increasing economic interaction with Asia in the 1960s, specifically Japan, highlighted the contradictions of a racist immigration policy favouring 'whites'. Predating London's work, a forum presented by the Australian Institute of International Affairs in 1963 entitled *Living with Asia* brought together leading political and civic actors to discuss Australia's 'cultural protectionism' *vis-à-vis* trade relations with Asia.[6] The White Australia Policy was officially abolished by the 1970s but not due to engagement with Japan *per se*, that country itself a largely monocultural nation-state. A cacophony of factors were also influential, for instance, the inclusion of Aborigines in both wartime economy and postwar growth, the US civil rights movement and ongoing local resistance to racism, the experience of globalisation through the emergence of mass media reporting the horrors of Vietnam, the effect of a large postwar generation with access to greater economic and social opportunity.[7] Nevertheless, both Barwick's and London's address to the Australian Institute of International Affairs are artefacts of the time. They anticipate an emergent relationship between the domestic and regional politics of identity in the context of economic globalisation.

Dalrymple's metaphor of 'continental drift'[8] posits a serendipity of geography (i.e. in a region of rapid and foreseeable growth) against geopolitical security as an undeniable determinant in Australia's need to engage with Asia. From a defence or security perspective, cooperation with Asian countries up to the 1970s were dominated by containing Asian communism and defending the separateness of Australia, a point well made by the landmark *Dibb Report* on Australia's defence strategy.[9] Australia's geospatial and geotemporal proximity to the Asian region did give it opportunity and imperative for broader engagement, a virtue which became a key selling point for Bob Hawke and Paul Keating throughout their terms as prime minister. But arguments about the primacy of geopolitical and national security as causal of the *engagement with Asia* thesis are rendered secondary as the volume of trade and investment and regional labour flows between Australia and Asia and Asian economic growth realise greater potential. Considering the converse, that is, whether a lack of Asian economic growth would have produced the same level of rapid political, social and cultural engagement the Hawke and Keating governments pursued, further illustrates the point that geography alone, or even geopolitical security was not the principle impetus for engagement in the 1980s.[10] The massive strategic presence of the US military in the Philippines and Japan in particular was a more significant security apparatus upon which Australia could rely. However, as a longstanding Australia–US military alliance (the

ANZUS Treaty, also including New Zealand) showed signs of tension in 1984–85,[11] along with the thawing of Cold War brinkmanship through Gobachev's *Glasnost*, Deng Xiaoping's *Gaige Kaifang* and embrace of the market, and the historical lack of regional military unanimity, geostrategic security in material terms complemented rather than drove Australia's engagement with Asia in the 1980s. Australia's economic desire to integrate with Asia provided opportunities for, and actually necessitated deconstructing military geopolitical allegiances as the main determinant of foreign relations.[12]

In the 20 years prior to more determined regional economic engagement under Hawke and Keating, growth across Asia had been occurring apace, albeit from a low base. Between 1960 and 1980, while Australia sustained an average growth rate of 2.7% per capita of GNP, emerging economies such as Singapore, Taiwan and Korea all averaged above 7% and Thailand 4.7%.[13] Over the decade 1983–93, the Hawke and Keating Labor governments having introduced a suite of new global market economy policies, Australia did manage an average growth rate of 3.4%, slightly above OECD averages of 2.8%.[14] This was still short of the scale and volume of growth throughout the region (Table 7.1). Growth in many countries was nonetheless erratic rather than sustained year on year, highlighting that many developing economies were subject to external global events. Much of the regional growth was a cascade effect of growth initially in Japan which invested some its increasing stocks of capital in regional neighbouring countries of Indonesia, Korea and Thailand, mostly to resource its own material needs and also partly through a regional strategy to contain Communism in the 1950s and 1960s.[15]

Relative national growth rates however only provide a *motive* for Australia's globalising economy towards Asia and a heuristic point of analysis. Trade and investment volumes between Australia and the rest of the region detail a clearer picture of where Australia's fortunes were turning: while a clear majority of exports were sent to the UK and Europe throughout the 1950s, with only 14% of export trade going to Japan and East Asia at that time, by 1984 the volume of exports to Japan and East Asia jumped to 46%, mostly at the expense of trade with the UK and Europe. A similar story applies for imports.[16] The 30-year period from the 1950s witnessed a major turnaround in economic relationships, and into the 1960s at least, Japan drove much regional growth in trade as it did in investment. By the 1980s, Japan's growth was established while the export-oriented strategies of South East Asia, represented largely by the ASEAN bloc, delivered some staggering if erratic export growth rates (Table 7.2).

Australian business borrowed significant sums to fuel its growth and to reinvest in other overseas ventures from the 1980s and importantly much of the money it borrowed again changed in provenance from the UK and USA to Japan, such that by 1992, Japan had trebled its status as the largest single country creditor providing 21% of total foreign borrowing.

Table 7.1 Real GDP growth (annual % change), 1983–95

Country	1983	1984	1985	1986	1987	1988	1989	1990	1991	1992	1993	1994	1995
Australia	−0.5	6.4	5.7	2.1	4.4	4	4.6	1.6	−1.3	2.1	3.9	5	3.5
China	10.9	15.2	13.5	8.9	11.6	11.3	4.1	3.8	9.2	14.2	14	13.1	10.9
Hong Kong	5.8	1	0.7	11	13.4	8.4	2.2	3.9	5.7	6.1	6	6	2.3
Indonesia	4.2	7	2.5	5.9	4.9	5.8	7.5	7.2	7	6.5	6.8	7.5	8.2
Japan	1.6	3.1	5.1	3	3.8	6.8	5.3	5.2	3.4	1	0.2	1.1	2
Sth Korea	10.8	8.1	6.8	10.6	11.1	10.6	6.7	9.2	9.4	5.9	6.1	8.5	9.2
Malaysia	6.3	7.8	−0.9	1.2	5.4	9.9	9.1	9	9.5	8.9	9.9	9.2	9.8
Philippines	1.9	−7.3	−7.3	3.4	4.3	6.8	6.2	3	−0.6	0.3	2.1	4.4	4.7
Singapore	8.5	8.3	−1.4	2.1	9.8	11.5	10	9.2	6.6	6.3	11.7	11.6	8.2
Taiwan	8.3	10.7	5	11.5	12.7	8	8.5	5.7	7.6	7.8	6.9	7.4	6.5
Thailand	5.6	5.8	4.6	5.5	9.5	13.3	12.2	11.6	8.1	8.1	8.3	9	9.2
Vietnam	7.1	8.4	5.6	3.4	2.5	5.1	7.8	5	5.8	8.7	8.1	8.8	9.5
UK	3.6	2.7	3.6	4	4.6	5	2.3	0.8	−1.4	0.1	2.2	4.3	3
USA	4.5	7.2	4.1	3.5	3.4	4.1	3.5	1.9	−0.2	3.3	2.7	4	2.5
New Zealand	−0.1	6.9	1.2	1.8	0.8	0	0.8	0.1	−1.7	0.8	5.2	5.9	4.3

Source: *IMF Data Mapper – World Economic Outlook* 2009, http://www.imf.org/external/datamapper (accessed 31 August 2009).

Terms of engagement I 109

Table 7.2 South East Asian economies: annual export growth (%), 1980–94

	1980	1985	1990	1991	1992	1993	1994
Indonesia	23.8	−6.5	16.7	10.5	14.0	8.3	9.3
Malaysia	16.8	−7.2	16.0	16.9	16.8	15.6	20.3
Philippines	25.7	−14.1	5.1	7.3	9.1	15.6	20.5
Singapore	36.1	5.4	17.9	12.0	7.6	17.0	32.3
Thailand	28.7	−3.8	15.2	24.1	13.4	13.4	19.5
Vietnam	n/a	n/a	15.9	46.1	19.2	21.0	22.0

Adapted from: DFAT-East Asia Analytical Unit (1995) *Growth Triangles of South East Asia*, Canberra: Commonwealth of Australia, see Table 2.3. NB: This table is not inclusive of all South East Asian countries, e.g. Brunei.

Table 7.3 Percentage share of total foreign borrowing from creditors, 1978–92 (7-year intervals)

Creditor	June 1978	June 1985	June 1992
Japan	7	18	21
UK	24	16	10
USA	31	21	15
ASEAN	2	13	3
International Capital Markets	n/a	7	27

Source: Griffin-Warwicke, J. (1992) *Australian Economic Indicators*, ABS 1350.0, November, Canberra: AGPS.

Both the USA and UK's supply of loan credit more than halved in the same period (Table 7.3).

The ASEAN figure of 1985 also highlights a massive 650% growth in its supply as a creditor for foreign loans from 1978. This figure reduced almost to the same low rate by 1992, with various factors including the Stock Market crash of October 1987, an appreciation of the Australian Dollar in 1989 and changing interest rates affecting the best source for loans. In fact, there was a significant depreciation of the US dollar against the Yen following the Plaza Accord of September 1985. This was in large measure a strategic realignment to kick-start US competitiveness against the Yen. For a brief period circa 1985, many ASEAN currencies which were linked to the US Dollar also depreciated, meaning it was cheaper to buy these currencies.[17]

On the supply side, despite their relative impoverishment it was certainly in many ASEAN countries' national interest to loan to Australia given its ability to pay. The initial monetary policies of the Hawke–Keating government clearly favoured borrowing to underpin Australia's restructuring and expansion (as discussed later in this section). With interest rates in Japan generally lower than the UK and US (Table 7.4), Australia's generally

110 *Terms of engagement I*

Table 7.4 Comparative immediate interest rates (%) (Call Money & Interbank Rate)

	1983	1985	1987	1989	1991	1993	1995
Japan	n/a	8.243	3.958	6.448	6.310	2.442	0.459
UK	8.99	11.5	8.51	14.98	10.72	5.88	6.69
USA	9.47	8.27	6.77	8.45	4.43	2.96	5.6
Australia	11.88	16.72	11.92	16.93	8.19	4.88	7.52

Source: *OECD – Main Economic Indicators*. Data extracted on 25 August 2009 from http://stats.oecd.org. Australian rate compared and sourced as 90-day bill rate, from RBA (n.d. 1997) Table 3.22b.

higher interest rates throughout the period (e.g. the loan rate to large business averaging 17.5% between 1983 and 1995),[18] and other factors such as Japan's increasing ability to loan more particularly after the Plaza Accord, Australia rapidly evolved a symbiotic relationship with that country's finances, steadily beyond the ASEAN states. Notably, the Australian private sector was responsible for the lion's share of all foreign borrowing from 1983 onwards.[19]

The fact that the majority of loans were short term[20] and were largely private sector might indicate that the financial 'Asianisation' of Australia was not occurring as systematically as some warned at the time. For example, while debt servicing did contribute negatively to Australia's current account and therefore trade terms from 1983 to 1993, Australian companies were drawing on Asia-based short-term capital and favourable interest rates opportunistically and investing not necessarily in Australia but also in third countries including the USA and UK. A servicing of longer-term borrowing from Japan and other economies of Asia might reinforce claims made by critics on both the political Left and Right that Australia would suffer through financial indenture. But an effect, intended or otherwise, following the Plaza Accord was a circulation of finance capital out of Japan, via Australia, and back to the US. Financial speculators based in Australia stood to make gains by borrowing high value Yen at low interest rates and reinvesting in the large and sophisticated US manufacturing sector which had higher trade deficit with Japan.[21]

Loans, then, explain an exploitation of growth and capacity in Asia with some benefit to current accounts of creditor countries. An issue was that most of Australia's foreign debt during the 1980s was held in the private sector. From the Left, a main critique was that *foreign investment* and *control* was considered bad for future equity, jobs and Australia's standard of living.[22] This raises the issue of capitalist elites' self-interest versus a national interest as noted in Chapter 5. It also puts a perspective on Australian government attempts to woo Asian business migrants with capital in large numbers from the mid-1980s who could either invest in fixed assets in Australia for production or repatriate overseas investment returns to their new country of citizenship. Further discussion on financial 'lieutenants' and entrepreneurs in Australia occurs in later chapters.

Foreign Direct Investment (FDI) in the form of loans and investment on existing ventures and securities rather than fixed stock was significant for Australia. This partially explains the role of finance capital linking Australia with the rest of Asia throughout the 1980s as foreign ownership restrictions were slackened.[23] At the time the ALP gained government in 1983 annual foreign investment in Australia averaged approximately \$8.7 billion. Between 1989 to 1994 annual foreign investment into Australia averaged A\$20 billion per annum, most of it from private enterprise. Equity and portfolio investment including debt servicing were the chief 'commodities' attracting investment throughout this period.[24] Investment by country is detailed in Table 7.5, from the beginning of the Labor government period to Australia's recession of 1991–92. Advanced economies are clear majority investors, but Japan's total investment expands almost fivefold; Hong Kong fourfold. ASEAN other (than Singapore) doubles by the end of the period although remains comparatively small. The growth rates are important, but so too is the historical basis of advanced capitalist capacities to circulate (invest) for greater accumulation of capital. Singapore and ASEAN fail to sustain FDI investment but clearly Australia was expected to provide returns given the cumulative rise in investment from the advanced capitalist economies.

Data on FDI from the tables above provide a range of possibilities for interpretation. Certainly, the proposed growth in Japanese investment in the early to mid-1980s is significant, but so too is the investment from the USA and the UK in overall terms. While official British interest in Australian governance and economic affairs clearly receded from the 1970s, with much of the FDI through private investment, it is clear that UK companies remained keen to invest in the ex-colony, as were US interests. Japan's investment is significant, relatively so is Singapore's, but equally so is the combined European investment. The mid-1980s period is important in understanding the high level of FDI activity in part because of the series of economic deregulation measures introduced by Keating (as Federal Treasurer) initially in 1983, namely, the floating of the Australian dollar (removing a centrally determined exchange rate), allowing foreign banks and other financial institutions to trade in Australia, and removing a cap on interest rates.[25] In short, borrowing money was cheap, deregulated to be in ready supply, whereas previous government monetary policy favoured equity investment in Australia particularly by Australian companies, a policy the Whitlam government initially pursued.[26]

Fear then that the Australian nation-state would suffer under a wave of Asian finance[27] far beyond the colonial domination of its former British rulers are not borne out by the figures. A sectoral analysis of investment does show particular interest by Japanese and ASEAN investors in tourism,

Table 7.5 Cumulative level of FDI by country of investor (A$billion – proposed)[a]

	1983–84	1984–85	1985–86	1986–87	1987–88	1988–89	1989–90	1990–91	1991–92	1992–93
USA	19.9	26.8	31.9	41.4	40.2	47.4	46.8	54.6	58.7	62.6
UK	20.4	26.1	29.3	37.3	44.5	48.9	47.8	51.5	56.1	60.3
Japan	10.8	16.2	20.8	21.4	29.8	39.1	48.0	51.0	52.1	54.1
Singapore	6.6	8.9	8.3	9.4	6.9	6.8	6.6	5.6	6.8	7.7
Hong Kong	2.5	3.4	3.0	3.0	4.8	6.8	7.4	9.7	10.7	11.5
ASEAN other^	0.6	0.8	0.7	1.1	1.3	0.7	1.1	1.1	1.2	2.7*
European^	11.3	14.2	19.2	24	24.4	25	28.5	27.3	27	n/a

Notes

a FIRB Reports 1987–88, 1989–90, 1993–94, Canberra: Commonwealth of Australia. NB: Figures are 'proposed', as FDI approvals in any one year does not mean or equate with full investment per proposal.

* Includes Malaysia, with investment of $1.1 billion.

^ Composite of individual investments from Germany, France, Switzerland, Benelux, Sweden. Figures for early 1990s were grouped under 'Other' and not reported individually, however, FDI averaged only 5.3 for combined 'Other' category during this period.

Terms of engagement I   113

real estate and minerals development, while the USA and UK were the lead investors in manufacturing although with substantial stakes in those other sectors dominated by Asian investors.[28] Right-wing critiques of Asian investment were concerned with national identity, as were left-wing critiques, but the latter were couched more in concern for the neoliberal, anti-Union, anti-welfare, corporate business models creeping into Australian workplaces and ultimately a way of life. Equally, however, one could argue from the data in Table 7.5 that neoliberal, corporate models were just as threatening from UK (Thatcherite) and US (Reaganite) neoliberal investment regimes, so motives for arguments about the greater perils of Asian capitalism[29] are questionable.

Resistance in the 1980s and 1990s to the kinds of authoritarianism outside the global North but in support of neoliberal global market economy was notable. NGOs and trade unions were not absent from Asian countries – Japan, Korea, Taiwan and the Philippines in particular experienced significant and sometimes militant mobilisations by social organisations opposed to the working conditions and demands of transnational capital State–corporate joint development.[30] Reviewing the figures on international creditors (Table 7.3) it should be noted that in 1985 while only 7% of foreign loans came from conglomerates, within seven years 27% of foreign loans emanated from such sources.[31] The growth in TNCs assembling global value chains but increasingly underwritten by interest-bearing capital is discussed in earlier chapters. To reiterate a key point, TNCs were at the forefront of the neoliberalisation of work, culture and society for countries such as Australia. Neoliberal market economics, not Asian finance, were the real threat to Australian working conditions and 'way of life'. What's more, concerns by some about Asian capital leading to ownership of Australia and threatening a way of life fails to consider that Australia invested in and had healthy *export* trade with Asian countries, especially with Japan, from the 1970s onwards. In 1988, Australia was the fifth-largest investor in both Indonesia and Hong Kong, sixth-largest in Malaysia, seventh-largest in the Philippines and eighth-largest investor in both the US and Singapore; It dominated investment in Papua New Guinea and was the largest investor in New Zealand.[32] An argument could equally apply that Australia was threatening a way of life of these countries with such 'counter-investment'. Likewise, Japan was the dominant investor throughout the region; Taiwan was the second-largest investor in the Philippines, Thailand and in Malaysian manufacturing in 1988 and 1999; Singapore the largest investor in Malaysian manufacturing, and fourth-largest in China.[33] A better approach then to understanding the importance of remarkable economic growth throughout Asia and concomitant social transformations is through consideration of *intra-regional* investment and development, of which Australia was one of many players. In this case, the regional dynamism can be better understood as a feature of globalisation and individual nation-state motives and prospects made more

114 *Terms of engagement I*

complex through multilateral dependencies. This concurs with the earlier analysis of global value chains emerging as a prevalent form of transnational production. The Labour Government in Australia was unapologetic about being a part of a 'brave new world' of market capital:

> *'Mr Hawke and Mr Keating have led a revolution in the Labor Party, born of the need to change Australia's international competitiveness... The Opposition's problem is that Labor is doing all the things that the Liberals should have done long ago'.*

[Keating]: Oh, ho, ho, ho. That quote is from *The Economist*'s survey on Australia dated 6 May 1989. Everyone in the world is a wake up to the Opposition ... We have had to pick up the pieces and repair in six years the indolence of 25 years. That is the truth about this country's current situation ... This Government has presided over the biggest shift in fiscal policy in any Organisation for Economic Co-operation and Development (OECD) country.[34]

Access to finance for start-up ventures is an important ingredient in a deregulated or privatised market economy, including for ethnic business.[35] Keating's financial deregulation measures as both Treasurer and Prime Minister did feed the climate for entrepreneurial activity to develop. Importantly, allowing foreign banks and financial institutions to establish operations in Australia was decisive in giving access to foreign venture capital, particularly for overseas ventures. The injection of foreign-owned banks into Australia from the early 1980s made this possible and adds a dimension to any claims that Keating's policy was simply to bring competition to the finance sector. Foreign Direct Investment in Australia, as has been shown, included substantial finance capital, while the presence of Foreign Banks also enhanced opportunities for foreign companies to invest in Australia by facilitating the transaction relationship between overseas investor and their local context.

Hawke and Keating – pursuing competitive advantage and the Region

Australia's exports were firmly geared towards East Asia by the time the Labor Party won government in 1983. As already noted in this chapter, there was a massive jump in export trade going to Japan and East Asia, from 14% in the 1950s to 46% by the early 1980s. Prime Minister Bob Hawke and Treasurer (and later Prime Minister) Paul Keating understood this economic growth across Asia in more radical terms than their conservative predecessor, although Hawke and Keating's separate terms as Prime Minister were also distinct on this matter. Both embraced Asia to define a response to economic, social and cultural transformations of

Terms of engagement I 115

globalisation, while their vision about Australia and Asia took different turns throughout their combined 13-year reign from 1983. It is clearer in retrospect that from the outset the Hawke and Keating Labor leadership carried on the globalising impetus of 1970s Whitlamite economics, although reducing tariffs was one area they initially feared to tread. The brief tenure of the Whitlam government, or rather its severe December 1975 election loss, scarred Labor Party economic thinking for some time and its commitment to reducing protection was shelved for some years.[36] Hawke and Keating devised other ways of stripping back what they saw as protected, inefficient and therefore overpaid production relative to their Asian neighbours – the 1983 Accord on wages and prices with trade unions and the floating of the dollar delivered micro economic consequences to individual industry sectors by demanding greater productivity, just as a tariff cut would have done across the board. The political mantra that reverberated throughout the Hawke–Keating era was competitiveness and productivity, echoing a defining discourse of economic globalisation:

> We have got to realise that we are in a new ballgame and if we play it hard and play it cooperatively, we will win *(Bob Hawke)*.[37]

> As in all nations before it, the pursuit of trade and competition has instilled in Australia a thirst for greater efficiency at home and a larger dominion abroad *(Paul Keating)*.[38]

Labor government policy was by no means the social antipathy of Thatcherism experienced in the UK at the time. Hawke–Keating Labor was a hybrid of old and new economics, old and new politics in the early 1980s, although, neoliberalism (or economic rationalism as it was otherwise known) became a more distinguishing feature. The abandonment of the Party's core principle by the Labor Party's triennial National Conference in 1986 of the 'socialisation of industry' for distributive equality, and the strategies of control over trade union wage claims through a Prices and Incomes Accord were important markers alongside the deregulated financial regime.[39] The pervasiveness of the competition-productivity mantra extended into the arenas of immigration, multiculturalism and a new national identity, inevitably leading to the concept of productive diversity and the entrepreneurial possibilities of a diverse population, increasingly with ties to Asia. Multiculturalism's history at this point becomes markedly intertwined with economic restructuring for regional engagement. What follows is a brief account of key responses to economic change impacting upon Australia's national and regional identity making.

Shortly after his election in November 1983, Hawke saw opportunity to capitalise on mutual concern about the General Agreement on Tariffs and Trade (GATT) among regional governments, addressing the Thai Chamber of Commerce on suitable multilateral cooperation between Australia and

116 *Terms of engagement I*

other countries of the region.[40] A much closer relationship between Australia's economy and those Newly Industrialising Countries (NICs) of Asia was envisaged in this initiative. Two months later, the Government hosted the ASEAN–Australia forum in January 1984. Remarkably, then Foreign Minister Bill Hayden's address to the forum claimed 'Australia's long term future is as a Eurasian country'.[41] Whether Hayden meant Australia's ethnic demographic would reflect that of other nations of Asia is unclear. It does reflect a static view of Asia, and an endorsement of Asia's apparent model of economic growth. Hayden's statement was somewhat ahead of its time, and not just in terms of international relations. The year 1984 showed how ambivalent Australia was to Asia as the infamous 'Blainey debate' emerged.[42] What is also significant is how rapidly and decisively Government discourse and rhetoric changed to promote the Australia-Asia economic and cultural connection. The Labor Government's early attempt at staking a claim in the prosperity of the region through such cooperative fora as the ASEAN–Australia forum was a shape of things to come – regional blocs dominated Government thinking throughout the period of their incumbency. The Pacific Economic Cooperation Conference (PECC), the Cairns Group of GATT, the Council for Security Cooperation in the Asia Pacific (CSCAP) and APEC are testimony to Australia's strategic attempts to participate in, influence and control regional transformation.[43]

The notion of a regional bloc was not of course new. Modern regional and global economic systems were under consideration since the end of the Second World War.[44] The steady progression of the European Economic Community (EEC) and the Common Market from the 1960s provided a contemporary example of how the global political economy might be re-organised around regions, notwithstanding the geopolitical and cultural alchemy required to re-fashion Europe's boundaries to achieve this. Meanwhile, ASEAN had existed since the 1960s, Australia had been invited as a full member of the Economic Commission for Asia and the Far East (ECAPE) in 1963,[45] and the PECC in 1980 was the culmination of almost two decades of work, which in turn laid some foundations for the formulation of APEC in 1989. What vexed the Labor government was not only the fact that being shut out of the European Economic Community and no longer a client in the UK colonial economy left it without a major preferred 'natural' market, but that the alternative of joining Asia proved to be a hard road, politically. This in part was because regional cooperation and cultural cohesion throughout Asia did not exist in any way like Australia hoped or believed it would.[46] Foreign Minister Hayden explained in the Parliament that:

> The political and economic implications of the European Common Market... create disadvantages for this country and ... are creating serious economic distortions within the European Community with consequences which will show up in the medium to longer

term as a result of the severe distortion of the use of economic resources.[47]

On ASEAN, Hayden explained in the same speech:

ASEAN at this point is an association reflecting very much shared political concerns and shared commercial concerns but it is certainly vastly different from the (European) Community in economic aspect. It is certainly not a Customs union, for instance, and is a long way from achieving that end.[48]

Despite the Labor government's approach to neoliberalisation both in terms of domestic production and its foreign economic relations, most if not all of countries of ASEAN as well as of Northeast Asia, were largely managed economies, with highly protected sectors of production and selected areas of export-oriented specialisation (particularly labour-intensive manufacturing) which were openly competitive. Japan's steel- and car-making industries are key examples of industries fostered locally through protection and government coordination to become export-oriented.[49] Australia's longstanding protectionism by contrast operated within a domestic *laissez-faire* approach, where profitability was not a matter of public directive but remained in the realm of private enterprise. Viewed as inflationary, domestic tariffs were targeted twice under Hawke and Keating for further cuts – in 1988 and 1991 – with Keating foreshadowing that 'general tariff rates will phase down over four years from 1992 to 1996 from 15 and 10 percent to a single rate of 5%'.[50] What was significant about many economies in the Asian region by the 1980s was a harmonisation of export-oriented industries, or a willingness to foster a competitive advantage through protection, rather than simply compete openly across the board.[51] To some extent this was dominated by Japan's economic interests and investments, but by the 1990s, the economies of the region found or were forced to find greater opportunities for exports alongside their own domestic consumption, pressured further by multilateral trade talks under GATT and through APEC.

The other significant feature of the region's economies facing Australia was their deregulated, low-wage, ostensibly neoliberal domestic policies towards labour in production. Organised labour was ineffective in many countries throughout Asia, although highly militant in some cases. Workforces were chronically underpaid and socially vulnerable with a large supply of the low-skilled.[52] Australia's immediate approach under Hawke was the Prices and Incomes Accord, which on the one hand, suggested a high degree of regulation, but typical of neoliberal policies, it was regulation ultimately in support of deregulation.[53] The move towards enterprise bargaining in Australia cemented with the Industrial Relations Reform Act, 1993, along with increasing legal frameworks and restrictions, such as secondary boycotts legislation turned the decade-long Accord in favour of private enterprise over organised labour.[54]

118 *Terms of engagement I*

The longstanding tradition of comparative wage justice, where wage increases in one industry would be a benchmark for other sectors was firmly in the Government's sights with the Accord and then Enterprise Bargaining.[55] To avoid any pressure on inflation, only fit and agile enterprises would be entitled to wage increases in this *centralised–decentralised* model of industrial relations. Wages and labour policy was not simply a matter of efficiency for employees and employers under arbitration, however:

> we said to the ACTU that it was our strong position that there had to be some adjustment of wages policy if we were to overcome the impact of devaluation on the economy and be able to capitalise on all the advantages. The ACTU accepted that there had to be some impact on wages policy but there certainly was a lack of willingness in the early stages to contemplate discounting on wage indexation increases. As we saw it, the wages policy had to be adjusted either by way of indexation or by way of forestalling productivity increases ... or a combination of both.[56]

What the then Minister for Employment and Industrial Relations Ralph Willis raises in this 1986 Parliamentary speech are the vagaries of international exchange rates on wage indexation, something no individual enterprise had any control over. So, while industry pattern bargaining or comparative wage justice was considered outmoded and antagonistic, the indiscriminate *pattern effects* of national monetary policy were allowable. This example underscores how 'centralised decentralisation' of wages policy in Australia became synonymous with neoliberalism in its valorising macro market forces over and above redistributive economics.

Decentralising the labour market was thus one of the most significant non-monetary macroeconomic polices the Hawke–Keating axis delivered in response to regional (low wage) competition. It wasn't until 1993 that non-Award agreements were fully endorsed by Keating.[57] All the while this market driven decentralisation was occurring, Australia did invest in key social welfare programmes such as Medicare and superannuation. Labor's traditional social welfare territory was not replaced wholesale by neoliberalism, although superannuation was contingent upon exchange rates, labour productivity gains and growth in national equities – none of which were secure in a global marketplace.

Remarkably, the restructuring and reorientation of Australia's economy was a political project for a market-based society driven by successive Labor Governments rather than neoconservatives or avowed neoliberal political contemporaries such as Thatcher or Reagan. Kelly's recent revision of Labor's changes to the Australian economy suggests that this was a patriotic, historically sound response based upon certain values of 'economic pragmatism, social egalitarianism and practical utility'.[58] Such values are creations to essentialise Australia's apparent success in the new global economy – 'Australian exceptionalism' is Kelly's ideal – at the same time denying arguments about neoliberalism. How any 'values' played a role in the political economy of Australia's regional trade terms is discussed in subsequent chapters.

Competition *from* Asia defined ALP policy making but so too did a desire to be a part of Asia: immigration from Asian countries continued to transform settlement patterns and historical expectations in Australia, to the point where government policy saw its own competitive advantage in being a hybrid of east and west in the region. This is the key to understanding the mixed rhetoric over the 13 years of Hawke–Keating governments on whether Australia was part of Asia and on what basis. A 1988 speech by then Minister for Employment, Education and Training, John Dawkins about Australia's future being in Asia sums up the economic determinism underpinning a call for links as deep as at the personal level:

> We need to develop political, commercial and personal links to the government, business and people of the nations to our north, not out of the goodness of our hearts or because we believe we should accommodate Asia especially, but because our survival and prosperity will depend on such links. We must look to our self interest in an increasingly competitive world. Convincing Australians that our future is in Asia should now be placed at the head of Labor's agenda.[59]

Dawkins's speech is particularly poignant for its date of delivery – Australia Day 1988, not coincidentally the year of Australia's Bicentennial. A year later, the *Garnaut Report*[60] unequivocally confirmed the trajectory of Australia's national project to 'enmesh' with Asia. One of the more influential reports on Federal Government orientations toward Asia, Garnaut was commissioned by the Hawke government in 1989 to map Australia's future economic directions. The report, *Australia and the North-East Asian Ascendancy* specifically argued for integration with a regional economic system. 1989 was also the year the APEC initiative was launched by Hawke, notably while visiting Korea.[61] The Garnaut Report could not have come at a better time for Hawke in confirming the need for APEC. The report also emboldened the Government's conviction in free trade as a panacea for Australia's inflation,[62] even while other governments continued to subsidise their own productive sectors. Speaking to the latest instalment in tariff reductions in the 1991 budget speech, Bob Hawke explained:

> with these tariff cuts, we demonstrate once again our commitment to liberalising international trade. The Government has been fortified in this approach by a number of recent reports, not least Dr Ross Garnaut's report *Australia and the Northeast Asian Ascendancy*. We

120   *Terms of engagement I*

have rejected the views of the so-called 'new protectionists'... [h] owever much our competitors might break or bend the principles of fair trade.[63]

While this statement serves to illustrate the ongoing influence of the Garnaut Report, the fact that Hawke spoke of *free* trade as *fair* trade is particularly noteworthy in this context, given that the world's trading nations were by no means presenting a level playing field. Nevertheless, faith in the Asian free market shaped much of the 1991 Budget. Ross Garnaut's work on this theme is more telling of his neoliberal predilections and the increasing momentum around Australia's free trade with Asia. Garnaut and Drysdale[64] subsequently presented a number of neoliberal preferences including 'open regionalism', reliance on market integration over intergovernmental integration, and rejecting discriminatory or quasi-protectionist regional blocs (such as the EC/EU and the NAFTA and MERCOSUR). The kind of regionalism presented by Garnaut and Drysdale purported that social, cultural and political concerns are not requisite for a region or regionalism; these may follow market activity. Garnaut and Drysdale thus saw a role for government in fostering this to ensure trade is open and efficient. Unfortunately, the social, cultural and political concerns proved to be some of the more obstinate or defining problems of an Asia-Pacific economic bloc for Australia.

While Hawke presided over a period of 'catch up' with Asia, Keating as prime minster considered Australia's economic position improving from around 1993 with the conclusion of the Uruguay Round of GATT. Combined with US agreement to join in APEC, hosting the first meeting in Seattle in November 1993, Keating's longstanding desire and belief in multilateral free trade as the best option for Australia was given a fillip.[65] The USA was not originally a leading proponent of APEC. Australia saw US involvement as vital. Some authors, echoing the party political opposition to Keating's approach to Asia have claimed Keating was a convert to Asia only upon taking over the prime ministership and that his policy only represented an intensification of Hawke policy, not a different approach.[66] As Keating himself reflected some years later:

> When I became prime minister in 1991 the common accusation was that, because of my known personal interests in European arts and music, it must follow that I had no interest in Asia. It was a strange charge that you had to be a cultural orientalist to know where Australia's interests lay ... Later, the line from my political opponents changed to an assertion that I had an 'Asia only' policy – an obsession with it – and was ignoring Europe.[67]

Keating's monetary policy as Treasurer under Hawke clearly favoured engagement with Asia with regional economic growth in mind, although

Terms of engagement I   121

Keating made at least two definitive speeches to Asian audiences on the limits of what being an Asian country meant, the latter just prior to his electoral defeat in March 1996. On both occasions there was a consistent message:

> Claims that the Government is trying to turn Australia into an 'Asian country' are based on a misunderstanding of both my own approach and the direction of government policy ... Put simply, Australia is not, and can never be, an 'Asian nation' any more than we can – or want to be – European or North American or African.[68]

And in 1996, at a public address in Singapore: 'I have never believed that Australians should describe themselves as Asians or that Australia is or can become part of Asia.'[69] Keating clarified his position on engagement with Asia in the following recollection years later: 'because the stakes for Australia in Asia were, and are, so high, and because there were *powerful cultural and historical forces resisting this transition*, I wanted to make our [Australia's] intention abundantly clear.'[70]

The cultural and historical forces of resistance Keating refers to range from the labour tradition, dependency on the Commonwealth, and the social and cultural hangover of the White Australia Policy that could just as easily have ignored 'Asia' as a catalyst for change. The fact that a resistance was seen to exist – and judging by the interminable (un)popular sentiment in Australia about 'Asians' and about multiculturalism supporting Asian migration, it did exist – there is some rationale in Keating and the whole 13-year Labor period of government needing to elaborate both rhetoric and conviction about 'Australia as an Asian country', as Hayden initially put it.

The contrast between Hayden's opening gambit in at the ASEAN–Australia Forum in the early 1980s with Keating's 1996 statement is a palpable representation of the full term of Labor thinking on engagement with Asia – from naïveté about wanting to belong and be immediately Asian, to being Australia within an Asia more broadly defined. As his term continued, Keating was prepared to talk up Australia's independence more than Hawke, and while many observers have lauded Hawke's consensus approach to politics,[71] Keating proved to be more assertive of independence. The growing Republican movement and the High Court *Mabo* case on Native Title were major developments evincing a new confidence about Australia's identity making, underpinned by a growing economy. Keating's forces of historical and cultural resistance were no doubt rebuffed on these occasions. And while Hawke's term was preoccupied with building productivity and infrastructure capacity for better export performance, Keating saw Australia as much more capable of reverse engineering the foreign investment trend of the 1980s and pushing Australia's business investment potential in Asia:

122 *Terms of engagement I*

> The opportunities for Australian companies in the Asia Pacific region are boundless, and as we continue to transform ourselves into a competitive and sophisticated manufacturing nation ... we will begin to see the huge rewards to be reaped from the changes we made in the eighties.[72]

> We're not going to be making cameras out in Parramatta because we're not going to be able to make a camera competitively with lots of other countries. But we can put telephone technology into Indonesia and Thailand.[73]

To this extent Keating was given opportunity to be decidedly different from Hawke, while his apparent tactics of framing regional discourse around the 'Asia-Pacific', rather than South or Northeast Asia indicates that he did have one eye on domestic concerns about being Asia-centric, and the other on balancing Australia's role by playing off its separate but influential relationships with the US and with East Asian leaders.[74] Importantly, Keating's 1993 and 1996 election launches both opened with statements on foreign policy, underlying the export-oriented Asia focused programme he had pursued for some time.

The Labor government's efforts by 1995 did not seem to resonate with the Australian public however, with some consistent evidence from public opinion polls and ultimately the 1996 election defeat resolving that the Australian polity was not quite accepting of being part of Asia, or not yet.[75] That election should not be seen solely as won or lost on the issue of economic restructuring for Asian engagement. There was, however, a wave of anti-Asian sentiment ushered in via the election of right-wing populist politician Pauline Hanson in 1996. What Keating's demise on this count does confirm, along with a number of anti-Asian backlashes throughout the 1980s (with a third backlash via Pauline Hanson) is that the politics of Australian identity making, inextricably linked with Asian regional economic engagement under Labor, was a struggle over the State's role in shaping global relations of production: an attempt to account for culture and identity either as a factor in market competition or as a competitive component in (globalising) its material productive forces. This is taken up in detail in subsequent chapters, but Keating's Singapore speech of 1996 is insightful on this:

> More important over time, I think, will be where we stand on the larger debate not about 'Asian' or western values, but about values themselves and what the role of government should be in shaping them.

> Fundamentally it will be a debate between those who believe the main role of government is to get out of the way and let the market rip and those who consider that government provided it is operating with the

consent of the governed has a role in shaping and expressing the values of our community. Defined this way, the debate cuts across Asian and western societies alike.[76]

This is an exemplary statement about a Labor government in denial that it was bringing in marketisation yet still seeing a role for itself in shaping 'values' independent of that marketisation.

Conclusion

Reflecting on the argument thus far, it is no coincidence that the 1970s global economic crises allowed space for social and cultural gains, hard won after protracted and significant civil and controversial military conflict experienced in many Keynesian liberal democracies the previous decade or more. For a brief period, the gains in and through multicultural policy and migrant advocacy in the 1970s can be understood as one part of asserting the 'embedding' of the economy. By the early 1980s market economic forms sponsored by an emergent neoliberal ideology challenged publicly planned industrialism and organised labour (as well as welfare). It would be erroneous to see this social contest simply as 'double movement', or as a sequential social phenomenon in this sense. Any such notion of historical struggle between capital and its social control is best seen in this period as dynamic, or 'combined and uneven' dependent upon major turns in the macro political economy.

The role of key actors within government, particularly Prime Ministers Hawke and Keating, are evident. Of course, they were supported by a bureaucracy with leading policy advisers who together were instrumental in shifting Australia towards being a regionally competitive trading nation. These dynamics emanating from within certain government circles are an indicator of how Productive Diversity would later be conceptualised and utilised. While their administrations clearly pursued market-based solutions to economic and social problems, neither Hawke nor Keating demonstrated a Thatcherite position that society itself, its institutions and ideals were anathema. Neoliberalism as ideology reveals only part of the story with the actions of the Hawke–Keating period best seen as a variation of neoliberalism. Laborite concerns for a national form of competitive advantage within regional cooperation, coupled with macroeconomic interventions aiming to attract new sources of FDI reflect their party's approach to economic governance that was not of an ideal or pure *laissez faire* type.

Having outlined in this chapter key transformations in Australia's competitiveness as a frame for understanding multicultural policy making, Chapter 8 examines just how grounded or embedded cultural values were in notions of Australia's productiveness and competitiveness. It provides a basis for understanding the ideational limits to multiculturalism in Australia without also considering the emergent global political economy.

Notes

1 Fitzgerald was appointed by Gough Whitlam as Ambassador to China.
2 'How to Talk to Asia', *The Sydney Morning Herald*, 16 May 1978, and Jones, M, (1978) '600 Experts on Asian Studies Confer in Sydney', *The Sydney Morning Herald*, 15 May.
3 Fitzgerald, S. and Drysdale, E. (1980) *Asia in Australian Education: Report of the Committee on Asian Studies to the Asian Studies Association of Australia*, August, Canberra: Asian Studies Association of Australia, Committee on Asian Studies; King, R. (1997) 'Australians Studying Asia: The ASAA 1976–1997', Honours dissertation, University of New South Wales. http://coombs.anu.edu.au/SpecialProj/ASAA/King/King01.html (accessed 5 August 2009).
4 Cited in Milner, A. 'The Rhetoric of Asia', in Cotton, J. and Ravenhill, J. (eds) (1997) *Seeking Asian Engagement: Australia in World Affairs 1991–95*, Melbourne: Oxford University Press in association with Australian Institute of International Affairs, p. 33.
5 Kivisto, P. (2002) *Multiculturalism in a Global Society*, Oxford: Blackwell. Cf. London, H. (1970) *Non-White Immigration and the 'White Australia' Policy*, Sydney: Sydney University Press, pp. 179–204.
6 Barwick, Sir G., Cairns, J.F. Crawford, Sir J., Roces, A. and Kojima, K. (1963) *Living with Asia: A Discussion on Australia's Future*, Sydney: Australian Institute of International Affairs, NSW Branch.
7 The point here is not to settle on what led to the end of the White Australia Policy, but to point out that the social experience of nascent globalisation was broadly felt.
8 Dalrymple, R. (2003) *Continental Drift: Australia's Search for a Regional Identity*, Aldershot, Hants: Ashgate.
9 Dibb, P. (1986) *Review of Australia's Defense Capabilities: Report for the Minister for Defense* Canberra: AGPS.
10 Cotton, J. and Ravenhill, J. pose a similar comparison of logic, in Cotton, J. and Ravenhill, J. (eds) (1997).
11 The MX missile 'crisis', for example, negotiations over US bases in Australia, New Zealand's opposition to US nuclear capability all showed signs of a weakening in unanimity between the Korean-war era ANZUS pact signatories. See Carpenter, T. (1986) 'Pursuing a Strategic Divorce: The U.S. and the Anzus Alliance', *Cato Institute Policy Analysis*, No.67. Washington, DC: Cato Institute, http://www.cato.org/pubs/pas/pa067.html (accessed 12 May 2013).
12 Cotton, J. and Ravenhill, J., 'Australia's "Engagement with Asia"', in Cotton, J. and Ravenhill, J., (1997), pp. 4–7.
13 IMG Consultants-Australia New Zealand Business Council Ltd (1985) *The Role of Australia and New Zealand in the Asia and Pacific Region*, Canberra: Department of Trade, p. 4.
14 Wiseman, J. (1998), p. 46. IMF statistics produce a slightly lower figure of 3% for Australia, as per Table 1.
15 David, A and Wheelwright, T. (1989), p. 256.
16 Ibid., pp. 256–58.
17 Lim, H., 'Regional Trade Agreements and Conflict: The Case of Southeast Asia', in Rafi, S. (ed.) (2009) *Regional Trade Integration and Conflict Resolution*, Abingdon, UK and New York: Routledge, in association with the International Development Research Centre, Ottawa. The Plaza Accord was an agreement between the world's major economies to purposely devalue the US dollar, ratified at the Plaza Hotel, New York.

Terms of engagement I   125

18 Reserve Bank of Australia (1997) 'Australian Economic Statistics 1949–1950 to 1996–1997', *Occasional Paper No. 8*, http://www.rba.gov.au/statistics/frequency/occ-paper-8.html#section_3 (accessed 5 March 2010), Table, 3.21a.
19 Griffin-Warwicke, J. (1992), see Graph 9.
20 Griffin-Warwicke, J. (1992).
21 Ravenhill, J. (ed.) (2005) *Global Political Economy*, Oxford and New York: Oxford University Press. See especially the chapter by Hiscox, M.J , 'The Domestic Sources of Foreign Economic Policies' on the Plaza Accord.
22 David, A. and Wheelwright, T. (1989).
23 There are extensive micro- and macroeconomic foreign ownership rule changes detailed in the Foreign Investment Review Board (FIRB) reports produced by the Board for the Government. While they cannot be all detailed here, in sum, there were constant refinements to facilitating foreign investment by expanding investment market opportunities or lifting thresholds for which investment had to be reported. The intention of giving foreign capital freer access is clear. Specific references to FIRB reports consulted in this research follow.
24 FIRB (1994) *Foreign Investment Review Board Report*, 1993–94, Canberra: Commonwealth of Australia, p. 30.
25 These measures have since been analysed and cited so widely that they need no further explanation.
26 See *Hansard*, 26 September 1972., pp. 1925–28.
27 David, A. and Wheelwright, T. (1989).
28 FIRB Reports, 1998, 1990, 1994.
29 David, A. and Wheelrwright, T. (1989).
30 Rodan, G. (ed.) (1996) *Political Oppositions in Industrialising Asia*, London and New York: Routledge.
31 Griffin-Warwicke, J. (1992).
32 Walters, R. (1990) *Recent Developments in Asia Pacific Investment*, Canberra: DFAT.
33 Ibid., pp. 30–36.
34 Paul Keating, in 'Economic Strategy: Discussion of Matter of Public Importance', *Hansard*, 15 June 1989, p. 3557.
35 Greene, P.G. (1988) 'Dimensions of Perceived Entrepreneurial Obstacles', cited in Baughn, C.C. and Neupert, K.E. (2003) 'Culture and National Conditions Facilitating Entrepreneurial Start-ups', *Journal of International Entrepreneurship*, Vol. 1, pp. 313–30; Ibrahim and Galt (2003), p. 1109.
36 Leigh (2002). The ALP suffered a 30-seat loss in 1975, or only one-third of the House of Representatives, precipitated by its dismissal from Office by the Governor General.
37 Bob Hawke, cited in Steketee, M. (1986) 'Hawke Takes a Swipe at the Leaders of Business', *Sydney Morning Herald*, 5 July, p. 6.
38 Keating, P. (1991) 'Statement by the Treasurer The Honorable P.J. Keating MP: Building a Competitive Australia – Taxation Measures', in Bob Hawke, Paul Keating and John Button, 12 March, *Building a Competitive Australia*, Canberra: Department of Prime Minister and Cabinet/AGPS, p. 2.1.
39 Kelly, P. (1992) *The End of Certainty*, St Leonards, NSW: Allen & Unwin, e.g. p. 250; Pusey, M. (1991). Note that economic rationalism as it was used by the Labor Party in the early 1980s referred to economies of scale – see various entries in Australian *Hansard*, http://www.aph.gov.au/Parliamentary_Business/Hansard/Search (accessed 2 April 2020), notably those by Senator Barry Jones.
40 Bates, S. (1997) 'The Foreign Economic Policies of the Hawke and Keating Governments', in Lee, D. and Waters, C. (eds) *Evatt to Evans: The Labor Tradition in Australian Foreign Policy*, St Leonards, NSW: Allen & Unwin in

126 Terms of engagement I

association with the Department of International Relations, Research School of Pacific and Asian Studies, Australian National University, Canberra, p. 251.

41 Bill Hayden, cited in *Sydney Morning Herald*, 18 January 1984.

42 The 'Blainey debate' was ostensibly a public argument about Asian migrants and the limits not of multiculturalism, but of assimilation. It is discussed in Chapter 8.

43 Higgot, R.A and Nossal, K.R (1997) 'The International Politics of Liminality: Relocating Australia in the Asia Pacific', *Australian Journal of Political Science*, Vol. 32, No. 2, p. 169.

44 Cooper, in Garnaut, R. and Drysdale, P. (eds) (1994) *Asia Pacific Regionalism: Readings in International Economic Relations*, Sydney: Harper Educational Publishers in association with the Australia-Japan Research Centre, the Australian National University.

45 Barwick, Sir G. 'Ourselves and our Neighbours', in Barwick et al. (1963), p. 45. ECAPE, the Economic Commission for Asia and the Far East was a UN body.

46 The 'idea' of Asia is discussed in Chapter 8, concerning a cultural backlash.

47 Bill Hayden, cited in 'Questions Without Notice South Pacific Region: Economic and Political Developments', *Hansard*, 30 November 1983, p. 3053. System ID: chamber/hansardr/1983-11-30/0061.

48 Ibid.

49 Matthews, T. and Ravenhill, J. (1996) 'Australian Policy and Northeast Asian Economic Growth', in Robison, R. (ed.) *Pathways to Asia: The Politics of Engagement*, St Leonards, NSW: Allen & Unwin, pp. 131–70.

50 Keating, P., in Hawke, Bob, Keating, Paul and Button, John (1991), p. 3.4.

51 Rodan, G. (1996); Robison, R. 'Looking North: Myths and Strategies', in Robison, R. (ed.) (1996)., pp. 3–28.

52 Ibid.

53 Cahill, D. et al. (eds) (2013).

54 For a detailed account, see Ramsay, T. and Battin, T. (2005) 'Labor Party Ideology in the Early 1990s: Working Nation and Paths Not Taken', *Journal of Economic and Social Policy*, Vol. 9, No. 2, Article 9, http://epubs.scu.edu.au/jesp/vol9/iss2/9 (accessed 31 August 2010).

55 Kelty, B. (2003) 'The Accord, Industrial Relations and the Trade Union Movement', in Ryan, S. and Bramston, T. (ed.) *The Hawke Government: A Critical Retrospective*, Sydney: Pluto Press pp. 325–46.

56 Willis, R., cited in *Hansard*, 10 September 1986, 'New Prices and Incomes Accord: Employment Prospects Discussion of Matter of Public Importance', p. 648. System ID: chamber/hansardr/1985-09-10/0109.

57 The Award structure set minimum conditions and rights per sector or industry negotiated with trade unions and backed up by the Industrial Relations Commission arbitration processes. See Keating's Speech to the Victorian Branch of the Institute of Company Directors, 21 April 1993. See also Commonwealth of Australia, *Industrial Relations Act*, 1993; s3(a).

58 Kelly, P. (2009) *The March of the Patriots: The Struggle for Modern Australia*, Melbourne: Melbourne University Press, p. 267.

59 John Dawkins, (1988) 'Australia Statement 1988', 26 January, cited in Bates, S., p. 253.

60 Garnaut, R. (1989) *Australia and the Northeast Asian Ascendancy*, Canberra: AGPS. (Not to be confused with the vernacular 'Garnaut Report' which currently and more pervasively refers to his 2008 report on Climate Change.)

61 Bates, S., in Lee, D. and Waters, C. (eds) (1997), p. 251.

62 As noted previously, it took some time for the Labor Party to again embrace tariff cuts following the Whitlam government failure. See also Button, J. (1994)

Flying the Kite: Travels of an Australian Politician, Milson's Point, NWS: Random House. Button as former Industry Minister notes in his biography how Hawke and Keating initially wanted to emulate Scandinavian social democratic model, but by the mid-1980s pursued competitive advantage strategies with a preference for developing high value goods industries (ETMs).

63 Bob Hawke, (1991) (Budget) 'Statement by the Prime Minister', *Building a Competitive Australia*, Canberra: AGPS, p. 1.7.

64 Garnaut, R. and Drysdale, P. (eds) (1994). Peter Drysdale was then Director of Aust-Japan research Centre at ANU and Ross Garnaut professor of economics in the Research School of Pacific and Asian Studies, ANU.

65 Dalrymple, R. (2003), pp. 88–91; Keating, P. (2000) *Engagement: Australia Faces the Asia Pacific*, Sydney: Macmillan.

66 Smith, N. (2004) 'Investigating the Consumption of "Asianness" in Australia: Culture, Class and Capital'. Paper presented to the *15th Biennial Conference of the Asian Studies Association of Australia*, Canberra, 29 June–2 July; Dalrymple, R. (2003).

67 Keating, P. (2000), p. 17.

68 Ibid., pp. 20–21.

69 Keating, P. (1996) Speech by The Prime Minister, The Hon. P. J. Keating MP, The Singapore Lecture 'Australia, Asia and the New Regionalism', Singapore, 17 January, p. 6, https://pmtranscripts.pmc.gov.au/sites/default/files/original/00009905.pdf (accessed 13 April 2020).

70 Keating, P. (2000), p. 245 (my emphasis).

71 Bramston, T., 'The Hawke Leadership Model', in Ryan S. and Bramston, T. (eds) (2003), pp. 56–69.

72 Keating, P., 'Securing Our Future', Address to Corowa Shire Council centenary, Corowa, 31 July 1993, in Ryan, M. (ed.) (1995) *Advancing Australia: The Speeches of Paul Keating*, Sydney: Big Picture Publications, p. 163.

73 Keating, P., 'Doing the Placido Domingo', Address to the Canberra Press Gallery, 7 December 1990, in ibid., p. 5.

74 Dalrymple, R. (2003), pp. 92–94; Keating, P. (2000), chapter 4.

75 Dalrymple, R. (2003), pp. 103–106; Cotton and Ravenhill, in Cotton, J. and Ravenhill, J. (eds) (1997)., p. 12.

76 Keating, P. (1996).

8 Terms of engagement II
Resistance abroad and at home

Asia looms large in Australia's policy thinking about diversity. In normative terms, Asia is by no means homogeneous or self-identifying as a region, except it seems, in relation to colonialism and 20th-century western capitalism. There are historical precedents for pan-Asian societies, notably Chinese hegemony and the spread of Confucianism in the centuries before western colonialism arrived[1] or the dissemination of Buddhist and Islamic culture. But the 'idea of Asia', as Milner and Johnson describe it, has been contested throughout history.[2] Its reinvigoration within 20th-century globalisation was a distinct political project largely within ASEAN nations to define a form of unity, but this was certainly not shared by other countries such as Japan and China.[3] Chinese and Japanese economic, political and military/strategic self-sufficiency and mutual antagonism confounded any urgency for a political and cultural regionalism. Nevertheless, as the convergence of globalising forces in the 1980s intensified Australia's nation-state identity reformation, so too did the other countries of the region come to consider their individual statehood in collective terms. This is not to suggest that the politics of regional trade were benign, nor each country's position on regionalism static or harmonious. For example, within ASEAN, the ASEAN Free Trade Agreement of 1994 was preceded by severe ructions with both the Filipino and Thai governments embattled over their petrochemicals industries' vulnerability to Singapore, and Malaysia's insistence on protecting its nascent auto-manufacturing sector.[4]

One report commissioned by the Department of Foreign Affairs and Trade in 1985 presented the Australian Government with a strategic analysis that foreshadowed a bleaker future if intra-regional cooperation were to progress:

> While Australia and New Zealand would clearly gain from increased trade and specialization within Asian economies ... the gains from trade which might be obtained from closer ties between similarly endowed Asian economies is considerably less.[5]

Such was the early thinking of some Australian business strategists, self-confident that western economic control through divide and rule strategies were the preferred model of economics for the region. It typified the thinking that former diplomat to China Stephen Fitzgerald was to later lambast in his provocative testimony *Is Australia an Asian Country?* (1997), where trade and foreign affairs officials and other policy and business 'elites' failed to understand and transmit the 'Asianisation of Asia'.[6] This harsh assessment may have been true of domestic understandings of Asia and *Asianisation*, reflected in business links into (the rest of) Asia, but by 1994 'closer ties between similarly endowed Asian economies' was something for the government to celebrate once APEC had arrived:

> Some 60 per cent of APEC countries' trade is with other APEC members, and whereas in the past a great deal of the region's trade and investment was between the US and individual countries in East Asia, there is now rapidly growing trade and cross-investment between East Asian economies which have not previously had much to do directly with each other. Traditional notions of complementarity and competitiveness no longer have much application: everyone is doing business with everyone else, and doing well out of it.[7]

While APEC was vital for including Australia in a regional bloc with Japan, China and the US,[8] overt resistance to the Australian government's desire for belonging came largely from within ASEAN. If anything, Australia's decade-long claims for being part of the region confirmed by APEC in 1993 steeled Southeast Asian opposition.[9] ASEAN countries had long competed with each other for key export markets, such as for electronics, and as previously mentioned, were unable prior to the 1994 ASEAN Free Trade Agreement (AFTA) to resolve their own general mistrust of cooperating with each other economically.[10] The Hawke government was never in a position to pursue a divide and rule strategy, but its singular portrayal of Asia as a bloc to which it should belong (partly through its desire for an all-in multilateralism) contributed to an underestimation of the diversity of national politics and cultures with which it had to contend. By the 1990s, the tension around a proposed East Asian Economic Caucus (EAEC) within APEC also showed how persistent the issue of an exclusive bloc was both within and outside Australia, as did the development of AFTA (the EAEC proposal by Malaysia excluded Western countries). The desire by the Australian government to talk up the possibility of joining the Australia–New Zealand Closer Economic Relationship (CER) with the AFTA in 1994 exhibited Australia's zeal to be 'included' on all fronts. In 1994, Foreign Minister Evans chose his words carefully, but in addressing the inaugural ASEAN Regional Forum in Bangkok (a 'security' forum), talked of the benefits of a conjoint CER-AFTA, which incidentally, he reminded his audience, was first proposed by the Thais:

130   *Terms of engagement II*

> We see possibilities for the most fruitful cooperation in a linkage between AFTA and CER as has been proposed by the Deputy Prime Minister of Thailand, Dr. Supachai. The potential attractions are obvious – the joining of dynamic groups of economies of roughly equal size to create a market of some 335 million people. The pace with which such a link develops would of course be dependent on the wishes of the ASEAN countries, and we look forward to continuing our consultations in this respect.
>
> Let me make it clear, though, that Australia would bring to any such link an economy well prepared to contribute to our mutual advantage. The last decade of extensive restructuring by the Australian Government has so transformed our economy that partnership with our neighbours in South East Asia should now be seen by our neighbours as a very attractive proposition.[11]

With APEC having been secured, Foreign Minister Evans's proposal as a parlay to AFTA appears hypocritical given his and Keating's former rejection of the EAEC, made famous by the 'recalcitrant' remark about Malaysian Prime Minister Dr Mahathir subsequently failing to attend the first APEC summit. This was a major public leadership dispute between Australia and Malaysia ostensibly having built up over years of competing economic agenda and cultural animosities. Prior to Evans's July 1994 address in Bangkok, the annual ASEAN–Australia Forum in Canberra had already pursued specific cooperation measures through Phase III of the ASEAN–Australia Economic Cooperation Program (AAECP) to which Australia gave $32 million. A key platform was to be facilitation of joint ventures between government, academic institutions and private enterprises.[12] Economic cooperation was clearly as possible as it was desirable; Political and cultural belonging was not so assured. For as Australia began to talk of Asia as one and Australia as a part of that whole, other countries of Asia had not been inclined to present their futures in exactly the same way,[13] at least initially. On numerous occasions the Australian government came into conflict with its neighbours on the *culture* of regional belonging, ironically precipitating a counter discourse on a shared sense of values and purpose exclusively among Asian countries that otherwise had their own myriad bilateral and multilateral grievances. For instance, Japan's strained relations with China and Korea, China's bellicose relations with Taiwan and Hong Kong, Vietnam's relations with its client Cambodia, Communist insurgency and also the southern border wars between Muslim and Christian Filipinos, or the intermittent internecine racial and cultural conflicts within Indonesia and Malaysia and suppression of ethnic minorities (e.g. Aceh).

Singapore, Malaysia, Indonesia and China all came into conflict with Australia on matters of regional belonging. Although these incidents appeared to be triggered by independent events, the pressure of Australia's economic and cultural diplomacy inflated individual diplomatic events over time. This led countries, particularly Singapore, to an engagement with Australia's own sense of purpose. When the 'Blainey Debate' on Asian immigration flared in 1984, it did not ricochet throughout Asia in the same way it would four years later when the Liberal Leader John Howard stoked the embers of anti-Asian sentiment. Broinowski's account of an incipient racism against students from Asian countries from the late 1970s notwithstanding,[14] her detailed account of Asian perceptions of Australia suggest that from the latter half of 1980s and certainly the 1990s with the election of racist MP Pauline Hanson did Australia's domestic politics around race reverberate more widely in Asia. Regional politics correspondingly were as protected as were its economies in the early 1980s and any gain to be made from exploiting Australian domestic conflicts had yet to be realised. The effect of regional cooperation efforts was also a countervailing force in this respect.

The 1986 case of two Australians, Barlow and Chambers, being executed in Malaysia for drug trafficking offences was one of the earlier episodes where a division in cultural values caused a conflict. Prime Minister Hawke's reference to Malaysia's capital punishment approach as barbaric was constructed as insensitive and meddling, and typified much of the subsequent posturing by a small number of regional leaders whenever there was a cultural diplomatic incident. A more determined chorus of anti-western rhetoric evolved in the latter 1980s, led by the 'Singapore School' under Prime Minister Lee Kuan Yew, and became the doctrine of 'Asian values' or the 'Asian way'.[15] US hegemony, as much as Australia's moves, was responsible for generating this expression of counter-Orientalism by the Singapore School but, according to Lawson, Australia approached it mostly with 'kid gloves', and sometimes compliance, preferring to work within apparent Eastern sensibilities.[16] This didn't stop Australia from being a target. When Lee provocatively referred to Australia potentially becoming the 'poor white trash of Asia' initially in the early 1980s and then again in the early 1990s,[17] he drew a line in the sand on the matter of regional belonging while simultaneously diverting attention from the vagaries of authoritarian political rule employed by Singapore, Malaysia, China and elsewhere.

There is some consensus that the Asian Values campaign was merely political bluster or a smokescreen for authoritarian practices in some Asian countries.[18] Nevertheless, countries such as Singapore followed through with domestic social policy goals aimed to create or support what they fabricated as the pillars of an exclusive Asian society, with the idea of the 'family' being foundational. For example, Prime Minister Goh Chok Tong in his 1994 National Day speech foreshadowed a range of socially exclusionary policies he intended to pursue such as barring unmarried mothers from purchasing state housing, foisting responsibility for maintenance

132   Terms of engagement II

payments for aged parents upon their offspring, and restricting medical insurance for female civil servants to encourage the practice and belief that men should receive and disperse remuneration and support for their families.[19] Familial and social responsibility were strongly interlinked and backed up with punitive measures. Some of these policies could be critiqued as neoliberal, others neoconservative and patriarchal, but not necessarily or exclusively Asian or Singaporean. It is eventualities such as these that highlight how the cultural trade barrier between countries masked other economic concerns.

A distinction should be made here between the 'Asian values' of the 1980s–1990s, which were aiming to be exclusionary on distinctive cultural grounds, and the 'Asian way' of doing things, which was intended to express that an alternative worldview on matters such as universal human rights was both possible and necessary because of material historical factors. The Bangkok Declaration of 1993 being the more famous regional statement on the matter of human rights[20] was nevertheless drawing upon such precedents as those originating in the 1976 ASEAN Treaty of Amity and Cooperation. Signed at the first ASEAN Summit, that Treaty was to legally enforce peaceful coexistence through non-interference in the internal affairs of each other's country.[21] This 'Asian Way' or rather 'ASEAN Way' in 1976 had mutual security and economic development concerns rather than a fundamental ethics that might be construed as Asian Values. The simple irony of the 'Asian Way' is that it protected internal differences of countries rather than built similarity among its subscribers.

There were many in Australia who shared some of these Asian Values, not least the former Liberal Premier of Western Australia, Richard Court, who spoke encouragingly after visiting Singapore in 1994 that:

> They [Singaporeans] have entrenched a highly disciplined approach to law and order issues where everyone knows the ground rules ... There is no doubt that the discipline at a younger age has helped instil a strong sense of responsibility and pride in their country.[22]

Issues such as capital punishment were not far under the surface of conservative Australia, nor were other more extreme tenets of policing by force, exhibited in Queensland, for example, under Sir Joe Bjelke-Petersen. Australia also shared much in common with other countries in the region in manifestations of irregular and more questionable business practises: bias, favouritism, etc. existed in the economies of both centralised and liberal democratic nation-states.[23] Nevertheless, engagement with Asia in the 1980s and early 1990s presented itself as an 'identity divide' based on ethics and morality both in Australia and in its relationship with the rest of Asia.

For Australian leaders to sell the idea domestically of becoming an Asian nation in any form would become much less tenable as the political nature of regional belonging contended with economic downturns including recessions in 1981 and 1991, the metaphor as much as the reality of rescinding protectionism, and wholesale changes in the social relations of production from a primary goods and industrial mass manufacturing economy to more open (vulnerable), free trade economy characterised by self-reliant SMEs and largely in services. The results of such changes included mass job losses in large industry such as steel making and coal from the early 1980s – the steel industry in Australia's largest 'steel town' shed around 15% of jobs in 1983 alone, even though steel demand had not decreased.[24] Manufacturing job losses represented about 28% of total unemployed for the same year Australia wide, and averaged almost one quarter of all job losses from 1983 to 1990. Total unemployment averaged a relatively high 8.5% between 1982 and 1986 and always at least 1% higher for migrants.[25] An increase to 40% in part time over full time work and a decline in real wages in the decade to 1992 for 90% of wage earners, lower taxation meaning less public funding for services and tightening of welfare support[26] all made for a difficult political and social climate in which to sell an open relationship with Asian economies and societies.

While no political leader in Australia had ever entertained the idea of abandoning Western parliamentary democracy and its notions of individual freedom for a differently perceived Asian *political* way,[27] many did see the neoliberal socioeconomic way as more or less an Asian way; a decentralised, flexible way of workplace relations, of collective and individual diligence, of limited welfare. Lee Kuan Yew reiterated this 'Asian way' on a number of occasions, pontificating on the defectiveness of Australia's economic complacency:

> As we were upgrading our economies you were carrying on with your old ways ... Within five to seven years you can bring all the barriers down and being to mesh in. But it will be painful at the beginning... It does mean your unions have got to change their philosophy of life and management has got to get trim.[28]

The Tiananmen and Dili massacres notwithstanding, what defined Labor's embrace of the region was that it refrained in large measure from stoking the embers of the Asian values furnace with careful statements on human rights, lest it be denied its need to be part of the Asian 'economic miracle'.[29] What the Australian Government did do in its attempts to be included was valorise multiculturalism as both an example of its harmonious, egalitarian society and as productive asset abroad. Multiculturalism, Prime Minister Hawke claimed in 1988, was integral to 'Australia's relations with the Asian Pacific region'.[30] Prime Minister Keating in 1994 said 'while you had any basis of racial selection [in the immigration programme] you couldn't hope to be accepted as part of the region ... I think the multicultural feature of our country plays very well in the Asia-Pacific'.[31] Anything less than this would have defeated Australia's recruitment of business and skilled migrants from

134   *Terms of engagement II*

Asia. Foreign Minister Gareth Evans presented multiculturalism as a shared values concept in which:

> Malaysia, Singapore, Australia, Canada and the United States - have been prepared to recognise each other as proudly multicultural, rather than monocultural, in outlook. That phenomenon is being reinforced all the time by the high level of people-to-people exchange, particularly in tourism, education and, in our case, immigration, and over time this does work to pull the region together.[32]

Multiculturalism was not a moral 'value', but it did communicate a certain moral position, as well as promising a cultural brokering service for business in Asia. And while it may have been presented as an asset abroad, and at the very least confirmed that Australia was no longer promoting a 'White Australia', multiculturalism was mired in contest on the domestic front throughout the period of the Hawke and Keating governments largely because it was linked to the political economy of engaging with Asia. The following section discusses the domestic resistance and how labour ultimately resolved this by appealing to Australia's productiveness as a modern value rather than its European cultural heritage.

Asia at home – domestic contestation of the global political economy

The long-term vision of Australia's participatory role as an Asian nation in global trade, accompanied by immediate policy changes to effect this can be interpreted from the material changes in global economic production described in the previous chapter and more broadly in Chapter 4 on Global Value Chains. Australia's economic opportunities were being re-mapped prior to the Hawke government, but his and then Keating's administration were solely responsible for developing a wholesale programme of engagement, 'enmeshment', competition and cooperation with Asia's rapidly expanding economies and their large numbers of migrants (actual and prospective). Engagement with the people as much as the countries of the region was a constant throughout Hawke–Keating period, initially through family reunion of refugees from the conflict in Indochina and then later tourism and workforce-related migration. The 1981 Australian Census recorded just over 256,000 people born in countries of Asia, with Vietnamese being the largest single group at the time, accounting for 41,000.[33] These were mostly refugees fleeing either government persecution or poverty or displaced as a result of conflict between Vietnam and Cambodia. Within ten years, by 1991, the number of resident migrants and citizens from Asia had more than doubled to 563,000.[34] As a group, they were a perceived as a large visible minority, in numbers almost as large as the 660,000-strong Southern European cohort of mostly Italian, Greek and Maltese migrants who had been arriving since 1946.

The migration figures continued to show a majority of arrivals overall from UK and Europe in the first years of the Hawke Labor government, despite conservative pronouncements about the *Asianisation* of Australia. In fact, as Hawke pointed out at the time, the 45% of visas issued to UK/Europeans occurred 'despite a diminution of migrant applications from that region', thus repudiated 'claims of anti-British bias or anti-European bias' in Labor's migration programme.[35] The idea of a 'balance' or a ratio of Anglo to Asian migrants emerged as a point of demarcation between Labor and the Conservatives under the first Hawke government, and would become entrenched as a fault line between the two political camps throughout the 1980s and 1990s. After some infamous remarks by the ex-military Returned Serviceman's League (RSL) leadership on Asian immigration in 1982,[36] emerging reports on unemployment among Asian immigrants, notably refugees,[37] then the eruption of the 'Blainey Debate' about Asians and migrant 'ghettoization' on 17 March 1984 in rural Victoria, Bob Hawke challenged the idea of an 'ethnic balance' as a party political issue:

> The Leader of the Opposition (Mr Peacock) has in this place and in statements to the media indicated that he is not opposed to the present number of Asians coming into Australia. Indeed, he said on Nationwide on 8 May that the 'right number' of Asians was now coming in. He has however, expressed concern about the 'mix' or the 'balance', as he put it, of the present migrant intake and has called for an increase in European migration.[38]

The increasing intake of migrants from Asia was still not the key transformative issue in the first years of the Labor government driving attempts at regional integration. Domestic politics however construed Asian immigration as a problem for Australia, and as a corollary to post-industrial immigration, multiculturalism was also consistently attacked. Blainey continued throughout 1984 with alarmist claims that ghetto formation and racial unrest would follow[39] and released a book lamenting not only social change, but also the apparent loss of democracy, supplanted by a ministerial-bureaucratic immigration clique.[40] By the end of that year some 350 print media reports and 200 letters to editors had been published[41] casting the Blainey Debate as one of the more notorious yet defining features of Australia's nascent multiculturalism.

The Blainey Debate of 1984 and subsequent anti-Asian racism was the subject of intense scrutiny and analysis,[42] and does not require explicit detail here. The bedrock issue of the 'debate' that social cohesion was threatened implicitly by ethnic diversity, however, marks an important, if inadvertent turn in the acceptance of the assimilation of Australia's European immigrants – the 'marginal whites' as Stratton defined them.[43]

136   *Terms of engagement II*

Racism, rather than ethnicity was the critical issue, for the debate had, despite Blainey's own deeper pro-British desires[44] cemented the idea that Asians were different not just from the dominant Anglo-Australia but from the broad European makeup of Australia's ethno-cultural demographic. A frontier had been drawn and multiculturalism was the key rhetorical ordnance deployed to defend against the successive wave of racist attacks, nonetheless backed up by the 1975 Racial Discrimination Act as the more definitive weapon at the government's disposal.

The idea of multiculturalism was more positive than the punitive idea of a Racial Discrimination Act (RDA) and therefore the more obvious choice for political leaders to build a least-coercive consensus for the shift from one social order to another. The idea, for example, that Australia could be bludgeoned into social integration with Asia through legislative repression via the RDA or similar mechanisms would seem untenable. Pursuing actual legal charges against racists such as Blainey might also be counter-productive. Creating or manipulating a modern global productive culture as Hawke and Keating's governments did clearly suited the economic times. For that political reason the relationship between immigration and multiculturalism was necessary, a relationship the CAAIP Report was to criticise in 1988. This marks a fundamental distinction between the purpose of social cohesion and multiculturalism in the period. While these two approaches to population diversity 'management' suggest different ethics, they are each suited to specific economic purpose.[45]

The anti-Asian trend in Australia was also coupled with attacks on multiculturalism as elitist,[46] along with other claims that Australia would suffer ecologically because immigration was overpopulating Australia. A New Right had emerged in the public sphere but was a curious amalgam of neoliberal economic rationalists and historical nationalists.[47] It attacked those who were engineering the ambitious economic transformation of Australia with an 'Asian' social and cultural affinity, suggesting an alternative way for Australia that ignored the historical forces of production and consumption challenging Australia's *cultural* protectionism, while embracing neoliberal social relations of production. Then President of the conservative Liberal Party, John Elliot, was still calling for Australia to join the EEC (EU) as late as 1989, the same year Hawke announced the APEC initiative:

> Because we are so small we have to get ourselves in with a trading bloc, and it would be beneficial to be part of a much bigger global market. It doesn't mean you lose Asians or their trade; what membership of the EEC would do is give us access to the biggest market in the world, which we do not have now... Australia is the last bastion of Europe in Asia and the cultural differences would suggest that Australia would be a lot better off in the EEC.[48]

The desire for a familiar connection between culture, production and trade are laid bare in Elliot's comment. However, Australia's entrenched monolingualism, its history as a colonial outpost, its attraction of more and more migrants from the Asian region left it no more continental European than Asian by the end of the 1980s.

The year 1986 had been a turning point in the politics of neoliberalism *for* and *against* engagement with Asia, *for* and *against* multiculturalism. The post-Blainey right-wing criticism of multiculturalism and its connection to Asian migration unnerved the Labor government, despite their public statements. Under the guise of federal budget cuts, a policy of *mainstreaming* emerged which aimed to bring a range of services and access and equity provisions out of statutory orbit and within the official policy regime. The Australian Institute of Multicultural Affairs, originally established by former Prime Minister Fraser to redress, in his own words, 'the lack of information on multicultural developments in Australia and overseas',[49] was to be closed as an independent institute and a new government Office of Multicultural Affairs (OMA) established; English-as-a-second-language (ESL) funding in schools was halved; the multicultural broadcaster, SBS was to merge with the larger Australian Broadcasting Commission; and the Human Rights Commission, a key statutory body for migrant justice, was earmarked for closure.[50] Key bureaucrats at the time have since suggested that the reshaping of multicultural policy and advocacy services was inadvertent and simply part of a wider budget cutting exercise; a 'bureaucratic cock-up' according to one.[51] Given that a new ideology of *mainstreaming* accompanied the cuts, it is difficult to countenance a position that the cuts were unintentional or just a 'cock-up'. Mainstreaming was thought out, devised, and pre-empted the savaging of multicultural service provision. Regardless, the Labor government reversed most of its decisions after months of coordinated protestations mostly from ethnic representative organisations. It simultaneously announced it would hold a committee of inquiry into immigration, what was to become known as the Fitzgerald Inquiry, resulting in the *CAAIP Report* of 1988.[52] That report marks a major divide in the political economy of migration and multiculturalism in Australia and is analysed both below and in subsequent chapters.

Questioning the link between migration and multiculturalism

The CAAIP Report delivered to government on 16 May 1988 was notable for identifying a public conception about the link between immigration and multiculturalism as a problem, such that immigration levels and/or composition were not enjoying wide public support, while the government invariably managed or was seen to have managed immigration as a feature of multiculturalism or the desire for a culturally plural society. According to the report, no clear rationale for an immigration programme was evident in

138 *Terms of engagement II*

the 'public mind'.[53] CAAIP, through its Chair, Stephen Fitzgerald, suggested that a decoupling of the two in public policy would be desirable to allay public prejudice and keep the immigration programme on track CAAIP.[54] CAAIP spoke to social cohesion and suggested that through an assertion of a new Australian nationalism, 'multiculturalism might seem less divisive or threatening'.[55] CAAIP's timing in the year of Australia's bicentennial gave it further resonance and while celebrations of Anglo and European Australia at the expense of Black Australia were in full swing, multiculturalism became increasingly seen as a policy facilitating Asian migration. It should be noted that in the year leading up to CAAIP and subsequently in 1989 (the year of the *National Agenda for a Multicultural Australia*), 75% of business migrants emanated from Asia, the majority of these from Hong Kong.[56] John Howard, then leader of the conservative Liberal Party, exploited community division with his infamous remarks about social problems associated with Asian immigration.[57] And while racism again found voice through Howard, it also registered on the political Richter scale in parts of Asia.[58] Just as Australia saw fit to criticise the human rights standards of some Asian countries, so too Australia found itself on the diplomatic back foot: 1988 reinvigorated a backlash at home and galvanised a partisan backlash abroad which had yet to find a concerted voice in challenging Australia's economic and political motivations.

It was somewhat naïve for CAAIP to suggest that to de-link immigration from multiculturalism in broad policy settings was possible without also questioning Australia's globalising political economy and the real opposition to that in parts of Asia. As argued above, countries in the region had their own economic development concerns in mind when challenging Australian overtures. Multiculturalism as some virtue of the modern global world was a political policy tool in this respect. Fitzgerald was more than suspicious that immigration policy was being driven by an elite group of cosmopolitan cultural pluralists with the sole aim of engineering cultural diversity for its own sake. 'Immigration to Australia is about becoming Australian. It is not driven by multiculturalism'.[59] Fitzgerald's stance was clear, and counter interpreted by the pro-Asian regional economy camp as a throw-back to Australia's discriminatory assimilationism of decades past. What CAAIP proffered was a break from the more recent past, a portrayal and rejection of historical internecine wars between multiculturalist camps that had positioned ethnic affairs as the same kind of interest group politics for which Hawke and Keating had criticised the union movement.[60] CAAIP tried to hose down the bubbling racism and fear about Australia's (Asian) diversity, and to simultaneously neuter the ethnic communities and their generally left-wing fellow travellers as agents for change.[61]

This period between 1986 and 1988 was a high point in the challenge to Australia's desire to see itself as a modern and equal partner in Asia based on its cultural diversity, mainly because of competing oppositions to the government line. *Mainstreaming,* evident in the CAAIP Report, was not just a budget crisis response, although, one of the more extreme recommendations from CAAIP was that 'User pays must be applied to immigration services'.[62] *Mainstreaming* would also have the deliberate effect of moving cultural diversity policymaking away from the ethnic lobby groups and agencies and implant it firmly and separately within key service bureaucracies, moving policy firmly away from the ethnic structural pluralism model to a hegemonic, or corporate cultural pluralism.[63]

CAAIP led parliament to a new Migration Act which aimed to reduce bureaucratic influence in migrant selection and any perceived or real influence by ethnic lobby groups. In tandem with the establishment of the National Office of Overseas Skills Recognition (NOOSR), it provided not an equitable recognition, but a timely recognition of overseas qualifications.[64] To suggest, as some have done,[65] that the Federal Government distanced itself from CAAIP following further community outcry needs qualification: there remained a continuity in policy thinking insofar as the follow up 1989 *National Agenda for a Multicultural Australia* introduced economic efficiency and entrepreneurialism with diversity as key tenets of multiculturalism. Ethnicity was envisaged as individually ascribed, voluntary, a form of cultural pluralism. As has already been established in this chapter, an economic rationale for Hawke and Keating, however, was contextualised within the 'economic miracle' of Asian regional growth and not simply resistance to the ethnic lobby groups representing 'old multiculturalism'.

CAAIP's recommendations strongly affirmed the need for business and skilled migration to Australia. This however emanated from the Report's axis of individual or self-reliance and a 'user pays' neoliberal approach to migration services. It was not formulated explicitly to satisfy the Government's desire to attract business and skilled immigrants from Asia to realise business development and open trade engagement with the region.

The government response to what was a crisis of legitimacy for the idea of multiculturalism supporting regional engagement, was to take from the CAAIP Report the focus on the economic rationale for multiculturalism, as then Office of Multicultural Affairs (OMA) head, Peter Shergold, later explained:

> As long as multiculturalism was either seen as ethnic dancing or social welfare, it really wasn't going to get the support that it required at senior levels. Not just in PM and C (Department of Prime Minister and Cabinet) but in Finance and Treasury and so on. And so, there was a conscious campaign to give it that economic dimension which has now been taken up and elaborated and called *productive diversity* and so on.[66]

This transition from multiculturalism to Productive Diversity is the focus of Chapter 9.

140 *Terms of engagement II*

Identity, productivity and work ethic

The 1989 *National Agenda*'s emphasis on individual entrepreneurial citizenship which would be followed by the Productive Diversity agenda presented to Asian leaders and business sectors the kind of social and cultural organisation some Asian leaders had been warning was essential for Australia's inclusion as a regional *economic* player. As far back as 1963, addressing the Australian Institute of International Affairs, renowned Japanese economist Kiyoshi Kojima identified Australia's likely economic readjustment required to meet Japanese and then Asian growth, and implied the related social challenge when he portended:

> for you, as for us, changes are coming. We think you will be able to accept without dismay the unhappy tendencies in markets for your primary products if the shift you are now making to higher industrialization is wisely guided. *There are, of course, difficulties in your way*, such as the high wage factor.[67]

Unionisation and tariffs, the bedrock of Australian economic *and* cultural protection, were clearly in Kojima's sights. Lee Kuan Yew's comments 30 years later in 1992 about the 'painful process of catching up'[68] that Australia would have to go through were the bookend to Kiyoshi's original observation of Australia's path towards globalisation. Work ethic was central to this insofar as it represents the degree of social control, and while Hawke and Keating managed to deliver the Prices and Incomes Accord to wrest control of the social order from trade union industrial relations, the central business of immigration was initially confounded by both ethno-multiculturalism and the Blainey-ites. Its strategic ideological reframing into Productive Diversity is the story of this book.

Overall, the morality behind Lee Kuan Yew's Asian Values idea of a common Confucian heritage which served to exclude Australia,[69] among others, could have been mistaken just as easily for a Protestant work ethic. Indeed, an Asian work ethic was very much part of the Singapore School's critique of Australia's 'welfare dependency' and '[d]eep-seated problems of work ethic, productivity, enterprise' and 'feather-bedding'.[70] This, of course, runs counter to the classic argument by Weber on the unique contribution of Western Protestantism to work, discipline and capitalist economic production.[71] Claims that the Protestant Work Ethic is falsified because of the success of 'Eastern' or Asian socioeconomic productivity systems fail to admit that the political economy of authoritarian rule has certain universal precepts – primarily, the coercion and control of the individual as human resource for production, or more simply as Marx put it as early as 1867: 'The advance of capitalist production develops a working class, which, by education, tradition and habit, looks upon the requirements of that mode of production as self-evident natural laws'.[72] While the

Terms of engagement II   141

nature of hegemonic practices of both western and eastern forms of the work ethic might reside in specific historical discourses and degrees of coercion, they are singularly concerned with disciplining social forces of production and reproduction. Despite claims being made upon individual effort, in no way do either eastern or western forms of this ethic value individual practices or discourses on individual freedoms.[73]

The war of words between certain Asian countries and Australia can be seen as a form of cultural protectionism, but possibly also a counter to colonial and western hegemony that had dominated most of Asia for the best part of the 20th century. The politics of Japan as a key regional player are not explored here, but Australia's close economic relationship with Japan in the 1980s (see Chapter 7), as well as its strategic and historical alignment with the USA, were not factors necessarily in Australia's favour. Correspondingly, what emerges is that Asia was by no mean homogeneous, but subject to nation-state rivalries concerned about their economic positioning.

Australian government efforts to elide resistance from abroad and build a regional free market also speak to the Government's desire to gain and expand market access. The nature and scope of transnational production described in previous chapters had not yet materialised in Australia the mid-1980s. But as Australia's economy moved away from its protected mass industrial and unionised production, notably in manufacturing, as the small business sector grew and alongside a steady increase in the services sector for employment, sourcing labour for value in mass production was becoming a distant an option in Australia. Asia on the other hand had an abundance of cheap labour and had already showed signs of rapid (GDP) growth, out-competing Australia in mass manufactures.

Conclusion

The rapidity and extent of economic, as well as social and cultural change engineered by the Hawke and Keating years were especially controversial for doing what most expected of a conservative neoliberal government. A particular reading of globalisation by Australian government leaders viewed Asian economic growth as peculiar to that region's own neoliberal relations of production. What this suggests is that Australia did not pursue an ostensibly neoliberal market economy strategy simply out of intrinsic ideological choice but through an observation and interpretation of the region as more competitive and also a source of value. Labor government planning under Prime Ministers Hawke and then Keating still retained strategic thinking befitting their Keynesian nation-building heritage: occupational skills planning and population growth management continued to play a front and centre position in migration policy, regional engagement was as much about national competition as private enterprise. Regional economic competition and restructuring the domestic economy, however,

142 *Terms of engagement II*

within a neoliberal frame inextricably linked post-1988 migration and diversity policy to a new multiculturalism for self-reliance and opportunity in a global free market. Countering the resistance both abroad and at home required a new brand of multiculturalism, one being reconfigured from within Government as a new model of a globally connected, economically modern and productive Australia. The CAAIP Report was a policy catalyst for this.

What is also evident from Chapter 4 on Global Value Chains is that regionalisation, as an aspect of globalisation, challenged nation but reaffirmed a role for state. The powerful role of the state to create the consensus and motifs for the shifting economic relations becomes evident through the next stage of multicultural policy making: Productive Diversity. Here, the idea of values as fundamental to culture and identity is tuned on its head: the value of ideas fundamental to market economics, that is innovation and entrepreneurial know-how became the basis for affirming a new citizenship.

Notes

1 Frank, A.G. (1998) *ReOrient: Global Economy in the Asian Age*, Berkeley: University of California Press.
2 Milner, A. and Johnson, D. (2002) *The Idea of Asia*, Canberra: Faculty of Asian Studies, Australian National University, http://dspace.anu.edu.au/bitstream/1885/41891/1/idea.html (accessed 6 September 2009).
3 Milner, A. 'The Rhetoric of Asia', in Cotton, J. and Ravenhill, J. (eds) (1997), pp. 37–38; Fitzgerald, S. (1997) *Is Australia and Asian Country?* St Leonards, NSW: Allen & Unwin, pp. 42–43.
4 Lim, H., 'Regional Trade Agreements and Conflict: The Case of Southeast Asia', in Rafi, S. (ed.) (2009).
5 IMG Consultants-Australia New Zealand Business Council Ltd (1985).
6 Fitzgerald, S. (1997). By 'Asianisation of Asia', Fitzgerald meant that Australia and many other western countries were simply unaccustomed or unaware of the possibility that countries of Asia might be collaborating and converging to the extent they did.
7 Evans, G. (1995) 'Australia in East Asia and the Asia-Pacific: Beyond the Looking Glass', *Australian Journal of International Affairs*. Vol. 49. No. 1. May, p. 105.
8 Dalrymple, R. (2002).
9 Lee Kuan Yew's more provocative statements reported in Australia were in 1992 and 1994, including a reiteration of Australia as 'the poor white trash of Asia' statement. See Kelly, P. (2009), p. 464; see also Sheridan, G. (1997) *Tigers: Leaders of the New Asia-Pacific*, St Leonards, NSW: Allen & Unwin, pp. 70–72 for Singaporean accounts of political differences.
10 Lim, H., in Rafi, S. (ed.) (2009).
11 Statement by The Honourable Senator Gareth Evans Minister of Foreign Affairs of Australia Thailand, 26–28 July 1994, cited in ASEAN.org (2003), http://www.aseansec.org/4412.htm (accessed 12 September 2009).
12 Joint Press Release of the 16th ASEAN–Australia Forum, Canberra, Australia, 3–4 May 1994, http://www.aseansec.org/2222.htm (accessed 3 October 2009).

Terms of engagement II   143

13 Broinowski, A. (2003) *About Face: Asian Accounts of Australia*, Melbourne: Scribe Publications; Milner, A., 'The Idea of Asia', in Cotton, J. and Ravenhill, J. (eds) (1997).

14 Ibid., see especially pp. 128–30.

15 Jones, E. (1994) 'Asia's Fate: A Response to the Singapore School', *The National Interest*, Spring, Washington, DC: The Nixon Center. pp. 1–3.

16 Lawson, in Robison, R. (ed.) (1996), p. 1.

17 Kelly, P. (2009).

18 Robison, R., in Robison, R. (ed.) (1996).

19 Sheridan, G. (1997), pp. 75–77.

20 Milner (in Cotton, J. and Ravenhill, J. (eds) 1997) implies that the Bangkok Declaration Summit had been crafted to 'again' exclude Australia (p. 38). That summit of course drew Asian representation from as far afield as Iran and convened two months prior to the World Conference on Human Rights held in Vienna in June 1993. It would be inaccurate to see the Declaration and indeed the Summit as a reaction to Australian overtures.

21 Lim, H., in Rafi, S. (ed.) (2009).

22 Rodan, G. and Hewison, K., 'Clash of Cultures or Convergence of Political Ideology', in Robison, R. (ed.) (1996), p. 40.

23 Milner, A. and Quilty, M. (1996) *Comparing Cultures*, Melbourne, New York: Oxford University Press, see chapter 1.

24 Donaldson, M. and Donaldson, T. (1983) 'The Crisis in the Steel Industry', *Journal of Australian Political Economy*, Vol. 14, pp. 33–43.

25 ABS (various dates) *The Labour Force, Australia*, cat. 6203.0, various tables, Canberra: AGPS.

26 Wiseman, J. (1997), pp. 45–46, 62–63; Carney, T. and Hanks, P. (1994) *Social Security in Australia*, Australia: Oxford University Press.

27 Foreign Minister Evans went so far as to suggest that Frances Fukuyama's idea that 'absolute intellectual dominance of the political and economic philosophy of liberal democracy' was a truism. Evans, G. (1995)., p. 106.

28 Sheridan, G. (1997), p. 71.

29 Rodan, G. and Hewison, K. (1996), pp. 48–50. There are many examples also of federal ministers and diplomats bringing up human rights issues in the course of their foreign visits, e.g. Kelly, P. (1984) 'Hawke Raises S Korea's Human Rights Record', *Sydney Morning Herald*, 7 February, p. 2. In most cases Australia followed normal diplomatic protocols and showed that its approach was just as much concerned with saving face.

30 Hawke, R.J., cited in Putnis, P. (1989) 'Constructing Multiculturalism: Political and Popular Discourse', *Australian Journal of Communication*, No, 16, December, p. 162.

31 Paul Keating (1994), in Sheridan, G. (1997), p. 125.

32 Evans, G. (1995)., p. 106.

33 Census of Population and Housing, 30 June 1981 – *Summary Characteristics of Persons and Dwellings*. Table 8, p. 8. Note: some countries of the Middle East are included as part of Asia.

34 ABS (2008) 'Australian Historical Population Statistics: Table 9.19 Population (a), Sex and Country of Birth(b), States and Territories(c)', *1991 census*. Excluding Southern Asia (India, Pakistan, Nepal, Bangladesh, Bhutan, Afghanistan, The Maldives) – this statistical cohort would add an additional 109,000 to the figure.

35 Hawke, R.J. (1984) 'Immigration – Ministerial Statement', *Hansard*, 10 May. System ID: chamber/hansardr/1984-05-10/0084, p. 2226.

36 See *Sydney Morning Herald*, 8 July 1982, p. 10.

144 Terms of engagement II

37 See *Sydney Morning Herald*, 4 October 1983, p. 1.
38 Hawke, R.J. (1984), p. 2226.
39 Sheridan, G. (1994), pp. 5–6.
40 Blainey, G. (1984) *All for Australia*, Sydney: Methuen Haynes.
41 Markus, A. and Ricklefs, M.C. (eds) (1985) *Surrender Australia?* Sydney: George Allen & Unwin.
42 Castles, S. et al. (1992); Cope, B. and Morrissey, M. (1986) *The Blainey Debate and the Critics of Multiculturalism*, paper presented to the Australian Institute for Multicultural Affairs National Research Conference, Melbourne University, May. Annandale, NSW: Common Ground; Markus, A. and Ricklefs, M.C. (eds) (1985) pp. 119–42; Milne, F. and Shergold, P. (eds) (1985) *The Great Immigration Debate*, Sydney: FECCA. More recent works have articulated a historical or ideological relationship with *Hansonism*, e.g. Jupp, J. (2002) *From White Australia to Woomera: The Story of Australian Immigration*, Cambridge: Cambridge University Press, see chapter 6; Markus, A. (2001) *Race: John Howard and the Remaking of Australia*, Crows Nest, NSW: Allen & Unwin; see also Vasta, E. and Castles, S. (1996).
43 Stratton, J., in Hage, G. and Couch, R. (1999), p. 179.
44 Lewins, F. (1987) 'The Blainey Debate in Hindsight', *Australia and New Zealand Journal of Sociology*, Vol. 23, No. 2 pp. 261–73.
45 More recent critiques of the prevalence of anti-Asian sentiment, including the emergence of Hansonism and broader Anglo-centric nationalism, centre on a failure of multiculturalism as policy to address issues of race rather than ethnicity or culture. Ang, I. and Stratton, J. (1998) 'Multiculturalism in Crisis: The New Politics of Race and National Identity in Australia', *TOPIA Canadian Journal of Cultural Studies*, No.2, Spring. See esp. pp. 26–28.
46 Jupp, J. (1992), chapter 6.
47 Frankel, B. (1992) *From the Deserts Prophets Come: The Struggle to Reshape Australian Political Culture*, Melbourne: Arena Publications; Castles, S., Cope, B. et al. (1992), see chapters 6 and 7.
48 John Elliot, 2 March 1989, cited in David, A. and Wheelwright, T. (1989), p. 201.
49 Foster, L.E. and Stockley, D. (1998) *Australian Multiculturalism: A Documentary History and Critique*, Avon and Philadelphia: Multilingual Matters, p. 32.
50 Foster, L.E and Stockley, D. (1998), p. 36.
51 Peter Shergold (1992) 'The 1986 Budget Row', interview for *Making Multicultural Australia*, http://www.multiculturalaustralia.edu.au/library/media/Audio/id/413.The-1986-Budget-Row (accessed 3 October 2009).
52 CAAIP Report (1988) *Immigration: A Commitment to Australia – Committee to Advise on Australia's Immigration Policies*, Committee to Advise on Australia's Immigration Policies (Fitzgerald, S. chair). Canberra: AGPS.
53 Ibid., see executive summary, pp. 1–22, esp. p. 3.
54 Ibid., p. 10; Sheridan, G. (1994), p. 13; Kalantzis, in Ryan, S. and Bramston, T. (2003).
55 Fitzgerald, in Ryan, S. and Bramston, T. (2003), p. 319.
56 Kalantzis in ibid., p. 317.
57 Sheridan, G. (1994), ibid.
58 Broinowksi, A. (2003).
59 CAAIP Report (1988), p. 10.
60 Lopez, M. (2000a).
61 Ibid.
62 CAAIP (1988), p. 16.

Terms of engagement II 145

63 Cf. Lopez, M. (2000a), pp. 447–48.
64 Kalantzis, in Ryan, S. and Bramston, T. (2002), pp. 321–22.
65 Jupp, J. (1992).
66 Peter Shergold (1995 'At the Crossroads … Productive Diversity Dr Peter Shergold, Public Service Commissioner, on Multiculturalism and the Support Towards It', interview for *Making Multicultural Australia*, http://www.multiculturalaustralia.edu.au/library/media/Audio/id/608.At-the-crossroads-Productive-Diversity (accessed 3 April 2020).
67 Kojima, K. 'Australia's Image in Asia II', in Garfield, J. et al. (1963), p. 33 (my emphasis). Kojima's reputation for advancing theories of foreign direct investment and comparative advantage, informing much of Japan's economic growth for the rest of the Asian region is argued in Ozawa, T. (2007) 'Professor Kiyoshi Kojima's Contributions to FDI Theory: Trade, Structural Transformation, Growth, and Integration in East Asia', paper presented at the *2006 Annual Conference of the Japan Society of International Economics* (JSIE), at Nagoya University, Japan, 14–15 October 2006, http://app.cul.columbia.edu:8080/ac/bitstream/10022/AC:P:262/1/fulltext.pdf (accessed 12 July 2010).
68 Lee Kuan Yew interview in Sheridan, G. (1997), p. 71.
69 And there is some suggestion that Lee introduced the study and pursuit of Confucianism in 1982 cynically to appeal to intensifying links with Chinese trade and business; it was not an appeal to heritage for its own sake; see ibid., p. 68.
70 Lee Kuan Yew, 1992 interview cited in Sheridan, G. (1997), p. 72.
71 See Weber, M. (2009) *The Protestant Ethic and the Spirit of Capitalism with Other Writings on the Rise of the West*, trans. Stephen Kalberg, New York: Oxford University Press.
72 Marx, Karl (1976) *Capital: A Critique of Political Economy*, Vol. 1, Harmondsworth: Penguin, p. 899. NB: This is the Penguin edition as distinct from the 1986 Progress Publishers edition cited elsewhere. Different editions were consulted only as a matter of convenience when writing.
73 See also Kuhn, R. (2006) 'Introduction to Henryk Grossman's Critique of Franz Borkenau and Max Weber', *Journal of Classical Sociology*, Vol 6. No. 2, pp. 195–200.

9 Productive diversity
From moral values to market values

Immigration has always been an economic concern of Australian governments, whether in restricting Chinese merchants and labourers in the early 1900s, populating post-Second World War Australia for massive industrialisation, or facilitating Asian business migration in the 1980s and 1990s. Up to the mid-1980s, however, immigration policy did not systematically require nor mobilise ethnicity as a productive resource, nor was ethnicity important to national consumption. Indeed, for most of the 20th century, ethnic small business – a by-product more than intention of government- or industry-driven pattern migrations prior to neoliberal globalisation – was effectively a niche market in Australia. Only in the 1970s did this begin to change, initially in areas such as hospitality. At a micro-level, some ethnic small businesses catered to majority Anglo culture in Australia for a good part of the postwar period, the 'Italian fruit shop' and 'Greek milk bar' being the archetype.[1] Here a distinction between ethnic-owned, and ethnic-oriented small business can be made, the latter changing more circa 1980s, arguably as consumption of cultural diversity became more palatable in mainstream society, and also more in demand as a fetish of cosmopolitanism associated with a globalised economy. This aspect of culture, its fetishised consumption, is not a consideration of this chapter.

From the 1980s, what is clear is that the link between immigration, culture and economy became more complex, although no more deliberate than the desire for the 'Beautiful Balts' – those that apparently looked most like the ideal *White* person – from among the postwar displaced persons of Europe in the late 1940s.[2] Then Immigration Minister Arthur Calwell's selection of blond(e)-haired, blue-eyed displaced persons from the Baltic States, however, exhibited simplistic thinking about race-as-culture. Any complexities of identity were rendered irrelevant to the postwar industrial economic production for which Australia was then recruiting.

Forty years later, the new multicultural citizen that the 1989 *National Agenda for a Multicultural Australia* envisaged was not one who had migrated decades ago, suffered assimilative racism and yet earned their place in Australia's postwar nation building history. The *National Agenda,* drawing on the recommendations of Dr Stephen FitzGerald's CAAIP Report certainly did cater to such worthy migrants and their extended families. The public service

Productive diversity 147

remained responsive to those culturally and linguistically diverse citizens and residents, especially with an ageing and largely un- or de-skilled postwar migrant cohort expected to access health and community services in greater numbers.[3] Migrant social welfare policy in 1989, however, did not of itself require the fanfare and policy re-vamp attending the *National Agenda*, unless understood as a political pacifier to CAAIP's controversial attempts to decouple multiculturalism from immigration in policy and public affairs (as noted in the previous chapter). The CAAIP Report rankled migrant community organisations and particularly the left wing of Australia's polity in arguing that multiculturalism was not universally understood, with FitzGerald holding a view that multiculturalism was instead a concoction of progressive elites. Therefore, it was argued that immigration should be based on less ambitious social considerations and pursued for its economic growth benefits (see previous chapter).[4] In other words, migration was important but might be better served with domestic policies that favoured economic, social and cultural *integration* rather than the equal rights associated with pluralist multiculturalism. Social cohesion, according to the thrust of the CAAIP Report, was seen to be compromised following years of incendiary immigration debates and particularly anti-Asian racism. Senior ministers in the Hawke Labor government believed there were macroeconomic threats from continued high levels of migration[5] but these held no truck with the CAAIP Report. Nevertheless, that Report would not receive the imprimatur of the Hawke government:

> [CAAIP] was in my view extremely dangerous in terms of the way it would be seen as signaling the end of multiculturalism ...

> The Prime Minister decided to get involved in this and got involved in a way where he, in general, supported the policy positions put to him by the Office of Multicultural Affairs.[6]

A profound ideological change in multiculturalism was heralded by the 1989 *National Agenda for a Multicultural Australia*, although much of the *National Agenda's* detail had evolved from the prior FitzGerald Report and the establishment of the Office of Multicultural Affairs (OMA) and Bureau of Immigration Research (BIR). OMA's first director, Dr Peter Shergold, provided some insight in his reflections on his role in shaping a neo-multiculturalism:

> I was trying to do two things. One was to actually define and delimit what multicultural policy meant ... And the second thing was ... to also move it away, not only from cultural frivolity – that is to say, an emphasis on food and singing and dancing, which is very important – but also to move it away from an emphasis on social welfare.

> And therefore I took multicultural policy through the Office of Multicultural Affairs down a route that was fraught with some

148 *Productive diversity*

dangers but I thought was very important in terms of getting Australian society to understand its significance, which was to emphasise the economic benefits of a culturally diverse society and the way that those benefits needed to be enhanced through government policy – in other words, through a promotion of immigrant languages, *using immigrant networks for business purposes*, providing English language to the extent that it was needed to succeed in Australian society.[7]

Dr Shergold's comments affirm unequivocally the shift in multicultural policymaking under the Hawke Labor government, as well as the role of key bureaucrats in that process. Placing greater weight on the 'economic benefits of a culturally diverse society' represented part attempt to depoliticise the place of multiculturalism in the public mind and in social policymaking[8], and part attempt to support economic restructuring increasingly favouring the recruitment of skilled occupations and anti-protectionism. Mass unskilled labour migration which had been the bedrock of the Australian intake had become less tenable.[9] Neil Edwards, a successor to Dr Shergold as head of OMA from late 1990 to 1994, recalled of the shift to Productive Diversity policy from multiculturalism:

When Paul [Keating] became PM ... the message came back from his office ... was, 'Look Paul's view is this multiculturalism stuff is Bob's agenda'; ... So I was able to provide something new for Keating. To say, well look it's not about community relations stuff, it's not just about social equity, and it's certainly not about something which splits Australia's nationhood.[10]

Edwards further explains that the making of a new diversity policy as one wrapped up in the economics of immigration within a broader economic transformation:

in some respects the trade dimensions was a kind of obvious one ... The articulation of it was this ... the world economy is a global multiculture; we are a microcosm. We can make more of this than anybody else in the world. And if we don't the other global multicultures – Israel and Canada – will.[11]

Comments about moving multicultural policy away from 'cultural frivolity' accorded with previous critiques about the limitations of multiculturalism in Australia. A number of scholars had argued from the early 1980s that economic concerns were missing from the conceptualisation of multiculturalism. Class, racist labour market segmentation and a lack of political representation could not be adequately addressed by focusing on cultural inclusion and social acceptance alone.[12]

Productive diversity 149

The *National Agenda* then was not conceived of *solely* as a definitive public exercise in anti-racist morality. The 1975 Anti-Discrimination Act, the 1978 Galbally Report, the 1979 Australian Institute of Multicultural Affairs, the 1985 Access and Equity policies and strategy, the 1986 Human Rights and Equal Opportunities Commission, and the 1987 Office of Multicultural Affairs, among many other social policy achievements had already cemented a path. Certainly, 1988 was a flashpoint year for race relations in Australia, with the nation's bicentenary agenda becoming much more complex than a jingoistic manifestation of Anglo-Celtic colonialism – Indigenous claims on the nation's history and the greater acceptance and social mobility particularly of second generation migrants highlighted that the 1988 bicentenary had many manufacturers.[13] A second 'Blainey debate' and (then) Liberal Party Opposition Leader John Howard's infamous speech in Esperance, Western Australia against further Asian immigration also occurred at this time, along with veiled anti-Asian statements in the Liberal policy platform on migration.[14] The *National Agenda* then, was a timely reminder of the morality of acceptance and an affirmation of support for diversity.[15] But new in its message was a vision of what Australia *ought* to become: a modern productive nation-state where ethnoculture was subject to the needs of the (globalising) market as much as the needs of the state:

> Australia's present and future interests demand that governments fully recognise the reality and implications of that cultural diversity.
>
> It is to that end that successive Commonwealth governments, and most States, have introduced a range of multicultural policies – policies which will help us better manage our diversity in the interests of social cohesion and justice; and harness the skills, education and *entrepreneurial ability of all Australians for the national good.*[16]

This was a strategic reworking of multiculturalism befitting globalisation. Its early and enduring policy articulation by the Australian Council of Population and Ethnic Affairs focused on social cohesion, cultural identity, equality of opportunity and access, and equal participation in society,[17] as decidedly social concerns. And as a reaction to anti-Asian racism in Australia and as a recasting of social power blocs away from ethnic lobby groups[18], multicultural politics in the 1980s was defiant. But its 1989 neology as a marker of socioeconomic mobility through individualisation of cultural resources suited the economic logic of post-industrial globalisation, which for Australia was to be realised as part of the Asian economic community. Cultural diversity presented 'competitive advantage' and access to Asia's growth centres; racist *mono*culturalism belonged to the old economy and was an economic millstone abroad as much as at home.[19]

150   *Productive diversity*

In some key respects, the CAAIP Report prefigured the work of OMA and the *National Agenda*'s call for the 'right' to productive citizenship – but as an immigrant in spite of their ethnocultural heritage. FitzGerald argued strongly for skill and entrepreneurship, supported by 'youthfulness' and language ability as the sole determinants of the *immigration* programme.[20] In a section on 'Productivity', the FitzGerald Report declared five principles, including:

- Immigrants with entrepreneurial skills stimulate business formation, technological innovation and international competitiveness
- Because immigrants are under pressure to become established in a new environment they add drive and energy to the economy.[21]

Missing from Stephen FitzGerald's point is discussion of the pattern that saw many migrants 'under pressure' exploiting their own labour in the poorly integrated ethnic small business sector, working hard, yet still marginalised or experiencing downward mobility.[22]

FitzGerald's approach was ambivalent about *ethnoculture* prefiguring in any consideration of entrepreneurial opportunity. The migrant experience of relocating was viewed as their vitality and promise to contribute to economic growth. This was consistent with the overall logic of the Report's proposed severing of multiculturalism from immigration policy. Migration not multiculturalism was the factor that ought to be celebrated in FitzGerald's view. This position had political sympathisers wanting to reduce the political influence of the community sector, notably unions and ethnic lobby groups in Australia's political economy.[23] FitzGerald later confirmed his concern at the time of the CAAIP Report that multiculturalism was under a systemic influence:

> The idea that multiculturalism might have run its course was deeply offensive to vested interests of the kind which represent in my view the 'ism', the dogma – their vested interest in the sense that it was developing as an industry, it provided their employment, their rationale, their 'raison d'etre'.[24]

Where Productive Diversity would come to view opportunity in individual cultural assets relative to the marketplace, FitzGerald's productivity agenda had already built upon foundations for a new political economy of migrant Australia by interpreting skill (formal or experiential), 'business acumen and managerial ability' and 'personal characteristics of ingenuity or hard work' as having a 'multiplier effect' on the economy.[25] An emergent human capital theory which sat neatly with neoliberal ideas about the pre-eminence of the market sought to measure personal characteristics such as age, language and education in terms of economic inputs and outputs,[26] while measuring ethnoculture was largely understood in terms of general work ethic, not as a specific skill set. FitzGerald's suggested approach to migrant selection argued that policies and programmes had to choose for 'characteristics that stimulate growth' otherwise immigration overall would not be 'conducive to accelerated growth'.[27] There was no compelling evidence by the early 1980s to suggest that ethnoculture was or should be one of these characteristics, except perhaps how it might sustain domestic markets for small intra-ethnic consumables. Ethnoculture only becomes a significant issue through Productive Diversity, but corresponding with the scaling up of the business and professional migration programme of the latter 1980s. The Business Migration Program is discussed in Chapter 10. The next section explains how Productive Diversity was developed.

The co-construction of productive diversity

Productive Diversity emerged as a conceptual framework for this aspirational shift in multiculturalism, championed both implicitly by bureaucrats and politicians, transnational business interests and migrant leaders in pursuit of the sociocultural capital needed for Australia's global economic challenges, and explicitly in parliamentary statements and government-sponsored conferences and publications, notably with the support of the Committee for the Development of Australia (CEDA), a business-industry think tank. For example, the October 1992 conference, 'Productive Diversity in Business: Profiting from Australia's Multicultural Advantage' (OMA and CEDA, 1992)[28] and the October 1993 conference, 'Productive Diversity: Winning Business through Australia's Multicultural Competitive Advantage' (CEDA, 1993),[29] sponsored jointly by CEDA and Government advanced Productive Diversity as a key policy plank of a multicultural Australia. CEDA had been approached by OMA to help disseminate the idea among the business community and duly responded with visits and workshops for managers and owners of large companies to explain the value, as much as the virtue, of fostering and recognising diversity. Toni Fedderson, then Research Director at CEDA recalls that Neil Edwards from the OMA made the initial approach about productive diversity:

> So they [OMA] explained to me this policy of productive diversity and a little bit about its origins and they wanted CEDAs involvement in exploring that. So that fitted very well with what we might do in our Strategic Issues Forum or in any of our programs... So yes, after that we set up a series of forums.[30]

Toni Fedderson played a central role in fostering the idea among CEDA's core constituency:

> what I did initially was ring a lot of companies, the people I knew best, just to talk to them, to persuade them to come to a session ... A policy

152 *Productive diversity*

> that didn't, or a topic that didn't exactly fit their immediate business needs was ... a very hard sell initially.[31]

According to Neil Edwards, it wasn't until the 1992 conference that the idea really gained traction in business circles, supported by business media:

> We had the PM speak to a big dinner and the conference that followed...and we made sure we had Mike Stutchbury from the [Australian] Financial Review, [print media] and ... we got Terry McCann [from] the Australian; [print media]. We got the economic writers to be there and some of them got switched on; they could see an argument, they could see how it fitted in with a competitiveness case.[32]

On the uptake among the business sector, Edwards recalled 'within two or three years the BCA (Business Council of Australia) was using the language of Productive Diversity as a piece of natural language'.[33] Productive Diversity policymaking had a clear agenda to engage the business and financial elite in multiculturalism. Presented partly as a problem of economic output for private enterprise, business leaders – the owners of production – were in effect tasked with realising value from the individual skills and endowments of their culturally diverse workforces. Toni Fedderson's approach was more subtle and in no way deterministic: 'Productive Diversity [was] "where are you looking for your markets", and "if you are [looking], is it any point in using any of your, or referring to any of your staff members to get input from them"'[34]

Studies have questioned the uptake or implementation of Productive Diversity at the enterprise level.[35] Hawthorne's address to a conference on productive diversity in 1995 challenged the 'bureaucratically assigned value' to the idea and also noted the SME sector is 'not governed by EEO principles'.[36] Any limitation of its success in practice serves to highlight that Productive Diversity, as a top down, macroeconomic lens focusing attention on 'ethnocultural capital' for national productivity, shaped the political economy of citizenship and migration primarily.

Productive Diversity was created for the market, a point revealed not just in OMAs own statements but also in addresses to business by CEDA. While not disparaging of the value of political leadership, Fedderson did note that resistance to Productive Diversity was variously expressed by businesses who viewed a focus on employee ethnicity as either overly selective based on cultural background, or potentially divisive in terms of workplace harmony.[37] The idea that one's ethnocultural background now *should* be identified was at odds with the race debates of previous decades and Australia's postwar history of racial stereotyping and racism against non-White migrants. The fact that elements of the business sector did not understand productive diversity as a form of 'positive discrimination' or 'affirmative action', as Toni Fedderson likened it to,[38] highlights the

Productive diversity   153

constraints and limitations of the previous decade of policy and public debate about multiculturalism.

Hage's retailing of the 'stew that grew'[39] as a metaphor for a perceived bureaucratic instrumentalism ever managing the diversity quotient in a cultural melting pot is an apt parody. The role of government driving the political economy of diversity was not exclusively the domain of OMA, nor the Immigration Department. In concert with a suite of related government inquiries into business productivity over the period, but notably the Karpin Report (Karpin, 1995) into both gender and ethnicity in business, management and entrepreneurial leadership and training; two commissioned reports by influential global business consultants McKinsey and Co. (1993 and 1994) on exports, value adding and manufacturing, and the earlier Hilmer Report (Hilmer, 1993) which established market competition policy in Australia, business leadership was strongly identified as critical to realising the latent riches of a diverse population within the marketplace.[40] Indeed, as the Karpin Report made clear:

> Increasingly, diversity is about efficiency and the bottom line as well as equity. We need to exploit the talents and harness the capacities of all the population, rather than just a narrow range, if we are going to improve productivity across the board.[41]

Pre-dating the Karpin Report, the CEDA–OMA launch of Productive Diversity was similarly focused on leading enterprises and successful business leaders around issues of workplace relations, efficiency and realising intra-firm potential among its skill base. As Neil Edwards recalled of the challenge of promoting the idea, the discourse aimed to convince business that workplace investment 'was about releasing the productive capacity that [they] wouldn't otherwise have' and that 'this is what needs to be done, this is what leading Australian companies are doing, will be doing'.[42]

In addition to the efficiency-equity agenda larger and well-established Australian companies were urged to address, Productive Diversity also concerned smaller and medium enterprises particularly exporters. The SME sector was considered by government and business interests increasingly important to Australia's GDP in line with 'New Growth Theory' and deindustrialisation moves in the economy.[43] While exporting appears historically to have been regarded as a space for individual migrant entrepreneurs to gain maximum advantage from their apparent culturally informed trade links and other 'intangible' capital.[44] Preceding the Productive Diversity agenda, the 1991 Joint Parliamentary Inquiry into business migration criticised both the lack of export activity and the over-representation of services in migrants' business activity:

> Bearing in mind the limitations on the data, the Committee noted the proportion of business that were established in the service industry.

154   *Productive diversity*

This was a concern in view of the supposed emphasis of the BMP on the introduction of new technology, export expansion and import substitution.[45]

The Inquiry also noted that the only service of value was in providing jobs, that is, there was no value adding or transformative service activity.

Productive Diversity spoke differently to different constituencies in this respect. Export trade became a significant policy agenda in relation to migrant SMEs, although business migration programmes mandated job creation and technology transfer as additional criteria for approving visas for migrant entrepreneurs. The periodical, *Multicultural Marketing News*, itself a curio of the times, reported in 1988 that most business migrants expected to export to their countries of origin.[46] Former Immigration Minister (1993–96), Senator Nick Bolkus, noted the value and influence on policy making of entrepreneurial migrants using their knowledge of 'home' markets;[47] Neil Edwards retailed the importance of immigrant entrepreneurs to his efforts, noting the case of one migrant exemplar originally from the Middle East:

> He said 'I can do things for you in the Gulf, which is taking off, that you can't do without people like me … that's my business; my business is to be a trader' …

> This is globalisation as it was actually happening. And, we used him … we promoted what he was doing and … what was happening … among some of the entrepreneurs in the Vietnamese community, in the Turkish community.[48]

The persistent matter of marginal intra-ethnic domestic business activity typified by small scale Greek and Italian 'provedores'[49] did not rate as a significant issue for Productive Diversity. This accords with the contention at the beginning of this chapter that 'old multiculturalism' attended to the welfare and social mobility of postwar migrants and their second generation, while 'new multiculturalism' as Productive Diversity was the stuff of migrant entrepreneurs advancing Australia's export economy. Neil Edwards reflected on OMA's approach:

> In a sense the Greek and Italian communities, the wave had in a way passed. They'd already done their bit as it were and changed the nature of Australian society; they weren't as it were 'selling back to Greece and Italy' in the same way … it wasn't a real big market then.[50]

One additional point supports this contention and relates to Asian-Australians. As Inglis noted of the 1986 Census statistics, second and then third-generation Chinese tended to fare worse in earnings outcomes.[51] Language for third generation was not necessary a factor, but their

Productive diversity   155

motivation to work is discussed as a reason for this depleted outcome. Neither did second- and third-generation migrants have any international or in this case Chinese market knowledge *per se*. Productive Diversity did not speak to this constituency just as it didn't speak to the bulk of the Southern European migrants from the 1950s and 1960s and their second generation.

CEDA's role in the advancement of diversity and productivity remains important to understanding the evolution of the concept and its relationship to immigration policy. It also points to a certain status quo in Australia's political economy, despite the apparent historical shift in migrant social relations from assimilation through integration and then multiculturalism: for Government relationships with business development interests around population growth were only strengthened by the emergence of multiculturalism in its transformation into Productive Diversity. As a broad national lobby group CEDA had a long history of working with all Governments and their Parliamentary Oppositions regardless of political or economic persuasion.[52] That CEDA and the Department of Immigration had intensified in 1982 a decades'-old relationship which then carried on throughout the whole Labor years in government is noteworthy for the increased economic basis of the Government's articulation of *citizenship*, laying the foundations for the later concept of Productive Diversity.

As part of a collaboration commenced as early as April 1982 between the Immigration Department and CEDA on the 'Economics of Migration', CEDA produced a series of reports generally in favour of non-discriminatory migration programmes for economic growth, including in 1985 *The Economic Effects of Immigration on Australia: A Booklet of Summaries*.[53] That report proved immediately influential in the decision to increase the size and making more complex the shape of the 1986 Immigration Program.[54] Increases were foreshadowed for the next three years but the Concessional Category largely for extended family members was tightened by then Immigration Minister Hurford, whereby:

> Applicants will be required to achieve a pass mark of 70 points on the existing points system which relates to the age, employability, education and skill characteristics of the potential migrant ... In summary, the new Independent and Concessionary Migration Category brings benefits from the economic gains to Australia from the people likely to succeed in their migration applications, whilst recognising the economic and social advantages of the extended family nexus. *This Category is not one of entitlements but one of optimising human and economic realities.*[55]

The Minister's statement in support of the Government's immigration programme in 1986 cited the 'complex', 'econometric' pro-migration findings provided by CEDA jointly with his Department, including the

156 *Productive diversity*

focus on individual economic attributes of 'skill, education, age and self-sufficiency profiles of a particular intake are perhaps more important than the overall scale of any one intake.'[56] The individual skill levels even of those notionally under family-related migration programmes were factored into the Government's transformation of the economy supporting the push for productivity through labour flexibility and self-reliance. The effect was immediate, with Family Migration visa numbers reversing a year-on-year growth to a zenith of approximately 70,000 visas in mid-1987; dropping the following three years to approximately 50,000 by mid-1990.[57] This trend was not unique to Australia – Canada, for example, similarly engineered shifts in visa categories away from family reunion in favour of entrepreneurial migrant streams.[58]

As noted in Chapter 8 a very public anti-Asian racism debate competed with an evolving discourse of multiculturalism in the 1980s. This was noted by CEDA as a challenge to migration-based economic growth.[59] Capitalist development interests as much as the pro-globalisation Labor Government remained sensitive to the effect of domestic identity politics on national economic policy and planning. The 1985 CEDA report, *The Economic Effects of Immigration on Australia*, analysed the economic value of migration presenting evidence which on balance supported further immigration, but with an emphasis on 'skill' in programme intake. Arguing for the positive economic effect of migration rather than the more contentious social and cultural possibilities embodied in diversity was historically consistent, although potentially disingenuous to the civil rights advances in Australia since at least the 1970s.

Contemporaneous research into Labor governance characterised federal policy making as being influenced by a decidedly 'economic rationalist' mindset, noting that at least half of all senior bureaucrats across all portfolios were economists with similar cultural and class backgrounds.[60] Neil Edwards was unequivocal on the policy modus operandi, rejecting the economic rationalist label: 'I mean that's about as ahistorical a comment as you can possibly make ... we were all dealing with that [the economy]'.[61] Consideration of this point helps to explain not only the closeness of Government and Business relations (and not Government-migrant community relations) but a difference between the basic charge of 'economic rationalism' a form of 'efficiency', and the more contemporary notion of neoliberalism as a more encompassing ideology of market private property relations. Edwards' contention was that any policy has economic consequences and that the economy was so very central to policymaking across a range of social dimensions. Nevertheless, while the actual economic consequence of a particular policy might be a consideration for responsible policy making, the overarching test of economic rationalism, according to Pusey's discursive understanding, was whether this was within a broader goal of *redistributive* economics.[62] Edwards added, 'I'd go so far as to say we were quite conscious, I was quite conscious, I think Governments were

Productive diversity 157

quite conscious that the promotion of an economic agenda actually had a very positive social cohesion, social acceptance model in it'.[63] On his response to the degree of unemployment, including migrant unemployment during the 1992–93 Recession, Edwards suggested 'it's very Hawke–Keating era, but the best welfare is a job'.[64] Such statements point towards Labor's difficult political relationship with the emergent market economy and attendant neoliberalism. While not addressing the very consequences of privatised, market-driven policy making are typically the cause rather than the cure for social disadvantage, Edwards articulates a vestige of Keynesian social responsibility in the role for government to ameliorate that disadvantage. Both Edwards and Toni Fedderson of CEDA identified the recession of the early 1990s as a pressing concern, one which they saw diversity able to redress in some part; Edwards:

> I remember quite an intense discussion we had in a little office, one which I drove, when we were looking at what our activity was when I arrived. Just as the Australian economy was hitting levels of unemployment that it hadn't had, hadn't happened since the nineteen thirties. They weren't [Nineteen] Thirties levels, but these were unprecedented. And I said this is disgraceful. We have eleven percent of the Australian workforce out of work, and of that workforce, of that unemployed group we can be sure, we know that some NESB groups at levels of forty percent unemployment.
>
> So we had quite an intensive debate 'So what are we doing about this? How can we play into this, this is what we should be doing'. It was a good debate ... that had to be had inside of that multicultural policy world which tend to come from that social justice, social cohesion logic and was never quite certain about.[65]
>
> Having thought 'okay there's an economic dimension here which we need to use', that fits with the broader agenda of Australia's circumstances. Remember 1990 [*sic*], a very, a quite a deep and sharp recession; And the Government taking some pretty gutsy decisions to continue to cut tariffs in that environment, etcetera. There were some thoughts along the lines of well how do we make it show that Australia's multiculturalism can contribute rather than simply be a cost.

Fedderson likewise noted the broader economic context as a conditioning factor or imperative for engaging business about diversity:

> So, that was an absolutely critical time for Australia; and to come to CEDA in ninety one [1991] and to see the way people were coping with that [economic] change. So, the Productive Diversity policy came about

158 *Productive diversity*

> because there was... a lot of unemployment ... in particular I suppose amongst the more recently arrived immigrants who would have found it even tougher to get work.[66]

In the case of migrant labour, successive Labor governments were active in identifying employment disadvantage experienced by this cohort, with OMA and BIR/BIPR-commissioned reports providing substantial evidence on this point. The Government's more transformative concern, however, was in the market opportunities for diversity. It is only when one considers the specific (individualised) social relations of production within the emergent market economy, with its valorisation of entrepreneurialism, a growth in SMEs and the de-industrialisation of labour, a growth in business occupations in the migrant intake, and allowing international finance capital greater freedom of operation, *inter alia* – this context and not an emphasis on the surplus value of skilled immigrant labour as a whole indicates OMA-CEDA and the Labor Government's policy making was serving a neoliberal agenda, willingly or otherwise.

Regardless of the personal ideological disposition of Labor ministers and their senior bureaucrats, it is apparent that the developing economic valorisation of migrant labour was in part a response to the ostensibly racist resistance to the changing ethnocultural composition of the migrant intake from European to Asian. As a parry to an anti-immigration report suggesting that Australia's immigration programme 'added $8 billion to Australia's foreign indebtedness in 1987–88',[67] Immigration Minister Senator Robert Ray spoke to a demand for greater proof for sustaining an immigration programme. As one of his predecessors had done, Senator Ray drew upon the 1985 CEDA study for credibility on the matter:

> There are a variety of studies but there are no complete studies on the economics of migration and its benefits or detriment to the economy ... The Committee for Economic Development of Australia (CEDA) studied the matter four or five years ago. I know the study to which the honourable senator [Coulter] refers. Equally one could argue that immigration is our third biggest import. The average immigrant family is bringing in $70,000 ...
>
> One of the problems of people examining the economics of immigration is that they nearly all start off with a preconceived ideological position. I could quote the CEDA document in contrast to the study the honourable senator [Coulter] has outlined. Both have started from a different point. We need objective research in this.[68]

Senator Ray used this same speech to explain that he was setting up the Bureau of Immigration Research (BIR) to undertake comprehensive studies on immigration matters. In tandem with Office of Multicultural Affairs, the

Productive diversity 159

Federal Government was committing not insignificant resources to evidencing its diversity agenda.

What the 1985 CEDA study did note was that '[E]xpenditure by recently arrived immigrants, *partly financed by funds they bring with them*, can substantially increase the level of consumer demand, particularly in areas such as housing', and that 'immigration may lead to increased imports but also capital inflow' while 'the effect on exports is unclear'.[69] The identification of migrants' transferable savings and also their exporting potential both in research and in parliamentary statements spoke to an emergent discourse focussing on the financial worth of all prospective migrants *as individuals* and their individual value to the market in terms of their disposable income as well as labour earning and generating potential. Immigration Department records included data on the sum of money brought to Australia by each migrant category and these were occasionally reported to Parliament to help justify or amend the migration programme. For instance, the then Minister for Local Government, Senator Margaret Reynolds, in 1987 tabled Immigration Department figures highlighting that the 3500 business migration visas for 1986–87 accounted for approximately one quarter of all money transferred to Australia upon visa conferral, with family migration and concessional categories each transferring around another quarter. Approximately another 20% of direct funds transfer came from the independent, skilled and employer nominee categories, while the remainder of funds transferred (approximately 5%) from the humanitarian category.[70] Reynolds was particularly interested in promoting the business migration category in her Senate address but nonetheless saw fit to continue the credentialing of all migrants based upon their transferable savings and investments.

Evidence on the economic effects of migration in Australia remained limited and even contradictory in the early to mid-1980s, mirroring the emergent complexity of migrant political economy in the globalising market economy. The burgeoning of research into the economic benefits of migration during the Hawke Labor governments of the 1980s centred on analyses of 'capital widening' and 'capital deepening', or quantitative versus qualitative effects, with a mounting acceptance that *deepening* the skill base of the labour market through migration was essential to productivity.[71] Expanding demand through untargeted and mass migration (a capital widening approach) was being questioned as a means of economic growth partly because migrant-induced demand particularly for infrastructure, presented challenges that might offset productivity gains. Aiming to reduce or at least focus the migration programme, the FitzGerald Report also favoured a shift away from measuring migration by its relative demand or 'capital widening' effects, in claiming that '[T]he principal economic impact of immigration is through the workforce'.[72] This statement related to the Report's emphasis on skill and entrepreneurship as the best determinants for future immigration programmes, and so reinforced its argument for the shift away from family reunion, community building or a

160 *Productive diversity*

welfare basis for the programme as such approaches would have 'costs that have to be borne'.[73] Significantly, it did not view immigration as a substitute for training and re-training the existing and future Australian workforce.

In a 1988 submission to the CAAIP hearings, the Centre for International Economics argued for attracting technology (plant and equipment) transfers despite being seen as a form supply-side capital widening because in effect it led to a deepening of skill and productivity.[74] This point was more radically framed by the 1985 CEDA study by historicising technological advancement: Australia could adopt new technology 'earlier' (than otherwise expected) through direct transfers from migrant capitalists.[75] This suggested that a domestic-only approach to advancement could and perhaps should be circumvented, that investment finance should be pursued through migration regardless of domestic demand.[76] A continuum of research into immigration by CEDA, OMA and the Bureau of Immigration Research,[77] alongside numerous Government committees and departments, ultimately distilled individual migrant skill and market knowledge as an essential ingredient for Australia's emerging market economy, even though between one third and one half of all migrants to Australia since the 1950s happened to have a skilled qualification.[78]

Blending skill-driven 'human capital' migration with multiculturalism, but within a globalising market economy, produced the cocktail of Productive Diversity. Neil Edwards explained that the essence of the idea, still underdeveloped a year after the 1989 *National Agenda*'s announcement, began with policy statements and not hard evidence on the economic contributions of multiculturalism:

> There were some thoughts along the lines of 'well how do we make it show that Australia's multiculturalism can contribute rather than simply be a cost'. So the first thought was let's get something into the major economic statement that Hawke put out, about, it must have been about February 1991 ...

> I took the view that even if you haven't worked out what you're going to do, the smart thing to do is to ensure you're going to have one line in the statement that says... 'Australia's language and cultural diversity constitutes a competitive advantage that we can make something of'. Now, intuitively it's kind of there but there was no real detailed policy wrap. But that was the first point; that put a stake in the ground and that effectively said well here's a commitment, were going to do something about this. So, and that became a commitment of the Government. I got that written in one way or the other.[79]

As a broad national lobby group CEDA had a long history of working with all governments and their Parliamentary Oppositions regardless of political or economic persuasion.[80] That CEDA and the Department of Immigration had intensified in 1982 a decades old relationship which then carried on throughout the whole Labor years in government is noteworthy for the increased economic basis of the government's articulation of *citizenship*, laying the foundations for the later concept of Productive Diversity.

Developing a culture of productivity

Conceptually, Productive Diversity came to represent Labor Government and business investment thinking by the 1990s about multiculturalism and globalisation, focusing attention on migrant skills, ethnicity and entrepreneurship. After Prime Minster Hawke's statement in 1991 affirming in principle the economic benefits of diversity, OMA took up the task of producing the evidence in support of the claim:

> The next thing that we did was said 'well what is that going to be'. Pretty clearly you could talk up the trade advantage and we did a lot of looking for examples of people making use of the trade advantage, and we found them, particularly with Australian business working into new markets.[81]

This concurred with a greater emphasis on the quality and skill mobility of the workforce in the postindustrial global economy. Following anti-protectionist monetary and trade reform introduced by the Hawke government (e.g. tariff reductions, a floating exchange rate), transnational capital and global market forces were more influential upon productivity in Australia. So called innovations in customisation, niche marketing, value adding for competitive advantage – post-Fordist approaches to production – aimed to mobilise broader and deeper skill sets of individual workers, rather than requiring of them only a generic or singular skill set in a production line.[82] Such restructuring was not uniform and it is important to note that many SMEs were run with unskilled migrant labour, notably in the garment industry. The conditions and pay for such workers, the vast majority of whom were women, underscores both the continued limitations for migrant labour but also the exploitation by migrant entrepreneurs of 'their own' 'cultural capital'.

Productive Diversity clearly was not created in a political vacuum. Following a broader campaign to restructure Australia's overall economy supported by a 'productive culture' motif,[83] the discourse, rhetoric and actions of the Hawke and Keating governments confirm a deliberate turn in thinking about cultural diversity. This was supported by cumulative econometric analyses of the relative cost to benefit of leveraging economic productivity off skilled migrants, and notably, their ethnocultural capital (measured by birthplace or first language). It thus had built-in but untested assumptions about its market utility evident especially in the justifications for Australia's Business Migration Program, the focus of Chapter 10.

162 *Productive diversity*

Productivity as 'working smarter' for a global division of labour

Like other postindustrial economies adopting and adapting neoliberal views of a market driven global economy, Australian policy calls focused on mobilising individuals as innovators and market-seeking economic actors. Notwithstanding what has already been offered to substantiate this claim, the 1995 report to the Keating Government cited earlier, *Engineering Effective Innovation to Asia* is worth citing further:

> The lack of innovation in Australia appears in part due to the shortage of forward- looking and *entrepreneurial* individuals. They must have the expertise to evaluate a potential product for technological viability and carry the concept through to commercial viability. Such individuals who are capable of bringing together technology push with market pull are relatively rare in Australia, while common in the United States. They often have engineering backgrounds and enter management as chief executives of their own companies.
>
> By comparison, Australia has inherited from Britain a sharp divide between technological (scientific and engineering) and management (finance and marketing) cultures.[84]

The quote above concerning a role for engineering entrepreneurs and Asian markets views culture as instrumental in non-labour activities.

Government and business claims made for ethnoculture, and for a diversity of ethnocultures to be uniquely useful in production manifested as an absolute proposition: that whatever occupation people work in their ethnoculture can be 'harnessed', or otherwise underpins innovation. As an answer to de-industrialisation and labour restructuring towards skills and innovation this message was perhaps best captured in Australia's 1989 *National Agenda*'s appeal to the 'entrepreneurial ability of all Australians'.[85] That statement is an amorphous claim about value adding but one that envisaged productivity as an individual pursuit in a diverse market economy.

The formulation construed by the proponents and architects of Productive Diversity targeted 'ethnics' overtly to draw upon their cultural know-how and identity. This was an interpretation of both human and cultural capital theory valorising individual traits as assets which might be accumulated and further deployed. As per the premise of this book, valorising ethnoculture is suspect in definitional terms, as one's ethnicity cannot be further expanded (valorised) the way capital expands. Taksa and Groutsis claim this as an evidentiary point about commoditising migrants:

> [T]he management of cultural differences does not succeed in the long-term without reference to migrant workers as agents. As a corollary, we implicitly dispute the assumption that migrant workers' cultural

Productive diversity   163

knowledge and multi-lingual skills can be reduced to resources and assets solely for the benefit of business in the era of post-colonial globalisation.[86]

Human commoditisation in Taksa and Groutsis's argument is a form of essentialising human being and doing, in this instance in the area of post-industrial labour. However, the argument in this book is that ethnoculture and diversity can only really apply to product and process innovation and market transactions, that is, non-productive activity. Therefore, the extent to which ethnicity and diversity is useful and of any consistent *value* is problematised. Reiterating Marxist value theory, labour creates (and arguably surrenders) value through the process of producing commodities. Value is not the actual or rather, variable price commodities fetch. The opportunities for *labour* to apply any ethnocultural factors individually or in a diverse group are proscribed by labour's productive function. This is not so for competitive market activity.

An assumption encouraged by Government, business and corporate interests was that labour could and should metamorphose into 'knowledge workers' – to innovate in process and product, assuming greater responsibility for market knowledge. Where such activities are applied to employees in a firm, notionally considered labour because of wages earned for time spent working, this changing nature of 'work' traverses the basic labour/non-productive labour divide. Adam Smith's original observation of how workers in repetitive, divided production activities would innovate, if only to provide relief from the physical demands of labour is pertinent:

> But in the consequence of the division of labour, the whole of every man's attention come naturally to be directed towards some one very simple object. It is naturally to be expected therefore, that some one or other of those who are employed in each particular branch of labour should soon find out easier and readier methods of performing their own particular work, wherever the nature of it admits such improvement.[87]

This form of worker innovation may have increased relative surplus value through better production techniques, but it was neither requisite nor incumbent upon labour in process work and industrialised production to innovate. The *expectation* of worker as entrepreneur, or alert to sales opportunities or somehow adding value over and above the creation of actual products for consumption is a more recent contention. Whether that is reflective of the imperatives of a networked 'informational economy' as per Castells'[88] claim, a general feature of postindustrialism or, in fact, ongoing concentration of capital through highly flexible global value chain production is an important consideration, although not a mutually exclusive one.

The analysis of productivity discourse in earlier chapters indicated that whether within existing firms or as independent SME capitalists, innovation

164 *Productive diversity*

and entrepreneurialism came to popularise the Labor government's post-Fordist/post-Keynesian expectations of work and productivity. Forms of management to devolve responsibility in and for production in general became more important according to a range of sources.[89] Total Quality Management (TQM) emerged as one internationally pervasive principle that expected continuous process improvement strongly implicating (self) management in all levels of work.[90] 'Working smarter' and 'value adding' were important adages, repeated many times over in and by government, businesses and even trade unions. Separate statements by three Labor Government members from the period serve to illustrate, which retrospectively might be viewed as part of a historical chorus of global labour restructuring:

> As a nation we have to take advantage of opportunities for growth if we are to create wealth for ourselves and for future generations. By *working smarter* and more efficiently, we are becoming an increasingly competitive and efficient economy with a major export potential in supplying a broader range of goods and services.[91]

> Those in the Liberal Party have never learnt that what they should be doing nowadays is *working smarter*. We can work as hard as we like, but if we cannot *add value* to products we are not being very smart. That comes through all the time in the speeches, the old rhetoric, of those opposite.[92]

> To achieve change, we must mobilise our most valuable resource: the talents of the Australian people. This does not necessarily mean working harder; in Germany and Japan, both highly successful competitive countries, working hours are actually falling.

> But it does mean *working smarter* – working more effectively, using new materials, new production technologies and new management methods. It means being, like Germany and Japan, a clever country.[93]

This resonated with ethnocultural diversity in specific ways. Neil Edwards, former Head of OMA recalls how it was interpreted from his perspective:

> There was a little bit of support for that in some of the management literature going on that the time namely that led to the concept that while a monocultural team in a workplace might solve a problem quicker, the culturally diverse team might solve a problem better. Needless to say, we made as much of that as we possibly could.[94]

Here, the link between ethnicity, diversity and knowledge is made explicit.

Despite a reference to work teams, it is innovation for either process improvement or market opportunity to which this knowledge applies.

The importance placed upon on knowledge, of which ethnocultural know how is here a substrata, accords with various interpretations of a global neoliberal economic order following the New International Division of Labour and 1970s post-stagflation: for the Global North, the gradual transformation of labour under post-Fordist, market capitalism into quasi-entrepreneurialism via work regimes of continuous quality improvement; of 'adding value' and 'working smarter'; the growth in SME as the vehicle to entrepreneurial self-employment but also providing the outsourcing or contracting out for services in both the public and private sectors; and individualised contracts with performance commissions and other non-salaried remuneration.[95] Indeed, there was even a concerted attempt by influential business leaders in Australia to shift the very language used in industrial relations, such that 'wages' should be replaced by the now familiar 'benefits' or 'remuneration' supposedly to coax an individualised relationship with work.[96]

Analyses and opinions of Australian pro-development interests moved somewhat towards the OMA's productive culture approach to multiculturalism, striving to provide evidence linking multiculturalism, and not migration per se, with Australia's economic development – the CEDA-OMA national summits of 1992 and 1993 being two highly visible expressions of this.[97] OMA and the BIR produced and commissioned extensive research over their lifetime on migrant economics, although assumptions about ethnicity as a competitive advantage were mostly measured in gross terms, with the idea gaining more traction by 1994.[98] Reports from within related government departments, notably the 1994 *Australian Cultural Diversity and Export Growth*[99] likewise pursued econometric analyses of population source countries (where migrants were born) relative to export growth. McKinsey and Co.'s report to the Australian Manufacturing Council, also in 1994, looked at how overseas market linkages were harnessed at the firm level.[100] The 1995 OMA response to a National Multicultural Advisory Council Report on the future of multiculturalism similarly justified the utilisation of immigrants as entrepreneurs and trade facilitators on the basis that approximately 80% of Australia's trade at the time was with non-English-speaking, and principally Asian region countries.[101]

This ideational demarcation of working smarter rather than harder in this context can be viewed as a distinction between (labour) productivity and (market) competition, just as it can also be seen as a representation of the global division of productive labour and non-productive occupational forms. The argument throughout this book maintains that working smarter as a form of innovation for the market is of non-productive and market expanding activity.

166 *Productive diversity*

Conclusion

By the end of 1980s the Government's attempts at social consensus on the nation's future identity through its multicultural and citizenship policies began to exhibit increasingly neoliberal tendencies. Neil Edwards' account, however, is more equivocal: the *intention* of Productive Diversity was one of opportunity rather than disembedding market forces from social control. What is readily apparent is a consensus discourse from within ruling circles emphasising human agency to create and realise market opportunity. A difference can be seen here in the way the previous chapter described *productivity* as a form of individual responsibility, which was very much the view of the CAAIP Report. Whereas, the emergent discourse of Productive Diversity, which only really gathers impetus with OMA's Director Neil Edwards under Paul Keating's Prime Ministership, views ethnoculture much more in market terms for *opportunity*. One way this was conceived was in the efforts to target business migrants and independent professionals.

Of interest here is not only a government and business development alliance affirming a basic macroeconomic link between increasing the population and economic demand. Novelty also rests in the fact that cultural diversity, the *breadth and depth* of ethnicities Australia housed, was considered an economic asset, nonetheless measurable or assessable largely by a simplistic causal link between migrant birthplace, generic entrepreneurial skill capacity and country(ies) of business. Only a small proportion of that breadth of diversity in the 1980s came from Asia overall, yet it was the most rapidly increasing ethnogeographic sub-group which thus captured the most attention in the public mind during this period. In practice, Productive Diversity as it articulated with immigration programmes, particularly for business and professional skilled migrants, courted entrepreneurialism largely within a certain Asia Pacific milieu and so in one sense was not diverse at all.

Chapter 10 explores an aspect of the international division of non-productive and market expanding occupations, focusing on business and independent skilled migrants. This cohort became an *avant-garde* for a new approach to skilled migrant selection, where skill and entrepreneurialism to grow a globally connected SME sector became so in demand from the 1990s.

Notes

1 Collins, J. et al. (1995).
2 Bone, P., 'Bridging the Differences', *The Age*, 4 January 2003, http://www.theage.com.au/articles/2003/01/03/1041566221402.html (accessed 4 October 2010). In fact, Calwell had wanted to recruit Scandinavians as well as English migrants but was unable to attract sufficient interest.
3 Office of Multicultural Affairs (1992 reprint), pp. 29–31, 38–40.
4 CAAIP (1988).

Productive diversity   167

5 Freeman, G. (1992) 'Migration Policy and Politics in the Receiving States', *International Migration Review*, Vol. 26, No. 4, pp. 1150–51.

6 Peter Shergold (c.1995) 'FitzGerald Immigration Policy Review, 1988', *Making Multicultural Australia*, http://www.multiculturalaustralia.edu.au/library/media/Audio/id/589.FitzGerald-Immigration-Policy-Review-1988 (accessed 3 March 2010).

7 Peter Shergold (c.1995) (my emphasis).

8 CAAIP (1988); Lopez, M. (2000a)

9 See Norman, Neville R. and. Meikle, Kathryn F. (1985) (3 vols) *The Economic Effects of Immigration on Australia*, vols 1 and 2; and *The Economic Effects of Immigration on Australia: Booklet of Summaries*, Melbourne: Committee for Economic Development of Australia. This report was one of the most influential in reshaping Australia's migrant selection programmes based on points for a variety skills and economic viability.

10 Neil Edwards, Interview, 24 January 2012, Melbourne, Australia.

11 Ibid.

12 De Lepervanche, M. (1984) 'Immigrants and Ethnic Groups', in Encel, S. and Bryson, L. (eds) *Australian Society*, Melbourne: Longman Cheshire; Jakubowitz, A. (1984) 'Ethnicity, Multiculturalism and Neo-Conservatism', in Bottomley, G. and de Lepervanche, M. (eds) *Ethnicity, Class and Gender in Australia*, Sydney: George Allen & Unwin; Jayasuriya, L (1983) 'Multiculturalism: Fact, Policy or Rhetoric?' *The Nation is People*, The University of Western Australia, Nedlands; The Extension Service.

13 Pettman, J. (1988) 'Learning about Power and Powerlessness: Aborigines and White Australia's Bicentenary', *Race Class*, No. 29, pp. 69–85.

14 Grattan, M., 'Howard to Bolster His Front Bench', *The Age*, 16 September 1988.

15 A distinction is intended here between the conservative morality of tolerance (cf. Chapter 1, this volume) and the affirmative morality of Labor's collective social justice heritage.

16 OMA (1992 reprint), p. 1 (my emphasis).

17 Australian Council of Population and Ethnic Affairs (1982) *Multiculturalism for All Australians: Our Developing Nationhood*. Canberra: AGPS.

18 Lopez, M. (2000a).

19 Hay, I. (1996) *Managing Cultural Diversity: Opportunities for Enhancing the Competitive Advantage of Australian Business*, Canberra: AGPS; CEDA (1993) *Productive Diversity: Winning Business Through Australia's Multicultural Competitive Advantage* (conference proceedings) Brisbane: CEDA; P. Totaro, 'Anti-Australian Backlash Sweeps South East Asia', *Sydney Morning Herald*, 23 August 1988, p. 4.

20 CAAIP (1988), pp. 44–51.

21 Ibid., p. 39.

22 See Ho, C. and Alcorso, C. (2004) 'Migrants and Employment', *Journal of Sociology*, Vol. 40, No. 3, pp. 237–59; Collins, J. et al. (1995); Collins, J. (1995) 'Immigration and the Labor Government in Australia: 1983–95', *School of Finance and Economics Working Paper No.45*, March. Sydney: University of Technology Sydney.

23 Lopez, M. (2000a).

24 FitzGerald (1996), interview, *Making Multicultural Australia*, http://www.multiculturalaustralia.edu.au/library/media/Audio/id/416.FitzGerald-Immigration-Policy-Review-1988 (accessed 17 February 2020).

25 CAAIP (1988), p. 39.

26 See Becker, G.S. (1975).

168 *Productive diversity*

27 CAAIP (1988). p. 44.
28 OMA and CEDA (1992) *Productive Diversity in Business: Profiting from Australia's Multicultural Advantage Conference Outcomes,* Canberra: CEDA and OMA. Toni Fedderson notes in an interview for this work that the author of this was Louise Wilson.
29 CEDA (1993).
30 Toni Fedderson, Interview, 24 January 2012.
31 Ibid.
32 Neil Edwards, Interview, 24 January 2012, Melbourne, Australia.
33 Ibid.
34 Toni Fedderson, Interview, 24 January 2012.
35 J. Pyke (2005a) 'Productive Diversity: Which Companies are Active and Why', paper delivered at the Australian Social Policy Conference, University of NSW, July, http://www2.sprc.unsw.edu.au/ASPC2005/papers/Paper205.doc (accessed 1 June 2012). This is a version of Pyke's Master's thesis cited earlier.
36 Hawthorne, L. (1995) 'Productive Diversity: Reality or Rhetoric', paper presented at *Local Diversity, Global Connections: Communication, Culture and Business,* 9–11 November, Sydney.
37 Toni Fedderson, Interview, 24 January 2012.
38 Ibid.
39 Hage, G. (2000), pp. 128–30.
40 Karpin, D. (1995). *Enterprising Nation: Renewing Australia's Managers to Meet the Challenges of the Asia-Pacific Century,* Canberra: AGPS; Hilmer, F. (chair) (1993) *National Competition Policy,* Canberra: AGPS. Note that these reports were commissioned some time prior to their eventual publication – the Karpin commission commenced in 1991, Hilmer in 1992. The other key reports were the 1993 McKinsey publications: McKinsey & Co. (1993) *Emerging Exporters. Australia's High Value-Added Manufacturing Exporters,* Melbourne: McKinsey & Company and the Australian Manufacturing Council; McKinsey Report, McKinsey and Co. (1994) *The Wealth of Ideas: How Linkages Help Sustain Innovation and Growth – Report by the Australian Manufacturing Council Secretariat and McKinsey & Company to the Australian Manufacturing Council,* Melbourne: AMC. A more specific report on science and technology investment and leadership with comparison to Asian countries was also influential within the bureaucracy: James, M.L. (1995) 'Engineering Effective Innovation to Asia', *Research Paper No. 23, 1994/95,* Canberra: Department of Parliamentary Library.
41 Karpin, D. (1995).
42 Neil Edwards, Interview, 24 January 2012, Melbourne, Australia.
43 As noted in Chapter 4, based on neoclassical economic theory's stages of growth, after Paul Romer and Robert Lucas. See Landstrom, H. (2008), pp. 301–02; Devinney, T. and Kirchner, S. (1997), pp. 408–09.
44 The idea of tangible and intangible culture refers, in anthropological terms, to artefacts of a culture, whether physical and material, or residing in human practice and knowledge. The idea of cultural capital is discussed in a subsequent chapter.
45 Parliamentary Joint Committee of Public Accounts (1991) *Report 310: Business Migration Program,* Seventeenth Committee. Canberra: Commonwealth of Australia, p. 36.
46 'Big Bucks and Brainwaves From Business Migrants', *Multicultural Marketing News,* No. 1, June 1988, p. 3.
47 Nick Bolkus, Interview, 15 January 2012.
48 Neil Edwards, Interview, 24 January 2012, Melbourne, Australia.

Productive diversity 169

49 Collins, J. Gibson et al. (1995); aka suburban 'milk bar', delicatessen and fruit shop owners.
50 Neil Edwards, Interview, 24 January 2012, Melbourne, Australia.
51 Inglis, C. et al. (eds) (1992) *Asians in Australia: The Dynamics of Migration and Settlement*, Singapore: ISEAS. Note, the figures are for males; results for females are more variable.
52 Toni Fedderson, Interview, 24 January 2012.
53 Norman, N. and Miekle, K. (1985).; Norman, N. and Miekle, K. (1983) *Immigration: The Crunch Issues*, Melbourne: Committee for Economic Development of Australia, p. 5. Turner, D.E. and Norman, N. (1984) *Managers' Perceptions of the Migrant Worker: A Survey Contribution to the Economics of Immigration Project*, Melbourne: Committee for Economic Development of Australia. By way of footnote, the Australian Government's relationship with CEDA on immigration matters went back much further. In 1969, CEDA published a paper by then Liberal (Conservative) party immigration Minister Billy Snedden entitled 'Immigration and Australia's Future'. By and large the concern of the paper was Australia's population size and demography, with an acknowledgement that migrant civil rights were lacking for minority groups (1969, Supplementary Paper No. 22, Melbourne: CEDA).
54 Norman and Miekle (1985); Estimates Committee E 28/09/1989 Department of Immigration, Local Government and Ethnic Affairs Program 1 – Migration and Visitor Entry Subprogram 1.1 – Migration Planning, Population and Research, *Hansard*, http://parlinfo.aph.gov.au (accessed 1 August 2011). System ID: committees/estimate/ecomd890928a_ece.out/0011.
55 Chris Hurford, MHR, 'Migration Program 1986–87 Ministerial Statement', *Hansard*, 10 April 1986, p. 1969. Sourced online 1 August 2011. System ID: chamber/hansardr/1986-04-10/0001 (my emphasis).
56 Ibid.
57 See Figure 10.1 in this book for details.
58 Ley, D. (2003) 'Seeking Homo Economicus: The Canadian State and the Strange Story of the Business Immigration Program', *Annals of the Association of American Geographers*, Vol. 93, No. 2, June, pp. 426–44, http://www.jstor.org/stable/1515566, p. 8 (accessed 15 September 2010).
59 Norman and Miekle (1983); Blainey, G. (1984).
60 Pusey, M. (1991).
61 Neil Edwards, Interview, 24 January 2012, Melbourne, Australia. Edwards was responding directly to Pusey's work.
62 Pusey, M. (1991), see pp. 58–63.
63 Neil Edwards, Interview, 24 January 2012, Melbourne, Australia.
64 Ibid.
65 Ibid.
66 Toni Fedderson, Interview, 24 January 2012.
67 Senator Coulter in 'Questions without Notice' *Senate Hansard*, 6 October 1989, p. 1837. Sourced online 1 August 2011. System ID: chamber/hansards/1989-10-06/0084.
68 Senator Robert Ray, ibid.
69 Norman and Miekle (1985), pp. 1–2 (my emphasis).
70 Senator Margaret Reynolds, 'Appropriation Bill (No. 1) 1987–88' *Hansard*, 25 November 1987, p. 2434, http://parlinfo.aph.gov.au (accessed 1 August 2011). System ID: chamber/hansards/1987-11-25/0212.
71 Mayer, E. (1990) 'Immigration: Some Issues for Discussion', *EPAC Discussion Paper 90/05*, Canberra: AGPS, p. 5.
72 CAAIP (1988). p. 39.

170 *Productive diversity*

73 Ibid., p. 44. A curio within the Report itself relating to this set of themes raises questions about the tension that existed between the 'old' and 'neo-multiculturalists'. While the Report clearly states that 'To the extent that immigration has humanitarian and social rather than purely economic objectives.... immigration will have costs that have to be borne' (p. 44). On the facing page, a large *pull-quote* (a typesetting or desktop publishing device to highlight a point within the text), headlines with the selected text 'immigration has humanitarian and social rather than purely economic objectives' (p. 45); this is either poor editorship, taking the quote completely out of its context, or a deliberate counterpoint, not by the author, but by someone possibly within the bureaucracy or Government concerned with the market-oriented approach of the Report.

74 Centre for International Economics (1988) 'The Relationship between Immigration and Economic Performance', in CAAIP (1988) *Consultants' Reports*.

75 Norman, N. and Meikle, K. (1985) 'Summary', p. 1.

76 In a sense this questioned import substitution or emulation as a standard strategy for economic development – one which numerous South East Asian countries had been encouraged to do throughout the postwar decades. The relevance of import substitution is discussed in Chapter 10 in relation to the Business Migration Program. See Brunton, H.J. (1998) 'A Reconsideration of Import Substitution', *Journal of Economic Literature*, Vol. 36, No. 2, June.

77 See BIMPR (n.d.., c.1995) 'Skilled and Business Migration: An Annotated Bibliography', Library Bibliography Series, Canberra: AGPS. This catalogue from the BIMPR Library contains extensive (hundreds of) records and entries specifically on the topic.

78 Ibid., see table, p. 70.

79 Neil Edwards, Interview, 24 January 2012, Melbourne, Australia.

80 Toni Fedderson, Interview, 24 January 2012.

81 Neil Edwards, Interview, 24 January 2012, Melbourne, Australia.

82 Castells, M. (2000a); Cope, B. and Kalantzis, M. (1997). Note also the claim about the market assuming greater control of and responsibility for the economy can be corroborated in many ways, not least in the deregulation policies of successive governments and in the evidence of the current account deficit largely fuelled by private equity, as discussed in Chapter 8.

83 Foster, D. and Stockley, L. (1990) 'The Construction of a New Public Culture: Multiculturalism in an Australian Productive Culture', *ANZJS*, Vol. 26, No. 3, pp. 307–28.

84 James, M.L. (1995), p. 6.

85 OMA (1992 reprint).

86 Taksa, L. and Groutsis, D. (2010), p. 2.

87 Smith A. (1937 [1776]) *An Inquiry into the Nature and Causes of the Wealth of Nations,* New York: Random House, reproduced in part in Argyrous, G. and Stilwell, F. (eds) (2011) *Readings in Political Economy: Economics as a Social Science*, Prahran, VIC: Tilde Press, pp. 71–75.

88 Castells, M. (2000).

89 See Cope, B. and Kalantzis, M. (1997) for a detailed analysis of management ideas at the time. See also O'Brien, J. (1994) 'McKinsey, Hilmer and the BCA: The "New Management" Model of Labour Market Reform', *Journal of Industrial Relations*, December, for an account of Fred Hilmer, referred to in this chapter and Chapter 10 as a key Australian influence on new forms of management. See also Evans, 'Building a Competitive Australia, Ministerial

Productive diversity 171

Statement', *Hansard*, 12 March 1991. Sourced online 3 January 2013. System ID: chamber/hansards/1991-03-12/0034.

90 Cope, B. and Kalantzis, M. (1997); that is, in both labour and non-labour.

91 'Keynote Address by the Hon. Michael Lee, Federal Minister for Resources, at the Ceremony to Mark the Completion of the Construction of the Junee–Griffith Pipeline. Griffith – 9 November 1993', Press Release, *Hansard*. System ID: media/pressrel/1742717.

92 Hon Gear, G., 'Appropriation Bill (No. 1) 1989–90 Second Reading' *Hansard*, 29 August 1989, p. 527, *Hansard*. System ID: chamber/hansardr/1989-08-29/0057. For a selection of similar examples during the period, see also *Hansard*, Monday, 30 October 1989, p. 2058; *Hansard*, Wednesday, 6 March 1991, p. 1296; *Hansard*, Tuesday, 12 March 1991, p. 1649.

93 Evans, 'Building a Competitive Australia, Ministerial Statement', *Hansard*, 12 March 1991. Sourced online 3 January 2013. System ID: chamber/hansards/1991-03-12/0034.

94 Neil Edwards, Interview, 24 January 2012, Melbourne, Australia.

95 Howard, M.C. and King, J.E (2008) – see especially, pp. 173–76; Cope and Kalantzis (1997); Castells, M. (2000a).

96 Hilmer, F. (1989), p. 190.

97 OMA and CEDA (1992).; CEDA (1993).

98 Notable, also for its inductive approach to proving the value of diversity was OMA's Australian *Cultural Diversity and Export Growth* (1994).

99 Aislabie, C. et al. (1994) *Australian Cultural Diversity and Export Growth*, Canberra: AGPS.

100 McKinsey and Co. (1994).

101 OMA (1995) *Our Nation: Multicultural Australia and the 21st Century: The Government's Response to the Report of the National Multicultural Advisory Council's 'Multicultural Australia: The Next Steps, Towards and Beyond 2000*, Canberra: OMA.

10 The Business Migration Program
Entrepreneurs wanted

Historically, migrants have been well represented, especially in small business in Australia. These reasons, as noted in earlier chapters, are often structural in denying immigrants the same opportunities for socioeconomic advancement within the dominant host culture (e.g. language barriers); and personal, in as much as direct racism also stigmatises opportunity and motivation to participate in all job market opportunities.[1] As census data reveals, by 1991, male business migrants (self-employed or employer) exhibited a clear growth in numbers from previous years and decades. This is suggestive of a climate more suitable for business growth, although not exclusively ethnic business growth. But in all cases, by 1991 an absolute majority of overseas-born eligible male migrants remained *employees* of one sort or another. Collins has documented that many such migrants worked for other ethnically owned SMEs, suggesting the establishment of a viable migrant SME economy.[2]

Collins notes further that the 1991 Census data on migrant entrepreneurs recorded approximately 25% of the Greek-born male cohort, 26% of Italian, 24% of Dutch and of Taiwanese, 21% of Lebanese, and 11% of Indonesian and of Vietnamese-born males. Korean-born males at 30% of their total cohort were the largest (ethnic) group notionally considered business migrants or entrepreneurs.[3] This inter-ethnic difference is not unique to Australia and has been the subject of numerous studies to determine its effects on success or otherwise in business. Success is a loaded term here, as migrant business is by no means anodyne in terms of exploitation and marginalisation of 'co-ethnic' labour. Burnley's demographic analysis of 1991 census data aimed to assess the extent to which the 'global city' dynamic was evident in Sydney by looking at class and ethnicity distribution. He found that there was a greater percentage of managers and professionals from among the Asian migrant cohort resident in Sydney than there were managers and professionals from among both Australia and the UK resident cohort combined.[4]

Research on the political economy specifically of business migration programmes in Australia has focused on a range of issues, including: ethnic small business as a phenomenon of mass migration and macroeconomic readjustment; forms of economic transnationalism that concern local labour markets

The Business Migration Program   173

and the efficacy or disadvantages of specific ethnocultural groups, and;[5] on policy implications of independent and skilled migration but which does not encompass developer-entrepreneurs.[6] Other research has argued that the BMP was a capital investment scheme run from the wrong government department,[7] a point that apparently resurfaced in advice from the Department of Treasury Finance to Department of Immigration on the 'investment-linked' category within the later 1994 Business Skills Program.[8]

In all, detailed research on Australian business migration programmes has been concerned with understanding experiences of and opportunities for this category of migrants. Interpretations of 'human capital' or 'cultural capital' as a measurable value are implicit in some of this research, particularly in the analysis of language, interpersonal networks, entrepreneurial dispositions, and education and training as factors in business success.

Australia's business migration programme

Business migration programmes, which thrived from the mid-1980s in Australia, Canada, New Zealand in particular, aimed to capitalise on the idea of migrant entrepreneurship as a driver of growth for both domestic and export capital. There is a harmonious relationship between 'new growth theories' of small and medium enterprise-led growth and neoliberal ideology about market relations as social relations of production. As noted in earlier chapters, the small business sector grew significantly in the 1980s and 1990s in Australia, with much business growth in the services sector, just as it had been in the USA and elsewhere. Job creation was increasingly viewed through a shift towards SMEs for advanced neoliberal market economies (see Chapter 4 and Chapter 5),[9] and towards value-adding services at a time when the concentration of low-cost labour for industrial-scale production Global South was becoming more accessible. In other words, transnational production and the global capitalist elites and governments pursuing this did not create the concentration of low-cost labour as a feature of post-1970s globalisation but found ways of exploiting or advancing the global division of labour. The role of small and large enterprise entrepreneurs in accessing the concentrations of low-cost labour and in the circulation of this transnational capital, both in domestic markets and for further export is an important development. Australia's specialised business migration programme tells a unique story among the many countries in competition for entrepreneurs.

During the five years 1985 to 1989 inclusive, business and skilled migration (combined) was the only category to experience sustained growth (see Figures 10.2 and Figure 10.3). A doubling of business entrants each year to mid-1988, and then peaking at 10,000 by mid-1990 was a growth rate unmatched by any other visa category in the family reunion or skilled

174 *The Business Migration Program*

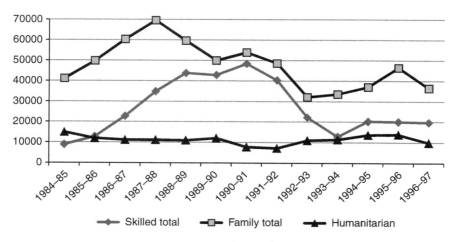

Figure 10.1 Main settler arrivals by visa category 1984–85 to 1994–95.[16]

stream.[10] This came with a significant relaxation of entry requirements and the privatisation of the accreditation process to migration agents that year.[11] Skilled independents, however, were the second-largest visa growth category and larger overall than the business category, peaking at 33,000 in mid-1991. This category also included professionals, SME entrepreneurs, etc.[12] Family reunion migration, meanwhile, remained highest in overall intake numbers, but was in relative decline for much of the same period.[13] Note, however, Collins' later survey of 1996 showing that an average 45% of small business operators of non-English speaking ethnicities had arrived on Family Reunion visas, and average 20% of small business operators of non-English speaking ethnicities had arrived on Skilled Independent visas.[14] Visa categories other than the specific business migrant sub-programme were also delivering entrepreneurs. In the case of family reunion, entry into small business was often the only employment option for these migrants due to structural barriers in the job market against those of non-English speaking background.

Immigration officials in certain overseas posts were reported as having said in 1988 they would 'give business migrants priority over those wishing to enter the country under non-business categories, including family reunions'.[15] Notably, this and similar statements were made in North America. Both the USA and Canada were viewed as competitors for the most desirable among this sought-after visa group.

Between 1992 and 1994, there was a rapid decline in all migration categories, which can be in part attributed to the recession, but also eligibility changes. The business migrant category dropped from 25% between 1990 and 1992 and shed around 50% in the following year to 3,607 entrants by mid-1993 before trending upwards again.[17] In 1993,

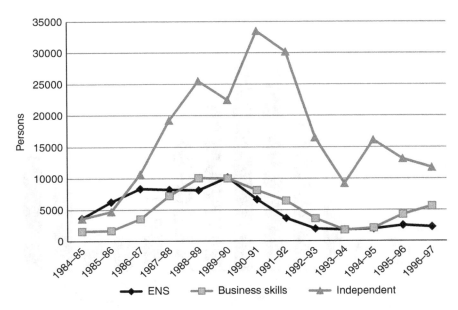

Figure 10.2 Skilled settler arrival by category (principle and secondary applicants), mid-1984 to mid-1994.[18]

following the recession, the number of immigrants (all visa categories), arriving from Asia almost halved from the approximately 61,000 arriving in 1990–91. The share of business migrants specifically from Asia is discussed further below.

Australia's Business Migration Program was one of three main sub-programmes of the permanent skilled migration category. That sub-programme transformed rapidly under the Hawke government in particular, as did the Independent migrant visa group. However, the latter category did not go through the same policy wrangling in an effort to expand market activity.

The BMP attracted limited scrutiny in parliament and the media until its up-scaling and liberalisation in 1988. Business migrants were labelled 'economic playmakers' according to one Labor Immigration Minister.[20] Their impact for a good part of the Labor period would be measured (simplistically) in their incoming numbers rather their financial turnover or business success, as well as their generic contribution to networking Australia's economy to Asia. The fact that business migrant activity was not, until a 1991 inquiry into the BMP, subject to any serious scrutiny only serves to highlight the laissez faire attitude or faith in wealthy entrepreneurs ready to flee less accommodating nation-states in Asia.

Australia had established as early as 1976 an Entrepreneurial Migration Category to encourage individuals preferably with at least $200,000 and

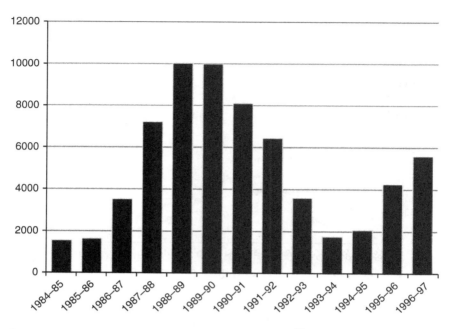

Figure 10.3 Business migrants mid-1984 to mid-1997.[19]

a business plan to migrate. According to then Minister for Immigration and Ethnic Affairs Ian McPhee in 1981, the scheme aimed 'to attract entrepreneurs whose investment and business skills will create more jobs'.[21] In April 1982, the Entrepreneurial Migration Category was re-badged the Business Migration Program (BMP) and set a higher asset test for intending business migrants.[22] The following year, under the new Labor government, the asset transfer requirement was reduced apparently on equity grounds such that $250,000 was considered a sufficient sum.[23] A few years later it increased again to between $450,000 and $1,000,000 depending on age and destination, and was crudely dubbed 'business multiculturalism' by one Labor Immigration Minister Mick Young.[24] Young's conflation of business migration and multiculturalism captured the policy moment.

The BMP had four main criteria used to attract and select migrants: establishing or improving a new industry; generating employment; export expansion; and technology transfer. The intent and stipulation was establishment of a business, expected within 24 months of migration, for the economic benefit of Australia.[25] A Parliamentary Inquiry into the success or otherwise of the Program was instigated in 1991, partly to resolve concerns around the system of accreditation of recruitment agents and the impact business migrants were achieving relative to their stated goals.[26] As

The Business Migration Program   177

summarised by one radio news report at the time, there were serious and indeed criminal allegations:

> Suspicions of wide-spread rorting were highlighted when the [1991] Public Accounts Committee held hearings as part of its inquiry into the program. Police intelligence units from Victoria and New South Wales said the program was being used by organised crime gangs, especially from Asia, to launder money and dodge tax bills in places like Hong Kong. They alleged large sums were being brought into Australia under the program, sunk into unused property, cleaned through non-existent transactions and then leaving the country.
>
> The scheme relied on agents and overseas sub-agents to help business migrants get into Australia and supposedly plough their money into worthwhile projects. But critics told the Committee these agents had a clear conflict of interest in making money out of whoever they could get into Australia.[27]

As noted in earlier chapters, a heightened and very public political debate about Asian migration to Australia flared up in 1988. The BMP was also a casualty of this debate and clearly a sensitive part of the immigration programme. Immigration Minister Robert Ray made it clear that the level of anti-Asian sentiment had a deleterious effect, financially as much as in attracting suitable candidates:

> As to whether that has gone on to harm our business migration program, I instinctively think, 'Yes, it has', but at this stage I cannot measure the extent. There are lags in the system of three to 10 months for approval. The evidence from business migration agents, especially in Hong Kong, Taiwan and Korea, is that their clientele is diminishing rather than growing. Whereas 70 people turned up to listen to the details at a business migration seminar in Seoul a year ago, only seven turned up at the most recent one. There is no overwhelming or compelling evidence yet, but we do not need much of a drop-off. We need only about 700 in a program of 12,000 not to come for it to cost this country $350m in terms of money brought in.[28]

The BMP Business Migration Program (BMP) had become a sensitive, high-stakes programme. As a result of the 1991 Inquiry, the BMP was re-engineered away from recruiting business people based upon their apparent prior success to recruiting skilled business talent with an emphasis that qualifications and not just experience through a visa points system. The aim was to circumvent subversion of the system by migrants and their agents. The CAAIP Report had recommended a points system for migrant entrepreneurs in 1988 which was initially rejected by the Minster for

178   *The Business Migration Program*

immigration in December that year,[29] so the idea of rationalising and measuring for entrepreneurial recruitment had emerged separate to concerns about corruption.

Throughout its nine years of growth up to the 1991 Inquiry, the BMP was interpreted differently by governments as economic and political circumstances changed. Import substitution, in particular, was not an official category for an enterprise proposition, but there appears some difference in understanding within government about this. Import substitution as a strategy typically relies on or accompanies protectionism according to Edwards.[30] It emerged as a development strategy for the Global South following the collapse of colonial trade system with the Second World War.[31] However, as previous chapters have made plain, from both Hawke's and Keating's point of view, and those supporting the restructuring of the Australian economy towards the global market place, export production, value adding with new technologies and techniques was required, import substitution was not. For a free-trade market economy, import substitution represented a strategy for internal demand only or as a form of protectionism, which had already begun to be wound down in Australia.[32] Trade flows through global value chains for mass consumer goods were a more important logic that helps explain why import substitution was not a viable category attracting business migrants going into the 1990s and beyond.

The importance of import substitution lingered at least within the minds of some officials within government as competition for manufactures and industry intensified through engagement with the new global, and specifically Asia's, economic growth.[33] What import substitution meant in political terms for factions of the Labor Party was an identification with the industrial labour movement to preserve certain sectors of the economy.[34] Import substitution was not requested officially in the application form *M.86 – Entrepreneur Eligibility Report* nor implied in the other application criteria noted above for the early part of the BMPs operation.[35] Yet, the 1991 Inquiry indicates that import substitution was included at least tacitly in the BMP rationale, if not in the actual selection of business cases. It is also worth noting that the first significant survey into the BMP commissioned by Government in 1989 states 'the replacement of imports' as one criterion for that study.[36] The survey failed to gain sufficient survey data on import substitution among all the business rationales surveyed. Following the 1991 Joint Parliamentary Inquiry, import substitution continued as an official purpose of the BMPs successor, the Business Skills Category.

The 1991 Joint Parliamentary Inquiry into the BMP had found that 45% of business migrants had established businesses within one year after arrival, increasing to 61% after two years; what the Inquiry was more concerned with was the fact that less than one-third of these business startups were 'export-oriented',[37] even though export development was only one of four stated criteria for eligibility as a business migrant. Import and export programmes and stimuli can exist side by side. However, Hawke and Keating's anti-protectionism and financial deregulation were public knowledge. Import substitution in this environment was not tenable.

The Business Migration Program clearly was a site of contest not just in terms of source countries for migrant intake, but a microcosm of the politics of Australia's economic direction under Labor. This tension between the intentions of business migrants and the expectations of the Australian government was further addressed by targeting the recruitment process. The burgeoning complement of migration agents based in the Asia Pacific region were subject to greater scrutiny and agent registration fees and non-refundable migrant applicant fees were levied.

Overall numbers for the BMP, while initially small, throughout the 1980s were dominated by migrants from countries of Asia. In 1987–88, for example, 80% of the approximately 1800 migrant entrepreneurs (principle applicants) that year came from Asia, largely Hong Kong and Taiwan.[38]

According to evidence admitted to the Joint Parliamentary Inquiry into the BMP in 1991, the scheme was introduced originally in the 1970s with European recruitment in mind, while its popularity and success in attracting business people from the Asia Pacific in the mid-1980s was viewed as a 'distortion' or possible deliberate bias of the BMP.[40] The original Entrepreneurial Migration Category between 1976 and 1981 under the

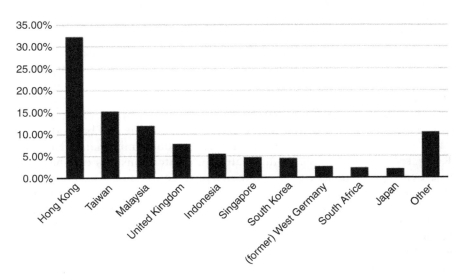

Figure 10.4 Business Migrant Program source countries, 1982–90: proportion of principal applicants.[39]

180   *The Business Migration Program*

conservative Fraser Liberal government was focused solely on the UK and other parts of Europe, corroborated by figures from the migration programme advertising budget of the Department of Immigration and Ethnic Affairs: up to December 1980 none of the $804,000 spent on promoting migration to Australia, including 'to attract entrepreneurs whose investment and business skills will create more jobs', went to countries other than Britain (90%), Germany, the Netherlands, Switzerland, Spain and Italy (10%).[41] However, it is a distortion to historicise the problems of the BMP under the Hawke Labor government as a scheme originally intended only for attracting business migrants from the UK/Europe. Claims of that nature presented to the 1991 BMP Senate Inquiry overstate the importance of the original hopes of the scheme from the late 1970s, deny that a pro-globalisation Labor government presided legitimately over the re-vamped BMP from 1983 onwards, and are contradicted by the reality that individual UK/European migrant entrepreneurs did not transfer themselves and their capital to Australia in meaningful proportions despite years of exclusive recruitment expenditure up to the early 1980s. In other words, even in its earlier years, the scheme never worked as originally anticipated anyway. The scheme under scrutiny in the 1991 Joint Parliamentary Inquiry was a scheme for the emerging regional and global reality for Australia. Advertising and promotions for the scheme by the mid-1980s continued in the UK, Germany and Switzerland, but now included Hong Kong and Malaysia.[42] Reports of recruitment initiatives in the Canada and the USA reveal how consulate staff were charged with hosting seminars to recruit potential entrepreneurs outside the better-resourced Asian posts. With only 60 such recruits (including family members) from the USA in 1987, for example, consulate staff played down any real success of the programme there: 'We don't expect a response now ... we're planting the seed to generate further interest in Australia', according to the Consulate's Robert Hillson.[43] More revealing was role of consulate staff in recruitment in the USA and Canada compared with the burgeoning and deregulated migrant recruitment agent industry in the Asian region.

The BMP was a political football since its inception in 1982, as migration generally would become throughout the decade and beyond. One case, that of Singaporean-born, Malaysian multi-millionaire Tan Sri Khoo Teck Puat that year, illuminates the contentiousness of what migrant entrepreneurs as citizens were meant to contribute. Khoo has been the subject of previous research in relation to wealthy migrant entrepreneurs, considered a 'success story' as a humanitarian visa entrant made good. More recent evidence since reveals that Khoo had previously bought the Australian Southern Pacific Hotel Corp in 1981,[44] having gained a migrant entrepreneur visa that year, and questions about his affiliations and intentions other than finance speculation were levelled at the then Liberal Government's support for the BMP. Using the case of Khoo, the Labor party (in opposition) questioned whether 'foreign

The Business Migration Program 181

nationals [could] purchase permanent residence under this program by purchasing Australian companies or business?'[45] When the Labor Party took government in 1983, left-wing Immigration Minister Stewart West reduced significantly the asset requirement for intending migrants under the BMP because 'it [had] allowed wealthy people to migrate who did not intend to set up a business'. Instead the BMP was to now give 'priority to businesses with employment or technology improving potential'.[46] This emanated from Labor's traditional left-leaning Keynesian approach to migration, marrying a desire for investment in jobs with social equity. The lower monetary threshold for applicants and corresponding rationale for encouraging smaller developers and local capacity building rather than global venture capital financiers did not prevail. Subsequent Labor government Immigration Ministers raised the monetary eligibility limit[47] along with policy and rhetoric to attract interest largely from Asian investors and major business operators.[48] The approach to business migrants initially introduced by Stewart West favouring a more equitable recruitment threshold while rebuffing speculative finance and investment was soon squared off by the ascendant, market-oriented Labor leadership of Hawke and Keating, which focused on improving access to Asian economies as well as liquidity through foreign investment. In the case of the BMP this included attracting a cadre of self-financed immigrant entrepreneurs. It wasn't until the 1991 Parliamentary Inquiry, and the effects of the 1991–92 recession, that business and independent migration was again subject to more stringent points systems and concerned more with regulating self-employed skilled individuals.[49]

Despite Khoo Teck Puat being from an Asian country, the Liberal Party in Opposition from 1983 chose to attack the BMP not on grounds of supporting venture capitalists but on the ethnic or nationality bias in the numbers of BMP visa holders. Criticisms of the Hawke Labor Government's Asia focus of the BMP echoed the undercurrent about Asian migration generally in Australia at the time, thus anti-Asian sentiment pervading conservative Australian politics did not leave self-supporting business migrants untouched. Parliamentary questions such as those in 1988 by then Shadow (Liberal Party) Home Affairs Minister and Asian migration phobic, Senator Jim Short (aka 'Semaphore Jim'),[50] aimed to stir up the issue – by no coincidence, in the same year John Howard infamously questioned Asian migration to Australia:

> Will the Minister confirm that the former Minister, Mr Young, issued an instruction to his consultant to increase the flow of business migrants from Europe and North America and to reduce the numbers being obtained from Asia? Is that instruction still in force?[51]

The Labor Government's response was tactfully anodyne:

182 *The Business Migration Program*

> We cast the business migration net as widely as possible to attract the best candidates from all parts of the world and from all types of industry. Since there has been no upper limit on the number of business migrants, there can be no discrimination on the basis of race or country of birth; nor should there be. Any people who meet the criteria are accepted, regardless of where they come from. An applicant from Asia and an applicant from Europe will each receive the same consideration.[52]

Applicants from Asia, however, were not given the same consideration in public debate. Along with reports emanating from source countries such as Hong Kong about racism as a barrier to business migrants,[53] the Labor Government continued with claims about the damage Australia's ongoing anti-Asian sentiment posed specifically to business migration. Minister for Immigration Minister Robert Ray in 1989:

> The program does have difficulties, but I want to stress too in fairness that the Asian migration debate is one of the factors operating in the business migration area … Those opposite [the Liberal Party] can make as much noise as they like. If they think that this debate has not affected our image and our reputation in places such as Hong Kong, they just happen to be wrong; it has.[54]

Business visa demand from Asia was a key factor throughout the 1980s as the figures from Figure 10.1 show. The 1991 Joint Parliamentary Inquiry into the BMP further noted that there were 'significant push factors' contributing particularly to Hong Kong and Taiwanese numbers – those push factors including the future of Hong Kong and Taiwan under the One China policy position.[55] An early example of migration and investment from Hong Kong was duly exploited by the Federal Labor Senators Devlin and Grimes in their government's quest to promote a pro-Asia business migration scheme in 1986:

> For some months I have been watching with interest the development of a specialist clothing factory, in fact a swimwear producing factory, in Launceston, Tasmania. The Shun Man company has been developing a factory and bringing in machinery. It looks as though it will employ in excess of 100 people when the factory is in full production. It is due to open next month. Mr Bill Cheung, who came out under the business migration program, obviously has considerable faith in the economy of Australia and in the work force in Tasmania. He was Hong Kong's third largest specialist swimwear manufacturer.[56]

The extent of business relocation from Hong Kong to Australia was in many cases not absolute or fixed and involved complex familial

The Business Migration Program 183

arrangements.[57] It also led to some large-scale relocation propositions that were strongly oriented to global business development. For example, a scheme proposed by Hong Kong businessmen in 1989 was presented to the Australian Government to establish a special zone in the Northern Territory and populate it with Hong Kong citizens to set up businesses.[58] Leasing land in such a fashion was not necessarily part of Australia's migration-led growth strategy although foreign investment and ownership by Asian capital was well established. The idea of a multi-function polis (or MFP) was perhaps the most ambitious, futuristic example proposed of foreign investment in Australian social and economic life.[59] There were, in fact, a growing number of globally resourced or oriented 'technology parks' in Australia at this time[60] (and beyond scope of discussion here, but relevant to Chapter 4 concerning Australia's connection with global value chains and high-end transnational production).

Throughout the 1980s, at least, the idea of housing foreign workers, or guest workers, remained outside the political economy of migration largely because of opposition by organised labour in Australia, as well as the Labor Party's commitment to citizenship as a basis for migration. Diversity policy in this sense was an important part of labour relations insofar as the union movement had long championed migrant identity, welfare and language rights as part of the social contract.[61] When it was raised as a serious recommendation by the FitzGgerald (CAAIP) Report, Prime Minister Hawke rejected the prospect, his *National Agenda for a Multicultural Australia* reinforcing the link between citizenship (permanency) and migration. The growth in temporary skilled and workforce migration would become more marked in the years following the Keating Labor Government as data below highlights.

The peak years for BMP visas issued were 1988 and 1989. In 1989, 103 respondents to a government-commissioned survey of business migrants revealed that approximately 70 migrant businesses – close to 82% of the sample – employed 1 to 10 people[62] While a small sample overall, the results indicate a significant trend towards small-scale operations. In a separate survey item, one-quarter, or 19 of 72 respondents who were in the small business category (1 to 10 employees) claimed to have a gross revenue well over $1 million, while the average turnover for all 72 businesses in 1988–89 was $1.1 million. What this means in adjusted terms is that *gross* profit was healthy: that is, in November 1989, the average private-sector wage was $22,708,[63] meaning that workers created around five times their value.

By 1992, applications had dropped markedly from Hong Kong, partly a result of the recession in Australia and a corresponding upturn in Hong Kong, and partly a re-tightening of recruitment and entry requirements following the 1991 Inquiry.[64] Nevertheless, Australia's orientation towards engagement with Asia in the 1980s was a corresponding pull factor facilitating Asian regional migration over business migration links

184 *The Business Migration Program*

with Europe or the USA. The significance of the Business Migration Program as it existed throughout the 1980s as a scheme for boosting Australia's complement of expatriate Asia-savvy capitalists was challenged by the 1991 Inquiry. But the resulting drop in applications from that region in 1992 engendered further criticism from the conservative Opposition as much as within the Government's own ranks, just as in 1988 when Senator Ray expressed concern about business migrant 'drop-off' following the embarrassing public debates about levels of Asian migration. Business migrants from certain parts of Asia were attracted by the BMP with its idealistic preference for exporters and finance entrepreneurs, along with a reasonably open citizenship policy. But the concern was about the quality of the cohort, given the worry about competition from Canada and New Zealand for the same migrants.[65] According to Neil Edwards, the pursuit of business migrants without a full appreciation of their contribution or the endurance of their extant national identities 'was almost a cargo cult' approach in the period up to the early 1990s.[66] Business migrants from Asia were fêted in expectation of bringing with them a material proportion of the growth occurring in the region.

The BMP was revamped in February 1992 as the Business Skills Program (BSP) and through the new points test aimed to avoid the *laissez-faire* approach to entrepreneur recruitment and selection based on the advice of private migration recruitment agents in the region; visa processing officials were relieved of individual character judgements about business acumen and instead were to rely on a points-based approach to skill or competency. The new BSP had an initial quota of 5,000 applicants, separate to the independent skilled category (self-employed professionals), which also attracted small business entrepreneurs in trades and services.[67]

Compared with Figure 10.4, the graph in Figure 10.5 indicates country of origin with the revised scheme introduced after the 1991 Parliamentary inquiry. Some changes are apparent: of note is the high application and visa issue rate for South African entrepreneurs, a statistic explained by the significant changes occurring in that country with the break-up of Apartheid and the consequences affecting white business dominance – 'capital flight' of White South Africans, in other words. Of more interest is the drop in Hong Kong approvals and relative to the number of Hong Kong applicants. Historically, the lead supplier of entrepreneurs for the previous decade of the 1980s, Hong Kong still topped the applicant list but not the approvals – by a significant margin: 158 applications but only 19 visas issued. Meanwhile, Malaysia emerged as the top source country in relative terms, with visa approval share more than double application share from would-be entrepreneurs. In actual numbers, there were 113 applications from and 76 approvals to Malaysia. That Malaysia and Indonesia were now contributing more entrepreneurs in this period in relative terms than under the pre-1991 period could be explained in a number of ways: simply a

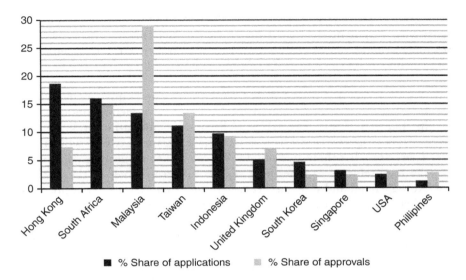

Figure 10.5 Share of BSC applications versus approvals by country of principal applicant: 17 Feb 1992–31 January 1994.[68]
Data selected from BSAP (1994), Annexure C – 'BSC Applications Lodged by Country', p. 64 and 'BSC Cases Visaed by Country', p. 65.

temporary spike or backlog processing by Australian immigration officials Australia recruiting business connections to source cheap labour and materials in those nearby countries. Or, given that Malaysia in particular was multi-ethnic, there may well have been Indian or Chinese diaspora applying from Malaysia, but ostensibly connected to economic development opportunities China or India. The ratio of successful applications for Malaysia warrants further investigation, as there may have been acute bilateral trade opportunities at this time. Technically, visas are issued on merit but Keating as Prime Minister had made significant efforts towards Southeast Asia during his term of office. Meanwhile, it was reported that the Hong Kong office took much longer than other visa issuing posts to process applications (see statement by Robert Ray, below). Bureaucracy may well have affected outcomes but deeper data on actual Immigration Department decision making for the time is not readily available.

Anecdotal evidence put to the Senate Estimates Committee in 1992 suggested that the scrapping of the BMP for the BSP had 'done some damage to the reputation of Australia as a desirable destination for business migrants', contributing significantly to a drop-off in applications, including from Hong Kong.[69] A tightening of the BMP to favour proven business skills and the monitoring of productive investment came with very poor timing as the 1991–92 recession lingered. Australia presented as a poor

186 *The Business Migration Program*

investment and migration destination at this time. Earlier, in 1989, Immigration Minister Robert Ray had flagged a similar concern about the sensitivity of potential Hong Kong business migrants to Australia's assessment criteria, suggesting that other destinations were luring these entrepreneurs away:

> A second factor is competition from New Zealand and Canada, which have far less rigorous requirements, not only in monetary amounts but in character checks, et cetera ... The business migration program this year has suffered, and I believe that the program next year will suffer. There are other things we can do. We can tinker around the edges with the requirements to ease them slightly-not ever to get to the level of New Zealand and Canada, because I think that they are economy class schemes and we are running a first class scheme.[70]

Given earlier criticisms about the apparent lack of proper accreditation and monitoring processes and potential rorting of the business entry category,[71] Senator Ray's portrait of the Australian system was somewhat overstated. What Robert Ray didn't point out was that, unlike Australia, the Canadian scheme did not automatically grant a visa at that time – success in implementing the stated business plan was the contingent factor for gaining residency and/or citizenship.[72]

Concern over competition for business migrants with countries such as Canada, the USA and New Zealand is telling of the Government's commodification of migrants as assets in a globalisation race. As the high point of Australian recruitment waned in 1991, Canada admitted 17,000 business migrants that year, the majority also from Asia.[73] What was peculiar to Australia's migrants was not simply their finance capital, but the way their role in facilitating and championing Australia's extensive economic, cultural and social engagement with the Asia Pacific region was construed. Comparisons with Canada's business and skilled migration programme serve to illuminate Australia's self-aggrandisement of its role as central to the Asian region, despite the fact Canada likewise bordered the Pacific and had in 1984 established an Asia Pacific Foundation to champion its own links.[74] When Australian Consulate staff charged with recruiting business migrations in Canada declared in 1988 that '[t]he western Pacific region is the fastest growing region in the world *and Australia is ideally suited as a base for the huge market place*', the competition for Asian entrepreneurs between Australia and Canada was evident.[75] As was the consulate's deliberate over-estimation of BMP numbers made clear to their Canadian competitors: 'The government will increase the number to 12,000 from July 1, 1988', then immigration officer Johann Jackson declared to Canadian media at an in-country trade seminar.[76] Immigration in Canberra may have been expecting figures that high but they did not reach that level. Nor was the figure quoted for

The Business Migration Program 187

Canadian audiences suggestive of the fact that only about 20–25% of annual figures were the principle applicants, the rest were family members. In all, 2,548 principle applicants were visaed in 1988–89.[77] Related reports in Canada's *Globe and Mail* cited Australian Immigration officials in 1988 as saying the BMP 'would match, if not go further, than similar campaigns in New Zealand, Canada and the United States to attract foreign wealth'.[78]

One challenge for the Immigration Department was that business migrant visa processing in Australia's key trade posts in the Asian region had a slow turnaround, compounding the concern over Canada and New Zealand as competitor destinations. In 1989, for example, average processing time for each application was seven months in Hong Kong, eight months in Singapore and five months in Kuala Lumpur, although applications processed in Athens, for example, took considerably longer, due in large part to even poorer resourcing in the European region.[79] As Immigration Minister Robert Ray lamented:

> I also went on to say in Hong Kong – it was not reported here – that the gap between the first approach and development of business migration applications by business migration agents and their lodging in our office is quite often 10 to 12 months.[80]

The administration of the BMP was a lengthy process relative to its competitors, and was critiqued for not being attuned to the way migrant entrepreneurs operated in the global economy. The 1991 Inquiry culminating in the new Business Skills Program did not acquiesce to the needs of capital by making it easier to bring foreign investment and cultural capital through entrepreneurs. It wasn't until after the 1991–92 recession that the Department of Immigration was again tasked with streamlining business migration for capital transfer through the 1994 Business Skills Assessment Panel, or Deveson Report.[81] 'World business is now extremely fluid', Labor Senator Mary Easson acknowledged in response to the Deveson Report on business migration. 'It is nothing today for a successful middle level business person to make a dozen or more overseas trips a year. This may result in that person being unable to qualify for the correct amount of time in Australia'.[82] Measures were subsequently endorsed by the Labor Government to exempt periodic stays outside Australia from residency requirements. Multiple re-entry visas were also made more available, but the lag in the administrative 'efficiencies' and stable policy relative to the introduction of the Business Migration Program highlight the tension caused by political opportunism for rapid engagement with regional economic growth and globalisation, and greater control of investment, business and skilled migration as part of Australia's productive capital.

Following the 1994 Deveson Report, ministers in the Keating Labor

188   *The Business Migration Program*

government were more confidently linking business migration to Asian growth:

> past business migration schemes emphasised a short-term focus; thus they were certain to fail. The new policies have been developed with a longer term vision, especially in the context of the internationalisation of the Australian economy and Australia's role in the Asia-Pacific region. As we are all aware, the Asia-Pacific region is the major growth area of the 1990s. In the period to the year 2000 Asia will have accounted for half of world GDP growth and half of world trade growth.[83]

Where the 1991 Parliamentary Inquiry into the BMP had identified the lack of export oriented startups, Keating's Labor government, post-recession, appeared to consolidate rather than extend risks:

> The business migration program is now called the business skills category. The category is concerned with the transfer of *business skills* which will benefit Australia in the medium term by adding to and diversifying Australia's existing pool of business expertise.[84]

A survey of 276 business migrant applicants between 1992 and 1994 reported to the Deveson review panel showed that 42% had net personal and business assets in excess of $1.5 million and were also 'involved in business overseas with turnover in excess of $A5 million'; overall, an average of $860,000 per individual was transferred to Australia 'despite there being no requirement to transfer funds prior to visa issue'.[85] Evidently, the post-1991 Business Skills Program was still approving wealthy entrepreneurs (by early 1990s standards) even if the revised focus on *business skill* through a points system and tightening of private migration agents' influence aimed to avoid undue emphasis on net wealth or investments.

Although the recession officially ran through 1991–92 (based on gross production figures), other indicators such as housing growth, finance credit and business confidence measures were still struggling by 1994.[86] The Deveson Report on business migration was as much a response to the recession as further streamlining of the programme to redress the more restrictive approach after the 1991 Senate Inquiry into the programme. Prime Minister Keating did state in his May 1994 *Working Nation* Policy Statement 'the complement to skill formation in the labour market is not going to come from migration. This time it has to come from training our own people, including those who are presently unemployed'.[87] The figures for the total *skilled* migrant category inclusive of business migrants and entrepreneurs told the opposite story, rising in 1995, ebbing somewhat in 1996, although still above 1994 levels.[88] The new (post-Deveson) Business Skills Category (BSC) originally planned for 1,600 principal applicant visas in their 1994–95 programme (it processed 2,087). This was the first year of

The Business Migration Program 189

growth in business migrant intake since the recession.[89] Notably, the business migration scheme also returned to allowing *business experience* and not just *skill* as a sub-category for visa assessment. Underscoring the interests of the market, the more fundamental change was in removing any requirement that the business migrant establish their activity in a designated industry sector, that is, those sectors of the economy government deemed to be in demand.[90]

Upon the advice of the Deveson Report, the new system rejected the idea that entrepreneurs be recruited for 'designated industry sectors', which had prevailed since the 1991 Inquiry.[91] The points system to obtain a visa removed any reference to this, opening the way for business in any aspect of the economy deemed fit by the applicant. Government devolved business planning further towards the market. The fault-line over business migrant skill or success saw a temporary redoubt with the 1991 Joint Parliamentary Inquiry into the BMP requiring a new emphasis on formal business qualifications, backed up by tighter assessment standards. That position was again wound back with the Deveson Report although was being undone well before that, in part due to the recession and the more pro-market Keating administration.

While most of the focus of the BMP, BSP and then BSC was on entrepreneurs, the programme issued sub-classes of visas relevant to transnational business development. A visa sub-category introduced in February 1992 singled out senior management of major or transnational firms (i.e. those with an annual turnover of $50 million). Visa sub-class 128 'Senior Executive' targeted management skill and business intelligence among corporate leadership as another way of attracting or importing knowledge and investment. Considering the international competition between Australia, Malaysia, Hong Kong and Singapore for attracting European, American and some North Asian transnational corporations to locate their Asia Pacific headquarters in the region, this was an important visa class.[92] The implication of the Senior Executive visa was in providing additional incentive for foreign business to set up operations in Australia. Senior Executive applicants were expected as with other business migrants to either establish a new business, or maintain equity in an Australian-based business in which they were also in a managerial position.[93] Separate rules applied for corporate executive foreign nationals *transferred* to Australia within their existing company. Following Keating's 1994 *Working Nation* statement, which included tax breaks for subsidiaries of global companies, revisions that same year to business migration visas for foreign national executives of large corporations relaxed rules for their temporary citizenship as a way of supporting the (re)location of regional business headquarters to Australia. As Immigration departmental bureaucrat David Wheen reported to Senate Estimates Committee in 1994:

> One of the issues involved in the establishment of the regional headquarters for the Asia-Pacific region of multinational companies in Australia is the movement of expatriate personnel to Australia to staff

190 *The Business Migration Program*

> those headquarters ... Rather than go through the normal market testing arrangements for those people who come into Australia as temporary residents, we would accept the decision of the national investment council ... company X can establish a regional headquarters in Australia and it must consist of a certain number of executive personnel. They would then have to meet the normal health and character requirements.[94]

Such resident-employees would not be subject to any other points testing with the expectation that 'a small number' would seek permanent residency while in Australia.[95] The competitive pursuit of foreign capital in the Asia Pacific extended special citizenship on the basis of one's position within a private company, notably a company expanding its global network within the region. There was no requirement to source local labour (in the form of local executives). Concern to facilitate corporate elites supports arguments raised in earlier chapters about the international division of labour and Australia's integration with global value chain production forms. The movement of elites became more pronounced with the rapid growth in temporary business migration in 1996. For instance, the Department of Immigration reported that '24 regional headquarters agreements approved in 1996–97 (up from 18 in 1995–96), leading to 204 permanent and 364 temporary visas issued, with 700 jobs created in 1996–97'.[96] While this now fell under the new conservative government of John Howard, the legacy of elite business migration had been well and truly established. Further discussion of temporary business migration and the circulation of business elites is presented below.

In effect, the post-Deveson programme was a turn to the opportunism of the pre-1991 BMP for regional engagement and investment. Australian business interests at the time were calling for more foreign investment, in part to counter the effects of the recession.[97] One additional way this was facilitated through the new BSC was via an 'investment linked' category which gave residency to business migrants who preferred to invest a sum between $750,000 and $2 million for a three-year period in identified securities with guaranteed rates of return.[98] This microeconomic reform measure was in part designed to stop the perceived transfer of money back out of Australia by entrepreneurs as well as to bring in greater finance capital post-recession. The expectation was that, after the three years, individuals would then invest in other activities they may have been involved in while qualifying for citizenship in Australia.[99] Such migrants were not assessed on their formal business skills in designated industry sectors but on their investment capital, while the business programme generally returned to assessing applicants based on proven success in business – a return to the BMP approach of the late 1980s but also of that advocated by the earlier CAAIP Report. The difference with the earlier approach of the BMP was that the new points system which, following the Deveson Report, was weighted towards prior business financial turnover and total labour costs (rather than actual number of employees) as a measure of the size of the business. The implication here is that *post*-Deveson,

The Business Migration Program 191

business migrants from low-wage economies were having to demonstrate either a greater number of employees (presumably indicating a larger business) to meet the new financial turnover threshold, or that the wages paid were relatively high. In fact, there was concern to filter business migrants who simply employed family members to bolster the size of their business. Clearly, the new BSC was not looking for family small business types but more ambitious entrepreneurs. The Deveson recommendations leaned towards a freer market approach and were duly supported by Government.

The Department of Immigration and Multicultural Affairs1996–97 Annual Report[100] lauded the following details of migrant business startups from 1994 to 1996:

- 82 per cent were engaged in business after 3 years, up from 79 per cent at 24 months and 54 per cent at 12 months.

This highlighted the time taken to establish a viable business due to policy and practice barriers to business creation and viability, but noting that ethno-culture can be a distinct disadvantage.[101] Three-quarters of businesses after three years were exporting and, importantly, 75% of all these businesses exported to South East Asia.[102] The report also noted that:

- Each new business employed an average 4.5 people; the same as at 24 months, but up from 3.7 people at 12 months.

In terms of employee numbers, business startups evidently remained in the 'Small' end of SMEs. However, this needs to be assessed relative to turnover. To wit:

- 18 per cent of exporting businesses had earnings worth more than $1 million.
- 30 per cent of businesses had an annual turnover of $1 million or more; up from 28 per cent at 24 months and 26 per cent at 12 months.

For some sense of scale, turnover of $1 million relative to average labour cost suggests labour was only 12.6% of annual turnover for the 30% of SMEs in their third year of operation.[103]

Overall, the picture is one of growth: those who migrated as business entrepreneurs, had 'delivered' despite the many years of adjustment to the programme, overt racism, structural forms of racism in terms of business information barriers in Australia,[104] and differing intentions of the migrants themselves.

There was some resistance expressed by members of the Deveson review panel and by the Department of Treasury to the idea of a business migrant investor category. That is, the granting of a permanent residency visa for those willing to deposit large sums of money capital in government

192 *The Business Migration Program*

approved securitised assets. Adoption by the Department of Immigration and Ethnic Affairs of a business investor visa was done without any strict cost–benefit analysis, emanating instead from submissions from the business community and parts of the Immigration and Ethnic Affairs bureaucracy that wealthy entrepreneurs were worth attracting 'to internationalise the Australian economy and to obtain a variety of economic benefits for the country', as justified by one senior DIEA bureaucrat.[105] Former Immigration and Ethnic Affairs Minister Nick Bolkus in the same Senate hearing reiterated a now-established sensibility that ethnoculture was a competitive asset for overseas business growth:

> The government was persuaded by the [Deveson] panel's argument ... that what you are talking about here are people who, given they have to prove a successful business background, are people with a role in the societies from which they come, with *business contacts, with cultural links and whatever, with cultural awareness* and that we should have one part of our program focusing on this ... It is a step that has a huge potential for us.[106]

Senator Bolkus's remark concerning the value of business migrants with 'cultural links and whatever, with cultural awareness' exemplify the kind of rationalisation the Labor Government-development lobby alliance jointly agreed about the importance of fostering and gaining competitive advantage in the regional and international market economy, particularly through its foreign affairs and trade arms. Senator Bolkus elsewhere noted in 1993 that Australia's export trade with the Asia Pacific had grown to be two and a half times as big as trade with the US and EU combined as a result of greater understanding of the Asia Pacific. Consequently, he identified the more complex, less tangible features of this general indicator of Asian engagement in his speech to the BIPR:

> In the context of the globalisation of markets, countries and companies with cross-cultural talents and skills have a competitive advantage over those that do not. This is due not only to language, but also to more intimate and direct knowledge of local practices, regulations and customs, particularly in the business environment. From an economic perspective, cultural skills also facilitate the acquisition of information.[107]

Bolkus' remarks here provide a more direct interpretation about know-how and knowledge of specific markets often termed a form of 'cultural capital'.

Economic citizenship

These statements highlight how government and the immigration bureaucracy conceptualised the ethnocultural character of its business migration planning in response to globalisation. Productive Diversity valorised ethnoculture but somewhat beyond what could be consistently measured as a contribution to productivity. Immigration officials were still reporting against Key Performance Indicators (KPIs) proposed originally by the CAAIP (FitzGerald) Report, such as the number of jobs for every business migrant (principal applicant) visaed.[108] Such a measure provides a basic indicator of business activity, but is not a reliable measure of diversity or cultural skills in operation. Nevertheless, the idea that 'cultural skills also facilitate the acquisition of information' had resonance and sophistication beyond CAAIP's pronouncements that immigrants are driven by character to work harder. At the same time, adopting Deveson's more *laissez-faire* approach to the business migrant profile, or devolving to the market the demands of migration, avoided a more complex rationalisation of what this meant for citizenship as an economic concern.

The 1989 *National Agenda*'s desire for primary affiliation to the Australian nation-state for all would-be citizens and residents did not factor in the transnational nature of global and indeed Asian regional commerce as it affected individual migrants' desires to build and maintain links across borders that weren't purely commercial. The idea that entrepreneurs might shift capital around or build business capacity in multiple countries did not sit well with the individual's obligations to the state inherent in the National Agenda, and so problematised the nation-state building dimension of Productive Diversity. Immigration rules regarding multiple re-entry visas for instance did differ for 'producers' and those considered 'traders', the latter under more the more rigid visa rules at one stage of the BSP.[109] More significantly, the investment programmes developed in 1994, following on from the tightening of accreditation and monitoring of entrepreneurial activity gradually introduced in the BSP post-1991, were in keeping with the idea that entrepreneurialism was bound by a notion of productive citizenship and therefore allegiance to the development of Australia as envisaged in the *National Agenda*. Indeed, investment in Australian securities may have afforded some control of perceived capital flight or fluidity. The Deveson Review committee also considered allowing transnational investment projects by migrant entrepreneurs but recommended against this. Likewise, an example of 30 Taiwanese-American entrepreneurs who returned to Taiwan '*en masse*' to establish a technology park in that country (drawing upon their US experience) was presented to the Australian Senate to characterise the new flexibility of global finance, but was never fully appreciated.[110] An inconsistency or hypocrisy in the Keating Government's desire to control migrant business reinvestment outside Australia is evident in immigration rules and visa classifications that facilitated transnational corporation (TNC) relocations to Australia. From 1994, TNC executive personnel (e.g. managers, marketing and sales) dispatched to Australia were to be granted temporary residency (with options for permanency) without any

194 The Business Migration Program

testing of supply in the domestic labour market.[111] In other words, by the mid-1990s, after several iterations of business migration schemes, Australia was keen to facilitate joint ventures *into* Australia, but less keen to allow incoming entrepreneur-citizens to invest or apply additional skills, experience and capital outside the country other than as exporters. This has implications for theorising transnational elites, in this case highlighting the degree of state control or interest in seeing such entrepreneurial types as an 'allocatable' resource.

The fact that permanent skilled and business migration encompassing domestic and foreign market entrepreneurs, dominated as it was from countries of Asia, was an ascendant feature of migration under the Hawke and Keating governments speaks not of consolidating the diversity inherited from Australia's migration history but of globalising its workforce, of endowing it economically with 'cultural capital' for a global – but also specifically regional – market. Correspondingly, the reductions and tightening of conditions for family migration streams during the period expose the retreat from diversity as a social and cultural endowment in its own right. For example, in 1993, unemployment and sickness benefits were made unavailable for migrants for the first six months of their residency. This was extended to two years in 1996.[112] While family migration was in overall gradual decline over a good part of the period of the Hawke and Keating governments, the effects of restricting welfare affected these migrants more so than business and employer-nominated skilled migrants who were essentially self-financed or arriving with the promise of a job. Thus, along with programmes to facilitate business migration were social policies designed to rationalise other migration categories.

While the state facilitated and strove to improve the capacity of its ethnocultural resources from the mid-1980s onwards, and did maintain refugee and family reunion migration streams, a neoliberal shift in migration and multiculturalism policy was manifest in the *transference of risk and responsibility* supply-side rather than demand-side, in particular, in the pursuit of individual migrants to grow the skilled and business visa categories. Risks and responsibilities were now the onus of the migrant of raising capital prior to entering the country, of funding one's own relocation, of establishing an appropriate or preferred business with the assistance of private migration agencies, possessing approved prior training and/or experience, self-supported welfare via 'wait listing',[113] and the implicit demand to be productive in a country where structural business barriers existed to anyone outside the dominant culture.[114]

One-time Labor Minister for Immigration, Mick Young, in 1987, invoked the 'hidden hand' of the market to make it clear how business migrants in particular were to take all risk and responsibility: '[p]rospective business immigrants will be protected from exploitation by normal market forces'.[115] In other words, the government would not be liable for the costs associated with failed bids to get a relevant visa even though that same

The Business Migration Program   195

government had completely deregulated the business migration accreditation process, leaving it open to serious corruption and incompetence.[116] Add to this the sentiment of the *National Agenda*, which transferred civic responsibility to *all* migrants, but realistically to those willing to contribute business capital *and* their individual ethnocultural resources as a citizen for the national good. Here had emerged a marked change to Australia's historical approach of garnering workers in job lots, skilled or unskilled, to fulfil national growth through the industrial economy. The message emanating from the *National Agenda for a Multicultural Australia* and then Productive Diversity was thus a mixed one in terms of citizenship – individuals had the right to private practice and enjoyment of ethnocultural heritage; however the private had become public inasmuch as ethnoculture was encouraged as a viable productive national good.

As Immigration and Ethnic Affairs Minister Nick Bolkus added in a 1994 Senate Estimates hearing, business migration 'complements the *productive diversity* agenda which the government has decided to mainstream'.[117] Productive Diversity had become a central principle for *immigration* as much as for the broader frame of *multiculturalism*; the distinction now being that there was a deliberate approach to sourcing value-adding increasingly in export trade through market activity from prospective migrants based upon a notion of their cultural capital. The fact is, even ethnic small business services, from tourism operators to lawyers and health services and the market in private 'foreign' schools for migrant children, were all now able to be seen as contributors in one way or another to the Productive Diversity agenda of harnessing cultural knowledge for global engagement and economic growth. Culture, more specifically ethnoculture, was viewed as a significant commodity in this respect, one which successive Australian governments were keen to somehow accumulate and exploit.

Temporary business migration and the post-Labour years

The Immigration Department's Annual report on business migrant outcomes from 1994 to 1996 (cited above) is presented as a positive story from the new conservative Howard Government elected in 1996. However, Prime Minister Howard had shown longstanding reticence towards engagement with Asia, which included his Ministers questioning the bias towards recruiting business people from that region. Howard's government also favoured temporary migration over permanent migration, evidenced by the massive growth in temporary business migrants commencing with his term of office in 1996. Temporary migration existed throughout the prior Labor government years, but following a review in the mid-1990s began to increase as the more significant source of business activity, measured in terms of migrant presence. In fact, around 200,000 temporary business visas were issued in 1995–96, a figure which steadily increased to around 530,000 by 2007–08.[118] Whereas *permanent* business entrants accounted for around 15% of the total intake in

196 *The Business Migration Program*

the first term of the Howard government, by 2007–08 they accounted for only 6%.[119] The matter of temporary migration is noted in Chapter 5 in relation to the circulation of the 'lieutenants of capital' (see also Figure 5.1). However, with the increase in temporary migration in line with greater engagement with transnational production, concepts of Productive Diversity that applied to permanent migration programmes do not apply in the same way.[120] In this case, it is insufficient to simply reduce the Howard government's move away from multiculturalism as a matter of social concern. There were strong economic motives in the desire to facilitate the free flow of capital and not bind it to matters of citizenship.

Nevertheless, Productive Diversity was reiterated in the Howard Government's re-visiting in 1999 of the decade-old *National Agenda for a Multicultural Australia* issued by then Prime Minster Hawke.[121] By 2001, however, diversity politics and globalisation were questioned following the attacks of 11 September 2001 on the USA. That event, and the series of Middle East conflicts that followed was a significant factor that undermined much of the political advance to embrace diversity in any pluralistic way.

Conclusion

The evolution and growth of business migration programmes concurred with a shift in multiculturalism from a social policy into an economic one (Productive Diversity). Productive Diversity clearly was a key part of this process in its description of culture as a tangible asset, something which is thought to both contain value and, through business migrants and entrepreneurs, add value within the logic of transnational or global value chain production. This adds more weight to claims that Australia was re-tooling its economy and re-shaping its terms of engagement for the global political economy. The growth in business and entrepreneurial migrants and skilled professionals more broadly also supports the contention that this was part of a global division of productive labour and non-productive and market expanding occupations. Entrepreneurs were being recruited for their potential to engage in export trade of some sort or another. They were not recruited for domestic internal and small-scale retail business as many preceding generations of migrants had found themselves working in. The identity and ethnocultural know-how of these new entrepreneurs becomes a key feature in justifying the scheme.

The influence of Labor Government ministers and their senior bureaucrats on immigration policy and discourse was decisive in linking multiculturalism to an issue of Australia's political economy. The direct contribution to development and production by able migrants enhanced by their ethnocultural links and capacities gained rapid currency in ministerial and bureaucratic circles. Self-reliance combined with the financial worth of migrants based upon their disposable cash and assets or the trade links and investment capital expected blended material and ideological rationales. A wholly other discourse not about belonging, not about social equality, but about

The Business Migration Program 197

engagement with the new global market economy can be traced through this period of multicultural policy making.

The value in deeper analysis of the development of the BMP-BSP-BSC resides in the fact that the Prime Minister's department, Foreign Affairs and Immigration bureaucracies in particular, exhibited a market faith in high-value business migration as much as small business creation in relation to Asia. That the Department of Treasury was at least one oppositional voice to the non-productive business investor visa category is significant in attempts to measure business visa planning. The Treasury was nevertheless overruled. Market knowledge of competitor nation-states and an entrepreneurial work ethic, although broad and ill-defined, were prime order factors in the multicultural and migration bureaucracies' intrinsic belief in the BMP.

At this point, the significance of Productive Diversity is apparent in the prosecution and validation of pro-market changes to migration programmes in Australia. Here was a conceptualisation of belonging that did not simply reify ethnoculture for competitive advantage but rather that market-oriented occupations and activity were important for Australia's globalising economy. In effect, non-productive market expanding occupations were more consistent with a value-adding strategy for transnational production. The migration and diversity policy developments in Australia during the Labour administrations from the early 1980s to mid-1990s indicate that the accumulation of entrepreneurial and skilled professional talent not only aimed to link Australia with Asia, but was consistent with a view that the economy was globally interconnected and pro-free trade, yet internationally segmented or partitioned at the level of labour. In recruiting and promoting the integration of certain categories and nationalities of migrants, valorising their expertise in market connections, as the evidence presented thus far demonstrates, the Government assisted deliberately the transformation of the social relations of production.

Considering the policy announcement made in the first year of Labor's 13-year term of office by its first minister for immigration, Stewart West, in 1983, about the need to approve business migrants who had employment generation and technology improving capacities rather than investment portfolios, a reasonably rapid turnaround from traditional Labor left views about the nature and value of investment is discernible. For the dominant view of the Hawke and Keating governments this turnaround was considered a matter of pragmatism.[122] It can also be seen as a radical experiment in market-based economics for the Australian Labor Party. The idea that certain migratory pull or push factors prevailed masks the one overarching pull factor facilitated by all willing governments: competition among nation-states in a global marketplace for economic agents.

Notes

1 Ibrahim, G. and Galt, G. (2003); Collins, J. (2003a); Collins, J. et al. (1995).
2 Collins, J. (2003a).

198 The Business Migration Program

3 See Table 4.7, p. 86; Collins, J., 'Asian Small Business in Australia', in Brownlee P. and Mitchell, C. (1998).

4 Burnley, I. 'Immigration and Globalisation? Affluence and Poverty among Immigrants from Asia in Metropolitan Sydney', in ibid.

5 Collins, J. in ibid.; Collins, J. (1991); Lever-Tracy, Constance et al. (1991) *Asian Entrepreneurs in Australia – Ethnic Small Business in the Chinese and Indian Communities of Brisbane and Sydney*, Canberra: AGPS, pp vi–xiv; Pookong, K., 'Australia's Business Migrants from Taiwan', in Zhuang, G. (ed.) (1998) *Ethnic Chinese at the Turn of the Centuries,* Fujian, China: Fujian Peoples Publishing House, pp. 564–82.

6 Iredale, R. (2001) 'Skilled Migration: The Rise of Temporary Migration and Its Implications', *CAPSTRANS/CEDA Policy Papers Series, Issue 6*, Wollongong: Committee for Economic Development of Australia and Centre for Asia Pacific Social Transformation Studies, University of Wollongong; Birrell, B. and Hawthorne, L. (1997) *Immigrants and the Professions in Australia,* Melbourne: Centre for Population and Urban Studies, Monash University; Iredale, R. and Appleyard, R. (eds) (2001) 'International Migration of the Highly Skilled', *International Migration,* Vol. 39, No. 5, Special Issue; Birrell, B. (2000) 'The Business Skills Program: Is It Delivering?', *People and Place,* Vol. 8, No. 4, pp. 36–42; Inglis, C. and Wu, C-T. (1991) 'Business Migration to Australia', *Conference on International Manpower Flows and Foreign Investment in Japan,* conference proceedings, 9–12 September, Paper #21, Tokyo and Hawaii: Nihon University and East–West Center.

7 Inglis, C. and Wu, C.-T. (1991).

8 Business Skills Assessment Panel (1994) *Migration of Business People to Australia: Directions for Change,* March, Canberra: Department of Immigration and Ethnic Affairs (aka *The Deveson Review*).

9 Waldinger, R. et al. (1990), p. 247; see also Collins, J. (1996) 'Ethnic Small Business and Employment Creation in Australia in the 1990s', *Working Paper No. 71,* December, Sydney: School of Finance and Economics, University of Technology.

10 Ongley, P. and Pearson, D. (1995) 'Post-1945 International Migration: New Zealand, Australia and Canada Compared', *International Migration Review,* Vol. 29, No. 3, Autumn.

11 Kingston, M. 'Exposed: The Big-Money Migration Rort', *Sydney Morning Herald,* 24 August 1988, p. 5.

12 Hugo, G. et al. (2001); see also Collins, J., 'Asian Small Business in Australia', in Brownlee, P. and Mitchell, C. (eds) (1998), p. 63. The Senate Estimates Committee inquired into the number of skilled or qualified engineers from India arriving in the early 1990s as independents, and heard that there was no labour market test for these migrants; they only need to meet the general application criteria (age, language ability, self-sufficiency, etc.). See 'Senate Estimates Committee F – Sub-program 2.1', *Hansard,* 2 September 1993.

13 See Figure 10.1 in this chapter, but see also Castles, S. et al. (1998) *Immigration and Australia: Myths and Realities,* St Leonards, Sydney: Allen & Unwin, p. 15.

14 Collins, J., 'Asian Small Business in Australia', in Brownlee P. and Mitchell, C. (eds) (1998), pp. 63–64.

15 'Australia Pushes Policy to Lure Rich Immigrants', *The Globe and Mail* (Canada), 3 May 1988, p. B28.

16 Sources: DIMIA (2002) *Australian Immigration Consolidated Statistics Number 21,* Canberra: AGPS, Table 2.7, p. 18; BIMPR (1995) *Australian Immigration Consolidated Statistics Number 18,* 1993–94, Canberra: AGPS,

The Business Migration Program   199

Table 2.11, p. 25; Figures include secondary or family members of principle visa applicant. Note, a separate category for New Zealand citizens is omitted from the data. This cohort is sizeable but their entry and resident rights vary distinctly from the other international migrant cohorts.

17 Ibid. See also Castles, S. et al. (1998). p. 15. A more dramatic drop in skilled/business migration occurred in 1984, corresponding again to a recession in Australia, although the overall numbers were small. See also DIMIA (2002), Table 6; Figure 2.7. Business migrant figures only began to recover in 1994–95. The *Deveson Report* suggests slightly upward trend, but see Figure 10.1 in this chapter.

18 DIMIA (2002); BIMPR (1995).

19 Ibid. Business migrant numbers averaged around 5,000 applicants between the years1998 and 2003. Note: figures include family members. Given the importance of family members to ethnic small business secondary applicants should not be discounted from the total. The capital and skills of spouses was requested information on business visa application forms.

20 Senator Nick Bolkus, 'Questions without Notice – Business Migration', *Hansard*, 5 December 1994, p. 3865, System ID: chamber/hansards/1994-12-05/0096.

21 Ian McPhee, MP, 'Answers to Questions – Expenditure on Advertising for Prospective Migrants', *Hansard*, 11 March 1981, p. 699.

22 Ibid. Note: the BMP underwent a number of name changes with different policy measures in each iteration. BMP is used in this first section to cover the three main iterations, Business Migration Program, Business Skills Program (BSP) and then Business Skills Category (BSC). In some cases the BSP and BSC are specifically mentioned.

23 Stewart West, MP, cited in *Hansard*, 18 May 1983, 'Australia's Immigration Policy and Program – Ministerial Statement', p. 662. System ID: chamber/hansardr/1983-05-18/0069.

24 Note that younger applicants incurred the lower amount, although all were subject to a 'settlement' fee of between $100,000 and $150,000, depending on which city they were to set up their business. A business migrant over 58 years of age, and setting in Sydney or Melbourne would be subject to the higher $1 million qualifying amount. Parliamentary Joint Committee of Public Accounts (1991), p. 21; Kingston, M. (1998), p. 5.

25 Parliamentary Joint Committee of Public Accounts (1991) paragraphs 3.6 and 4.1.

26 See Kingston, M. (1998), p. 5 for an account of alleged abuses of the scheme.

27 Williams, Evan and Murphy, Paul (1991) 'Background and Reasons for the Abolition of the Business Migration Program', PM – ABC Radio, 25 July. Transcript sourced via *Hansard*, 27 July 2011. System ID: media/radioprm/MAI00.

28 Ray, R. (1988) 'Questions without Notice – Family and Business Migrants', *Hansard*, 22 November, System ID: chamber/hansards/1988-11-22/0023.

29 Ray, R. (1988) 'Committee to Advise on Australia's Immigration Policies – Ministerial Statement', *Hansard*, 8 December. System ID: chamber/hansards/1988-12-08/0016. In fact, while there was no annual cap on the number of business migrant visas in the 1980s there was a *de facto* points system for entrepreneurs, even as early as 1982. For instance, chapter 20 of the migration Assessment Interview Guidelines for Immigration Officials explains that where an assessor is issuing points for a migrant applicant's skill level, 'Business Migrants receive full points on this factor'; under occupational demand 'Business migrants and employment nominees are classified as being in

200   The Business Migration Program

shortage'. Thus, business migrants automatically received 38 out of a required 60 points on these two counts. DIEA (1982) *Migrant Entry Handbook*, Canberra AGPS, p. 20. This information is noted here simply to ensure accuracy of the historical record: for it is readily assumed that the 1991 parliamentary Inquiry into the BMP brought the points system to the programme.

30 Edwards, S. (1993) 'Openness, Trade Liberalization and Growth in Developing Countries', *Journal of Economic Letters*, Vol. 31, No. 3, September.

31 Brunton, H.J. (1998).

32 Ibid.

33 See Chapter 7 in this volume. See also 'The Australian Manufacturing Revolution', *Australian Financial Review*, 11 May 1993, p. 1.

34 For the same reasoning, I suggest here, did the 1991 Inquiry also criticise the over-representation of business migrants in the services sector. In hindsight, services have become a viable and defining feature of market economies. Elements within the Labor Party did not view services as a sector of labour productivity and productive growth.

35 DIEA (1982) *Migrant Entry Handbook*, Attachment 3, ch. 10 – Form M.68 – Entrepreneur Eligibility Report, Canberra AGPS; Parliamentary Joint Committee of Public Accounts (1991), p. 20.

36 MSJ Keys Young Planners Pty Ltd (1989) *Expectations and Experiences: A Survey of Business Migrants*, Canberra: AGPS, pp. vii, xv.

37 Parliamentary Joint Committee of Public Accounts (1991).

38 Kingston, M. (1988), p. 5. Note that family members were counted in the BMP visa totals for each year. Principle applicant refers to the entrepreneur but may include a spouse or family member as a business partner.

39 Parliamentary Joint Committee of Public Accounts (1991), p. 30. See also Collins, J., 'Cosmopolitan Capitalists Down Under'; Rath, J. and Kloosterman, R., 'The Netherlands: A Dutch Treat', in Kloosterman, R. and Rath, J. (eds) (2003) *Immigrant Entrepreneurs: Venturing Abroad in an Age of Globalisation*, Oxford and New York: Berg, pp. 70, 142.

40 Parliamentary Joint Committee of Public Accounts (1991). pp. 29–30. That evidence was submitted by the conservative migration scholar, (then) Dr Robert Birrell.

41 Percentage share of migrant recruitment expenditure (rounded) from figures reported by Ian MacPhee, MP. Not all of the expenditure reported was specifically for recruitment of entrepreneurs; it supported campaigns for migrants overall. See also quote from Senator Ian MacPhee, 'Answers to Questions – Expenditure on Advertising for Prospective Immigrants (Question No. 579)', *Hansard*, 11 March 1981, p. 699. System ID: chamber/hansardr/1981-03-11/0100.

42 'Answers to Questions – Business Migration Program', *Hansard*, 13 March 1986, Question 3204. System ID: chamber/hansardr/1986-03-13/0162 p. 1388-.

43 Webster, B., 'Australia Looks for Entrepreneurs', *The Ottawa Citizen* (Ottawa), 24 March 1988, p. E8; 'Aussies Courting Business Enterprises', *The Vancouver Sun* (Vancouver, BC), 4 June 1988, p. H8.

44 The Telegraph (2004) 'Tan Sri Khoo Teck Puat', Obituaries, 2 March, http:// www.telegraph.co.uk/news/obituaries/1455763/Tan-Sri-Khoo-Teck-Puat.html (accessed 1 November 2010). Note: Khoo did not appear to come to Australia as a postwar refugee, as has been understood previously. See in Collins, J. (1991) *Migrants Hands*, p. 155. Note: 'Tan Sri' is an honorific title in Malay.

45 McLeay, L., in 'Answers to Questions – Procedural Text – Immigration: Business Migration Category', *Hansard*, 8 December 1982, p. 3139. System

ID: chamber/hansardr/1982-12-08/0262. Khoo was also named as a potential buyer for Sydney's retail business Grace Bros, and held personal wealth to the value of $400– $500 million. See 'Khoo Teck Puat Not Buying Grace Brothers of Sydney', *The Straits Times*, 15 December 1982, p. 28.

46 Stewart West, MP, cited in 'Australia's Immigration Policy and Program – Ministerial Statement', *Hansard*, 18 May 1983, p. 662. System ID: chamber/hansardr/1983-05-18/0069.

47 In 1988 this was $675,000, for example. See Senator Robert Ray, 'Questions without Notice – Business Migration Program', *Hansard*, 1 March 1989, p. 1047. System ID: chamber/hansards/1989-03-01/0047.

48 Kingston, M. (1988); Stewart West MP, cited in *Hansard*, 18 May 1983.

49 Freeman, G.P. (1992).

50 Nicknamed 'Semaphore Jim' because of his desire to send harsh 'signals to Asia' deterring refugees coming from the region; see Le, M. (2001) 'Migrants, Refugees and Multiculturalism: The Curious Ambivalence of Australia's Immigration Policy', *2001 Alfred Deakin Lecture*. Broadcast Monday 14 May 2001 on ABC Radio. Transcript, http://www.abc.net.au/rn/deakin/stories/s295948.htm (accessed 3 November 2010).

51 Senator J. Short, 'Australian Senate: Questions without Notice: Business Migration', *Hansard*, 23 August 1988, p. 79. System ID: chamber/hansards/1988-08-23/0048.

52 Senator Bill Reynolds, in ibid.

53 Grutzner, A. (1988) 'The Migrants Who Won't be Wooed – Hong Kong Businessmen are Worried about Migrating to Australia Due to Recent Racist Comments', *The Australian*, 29–30 October, p. 30.

54 Senator Robert Ray, in *Hansard*, 1 March 1989, 'Questions without Notice – Business Migration Program'. System ID: chamber/hansards/1989-03-01/0047.

55 Parliamentary Joint Committee of Public Accounts (1991). p. 30.

56 Senator Don Grimes, cited in 'Questions without Notice – Business Migration Program', *Hansard*, 23 October 1986, p. 1811. System ID: chamber/hansards/1986-10-23/0060. Note: Senator Devlin presented a 'Dorothy Dixer' to colleague Senator Grimes inviting comment on the Tasmanian example.

57 Pe-Pua, R. et al. (1996), *Astronaut Families and Parachute Children: The Cycle of Migration between Honk Kong and Australia*, Canberra: Bureau of Immigration, Multicultural and Population Research.

58 *Houston Chronicle*, 'Hong Kong Seeks to Move Some Business', 18 July 1989.

59 David, A. and Wheelwright, T. (1989).

60 Joseph (1994) 'New Ways to Make Technology Parks More Relevant', *Prometheus: Critical Studies in Innovation*, Vol. 12, No. 1. DOI: 10.1080/08109029408629377 (accessed 15 July 2013).

61 Lopez (2000a).

62 MSJ Keys Young Planners (1990), p. 49. Note: respondents were those who had arrived between July 1984 and December 1987. In fact, this allows for a greater rate of outcomes as recency of arrival is considered a factor in business establishment.

63 ABS (1990) *Average Weekly Earnings, States and Australia, November 1989*, Canberra: AGPS, Table 2, p. 4. Catalogue no. 6302.0. These figures are presented a heuristic comparison between turnover and wages for the period. Providing a comparative wage figure gives some sense of scale of gross profit only. Additional business costs can be calculated by including the going business loan rate (for advance purchase of capital) but unnecessary here to develop a model. Sector analysis of the business type would be required to develop a more detailed model.

202 *The Business Migration Program*

64 Estimates Committee E, 17/9/1992 Department of Immigration, Local Government and Ethnic Affairs – Program 1 – Migration – Subprogram 1.2 – Permanent Entry, *Hansard*, 17 September 1992, p. 174. System ID: committees/estimate/ecomw920917a_ece.out/0052 (accessed 13 January 2011).

65 Ray, R. (1988) 'Questions without Notice – Chinese Triads', *Hansard*, 1 November. System ID: chamber/hansards/1988-11-01/0040.

66 Neil Edwards, Interview, 24 January 2012.

67 Estimates Committee E, 17/9/1992 Department of Immigration, Local Government and Ethnic Affairs – Program 1-Migration – Subprogram 1.2-Permanent Entry *Hansard*, p. 174. System ID: committees/estimate/ecom-w920917a_ece.out/0052 (accessed 13 January 2011); Parliamentary Joint Committee of Public Accounts (1991).

68 Note: no 'application' figure for the Philippines was supplied in the BSAP data. It is reasonably inferred as below that of the lowest identified application source, which was the USA at 2.4 %. The figure derived here is the median between 0.1 and 2.3, where 2.4 was the lowest identified number available (USA). As a small proportion of applications and visas the Philippines is not a significant reportable outcome, although clearly as a ratio there proportionately more visas granted that applications received.

69 Senator David Kemp in Estimates Committee E, 17/9/1992 Department of Immigration, Local Government and Ethnic Affairs – Program 1 – Migration – Subprogram 1.2 – Permanent Entry *Hansard*, p. 174. System ID: committees/estimate/ecomw920917a_ece.out/0052 (accessed 13 January 2011).

70 Senator Robert Ray, in *Hansard*, 1 March 1989, p. 1047.

71 Palfreyman, R. and Rowe, J. 'Comment on the Shortcomings of the Now Abandoned Business Migration Scheme', *The World Today*, 26 July 1991, ABC Radio. Transcript available in *Hansard*. System ID: media/radioprm/5BI00.

72 Kingston, M. (1988).

73 Ongley, P. and Pearson, D. (1995) p. 771. Generally, in both countries' cases, the figures include families of the business migrant.

74 The Canadian Asia Pacific Foundation was established in 1984 as an independent think tank on relations. See http://www.asiapacific.ca; See also Yu, H. (2010) 'Global Migrants and the New Pacific Canada', *International Journal*, Vol. 64, No. 4, Autumn, pp. 1011–26 for an account of Canadian–Asia Pacific connections. See also a comparative analysis of Canada, Australia and New Zealand migration policy frames in Hiebert, D. et al. (2003).

75 *The Vancouver Sun*, 4 June 1988, p. E8.

76 Ibid. Attempts at recruiting in countries such as Canada and the USA may not necessarily only have been aimed at citizens of those countries – business migrants from Asia might be lured from their residencies in Canada to Australia tantamount to poaching.

77 Parliamentary Joint Committee of Public Accounts (1991). p. 20.

78 'Australia Pushes Policy to Lure Rich Immigrants', *The Globe and Mail* (Canada), 3 May 1988, p. B28.

79 See figures in 'Appropriation Bill (No. 3) 1989–90', *Hansard*, 24 May 1990, p. 967. System ID: chamber/hansards/1990-05-24/0076. The Hong Kong processing office had approximately 14 times the Australian salary budget, and Kuala Lumpur more than six times that of the Athens office, highlighting the concentration of effort in the Asian region.

80 Senator Robert Ray in *Hansard*, 1 March 1989.

81 Business Skills Assessment Panel (1994). Ivan Deveson, former CEO of Nissan

The Business Migration Program 203

Australia and Channel 7 Television was the Chair of the Panel and presented the findings to the Government.

82 Mary Easson, MHR in 'Appropriation Bill (No. 1) 1994–95', *Hansard*, 2 June 1994, p. 1288. System ID: chamber/hansardr/1994-06-02/0015.

83 Ibid.

84 Ibid. (my emphasis).

85 BSAP (1994), p. 8; Mary Easson, MHR, cited in 'Appropriation Bill (No. 1) 1994–95', *Hansard*, p. 1288.

86 Love, D. (2008) *Unfinished Business: Paul Keating's Interrupted Revolution*, Carlton, VIC, p. 162.

87 Cited in 'Legal and Constitutional Legislation Committee, 20/11/1995 Department of Immigration and Ethnic Affairs – Program 3 – Offshore program delivery – Subprogram 1.2 – Permanent Entry', *Hansard*, 20 November 1995, p. 174. System ID: committees/estimate/ecomw951120a_slc.out/0029.

88 See Figures 10.1–10.3, but also see also Riley, M. 'Migration Up by 10,000 Next Year', *Sydney Morning Herald*, 10 May 1994, p. 2.

89 BSAP (1994).

90 'Senate Estimates Committee F – DIEA', *Hansard*, 26 May 1994, p. 50. System ID: committees/estimate/ecomw940526a_ecf.out/0012; DIMIA (2002).

91 BSAP (1994), p. 2.

92 'Issues Watch: Regional Headquarters', *Business Asia*, Vol. 25, 6 December 1993, p. 11.

93 BSAP (1994), pp. 67–69.

94 David Wheen, in Senate Estimates Committee F – DIEA, *Hansard*, 26 May 1994. System ID: committees/estimate/ecomw940526a_ecf.out/0012.

95 Ibid.

96 DIC (1997) DIMA *Annual Report 1996–97 Sub-program 2.1: Economic Entry*, Canberra: Commonwealth of Australia, http://www.immi.gov.au/about/reports/annual/1996-97/html/prog2001.htm (accessed 1 September 2013).

97 BSAP (1994); Senate Estimates Committee F – DIEA, *Hansard*, 26 May 1994. System ID: committees/estimate/ecomw940526a_ecf.out/0012. See also Vanstone, A. (1994).

98 Launched on 22 March 1995; implemented 3 April – reported in the *South China Morning Post*, 23 March 1995, but curiously absent from Australian media at the time. The greater the sum transferred, the more points an applicant received to qualify for a visa.

99 BSAP (1994); Senate Estimates Committee F – DIEA, *Hansard*, 26 May 1994. System ID: committees/estimate/ecomw940526a_ecf.out/0012.

100 DIC (1997), p. 4. Note: following the change of government in 1996, the Department of Immigration and Multicultural Affairs became the Department of Citizenship (DIC).

101 Collins, J. (2003).

102 DIC (1997), p. 4.

103 ABS (1990) *Average Weekly Earnings, States and Australia, November 1996*, Canberra: AGPS, Table 2, p. 3. Catalogue no. 6302.0. A heuristic analysis of those 30% of business earning at least $1 million is offered here without knowing the details of each and every business: The average gross annual wage in the private sector, seasonally adjusted in November 1996 was $28,028. If, as stated, the average business employed 4.5 workers (in 1996) then gross labour cost was $126,000, leaving $874,000 gross surplus. A lower labour cost also translates into a lower company tax as Australia's corporate tax rate of 36% in 1995–96 included 20% as income tax transfer. See Parliamentary Research Service (1995) *Bills Digest, Nos. 93–94.1995 Income Tax Rates Amendment*

204 *The Business Migration Program*

Bill 1995 – *Taxation Laws Amendment (Budget Measures) Bill 1995* (25 May), Canberra: Department of Parliamentary Library, p. 2.

104 Collins, J. (2003).

105 Peter Hughes, Assistant Secretary, Migrant Entry and Citizenship Branch, cited in Senate Estimates Committee F – DIEA, *Hansard*, 26 May 1994. System ID: committees/estimate/ecomw940526a_ecf.out/0012.

106 Senator Nick Bolkus cited in Senate Estimates Committee F – DIEA, *Hansard*, 26 May 1994. System ID: committees/estimate/ecomw940526a_ecf.out/0012 (my emphasis).

107 Senator Nick Bolkus, 'Building on a Multicultural Australia', BIPR *Bulletin*, No. 9, July 1993, p. 10.

108 Senate Estimates Committee E, Department of Immigration, Local Government and Ethnic Affairs Program 1 – Migration and Visitor Entry Subprogram 1.1 – Migration Planning, Population and Research', *Hansard*, 28 September 1989. System ID: committees/estimate/ecomd890928a_ece.out/0011. In 1989 the KPI was 14 jobs for every BMP visa holder.

109 Estimates Committee F, Department of Immigration and Ethnic Affairs, *Hansard*, 2 September 1993.

110 Mary Easson, 'Appropriation Bill (No. 1) 1994–95' *Hansard*, 2 June 1994, p. 1288. System ID: chamber/hansardr/1994-06-02/0015.

111 Estimates Committee F, Department of Immigration and Ethnic Affairs, *Hansard*, 26 May 1994.

112 Castles, S. et al. (1998), p. 127.

113 Crock, M. (1998) *Immigration and Refugee Law in Australia*, Annandale, NSW: The Federation Press.

114 Castles, S. and Collins, J., in Cope, B. (ed.) (1992), notably pp. 142, 146–48 for an account of these barriers. Of course, generally risk and responsibility is a feature of private enterprise and the suggestion is not that business previously operated on other principles. What is important is the way migration came to be re-valued as an individual pursuit where skill and/or business capital were vital to qualifying as a settler and eventual citizen.

115 Cited in Kingston, M. (1988): p. 5. Note Mick Young's statements for the article occurred in November 1987.

116 In the years following Prime Minister Keating's government, this neoliberal logic would extend to a $1,000 processing fee for failed *refugee* applicants. See Joint Parliamentary Committee on Migration (1999) 'Reference: Review of Migration Regulation 4.31B. Hearing: Friday, 26 February 1999, Melbourne', *Hansard*. System ID: committees/commjnt/j0000080.sgm/0003 (accessed 29 November 2010).

117 Senator Nick Bolkus, cited in Estimates Committee F, Department of Immigration and Ethnic Affairs, *Hansard*, 26 May 1994 (my emphasis).

118 DIMIA (various dates) *Immigration Annual Report* and *Consolidated Statistics*, Canberra: AGPS.

119 ABS (2009) *Perspectives on Migrants, 2009, Cat. 3416.0*, Canberra: AGPS, p. 4.

120 Boucher, A. and Gest, P. (2014) 'Migration Studies at a Crossroads: A Critique of Immigration Regime Typologies', *Migration Studies*, Migration Studies Advance
Downloaded from http://migration.oxfordjournals.org (accessed 25 August 2014).

121 Bertone, S., in Jakubowicz, A. and Ho, C. (eds.) (2014).

122 Kelly, P. (1994).

11 Conclusion

The possibility of sourcing vast labour forces corralled into competing for the lowest available wage fuels the migration of echelons of corporate professionals, business makers, financiers and also substrates of management and operational leaders, and senior service personnel compelled and attracted to emulate and reinforce a global labour hierarchy.

By focusing on surplus value as the moral reading of this value creation system, I have deliberately drawn attention to the meaning of the word 'value' in Global Value Chains (GVCs). For it is abundantly evident that, worldwide, maximum value is extracted relative to the cost of labour to be reproduced to create the commodities delivered to the factory owners. If that is the case, if garment workers in Bangladesh or auto manufacturing workers in India, or mobile phone assembly workers in China struggle to hold onto a representative or even fair share of the value created by them each day, how much responsibility must governments like Australia take for orchestrating their own postindustrial migrant workforces to command the flow of goods and services through these value chains to fill the wells of the wealthy?

Of course, the recently exposed systemic theft of earnings of migrant tertiary students in certain global franchise industries in Australia represents another crisis in the morality of migration programs and a real contest of value.[1] While not the subject of this book, it is important to acknowledge this phenomenon and the excellent scholarly work pursuing it, illustrating also how value, social reproduction and migration intersect *within* economically rich and culturally diverse countries like Australia.[2]

The moral question posed by this book, then, is this: Are we asking 'highly skilled' migrants to be predators, seeking out the least cost route for commodity production and accumulation of value through their knowledge of the cultures and nations they have at one time migrated from? Put another way, *when migration recruits for talent and skill, it is recruiting for the right to control the labour supply of the Global South*. Migration can be viewed as a real way to ameliorate the lived experience of global maldistribution. But in an era where the Global North benefits from putting the Global South to work in more intricate and precarious ways, this is where the real source of 'ethnic surplus value' surely exists.

206 Conclusion

Hence, the approach taken in this book was to address this problem of theory as it first played out in the Australian political and economic context and the strata of occupations targeted by Australian migration policy in the new global market economy. Posed as a question, how was the economic value of ethnoculture and diversity construed through Productive Diversity and multiculturalism more broadly by Government? It is apparent that this value 'exists' principally in market relationships and acutely in the (global) exchange relations contesting capital's accumulation. Productivity and diversity did not mean actual value from ethnocultures in productive labour. Productive Diversity's claims on value were outside the realm of labour and its direct relationship to production. Here, two things coincide and reinforce this interpretation: first, the emphasis on value's circulation, exchange and accumulation through global trade, through value chains of small and large enterprise; and second, in response, the changing occupational profile and increasing circulation of business makers and managers and professional skilled migrants in and out of countries such as Australia.

The historical understanding of Australian multiculturalism is that it emerged from a legacy of migrant labour. In less than a decade, from the late 1970s and concurrent with the rise of the global market economy, Australia's ethnic *diversity* was conceptualised as uniquely useful for economic or competitive advantage for the global market economy. Entrepreneurialism as advantage was underlying or central to this rationale: whether 'working smarter' within firms or independently as business managers, entrepreneurs and globally engaged and mobile market professionals and corporate elites. Ethnoculture as localised know-how can be useful to gaining advantage in market exchange, but it cannot be reified as a category and contain material value on the factory floor.

To round off the theoretical point concerning the circulation and accumulation of capital, individuals and enterprises engaged in competitive trade problematises a view of Productive Diversity as a form of cultural agency. Gaining opportunity is theoretically possible from migrant entrepreneurs drawing, as required, upon their ethnocultural ties and heritage to identify and gain market share. This, however, posits migrant minorities, and indeed 'cultural capital', within a class agency distinct from minority migrant labour. To that extent Productive Diversity does not fulfil the promise of Cope and Kalantzis's ideal market of a *cooperative diversity*, nor does it sustain claims by Hage and others about ethnic labour's value exploitation and commodification. What emerges is a picture of divergent discourses, with Australian governments, concerned about the country's global market connectivity but in the midst of a postindustrial transformation, seeking to accumulate business and related expertise. During the 1980s and 1990s, this was sourced particularly from the growth region of Asia Pacific.

While Productive Diversity was an important policy moment for Australia, it has not attracted much analysis as a concern of political economy. From other disciplines and approaches, Hage offers one of a few attempts to explain the government's actual Productive Diversity policies but his description of this type of policy as the extraction of ethnic surplus value, and by a white managerial class is problematic. In Marxian political economy terms, Productive Diversity was not aimed at enhancing surplus value the way that policies supporting migration intakes of previous decades targeted migrants to do dangerous and dirty low-skill work at the lowest possible wage in Australia. Instead Productive Diversity as a government and business sector idea aimed at growing the economy through increasing trade opportunities – consistent with Labor government economic strategy at that time. Ethnoculture and diversity in this way become features *in* exchange, in the circulation and accumulation of value, rather than objects *of* exchange. For this reason, it is imprecise to see Productive Diversity as a *reification* of ethnoculture, something that is the commodity form exchanged. Fundamentally, as a matter of Marxian political economy commodification is not an appropriate conceptualisation for ethnoculture, except perhaps where it is represented in actual consumption.

Hage's broader and influential claims that Productive Diversity was essentially a 'White Fantasy' about management of non-Anglo 'ethnics' in the workplace is consistent with the proposition that social hierarchy reflects and maintains social reproduction. But migrant ethnoculture as a target of the Productive Diversity policy period was not devalued; rather, the contrary. Productive Diversity formed part of a process of emancipating minority cultures from social mores and hierarchies. Therefore, claims about exploitation of ethnocultural surplus labour founder. Even if Productive Diversity applied (only) to migrant *productive* labour in Australia, the argument here is that there is a significant contradiction in any claim about an emancipatory multiculturalist policy seeking exploitation of surplus value. Productive Diversity can, on the other hand, be viewed as supporting surplus value exploitation off-shore through transnational production links: that is, in promoting Australia's ethnocultural diversity for the exploitation of surplus value from low-wage labour found in the Global South.

As a policy accompanying or deriving a rationale from Australia's migration planning and intake, Productive Diversity advocated and organised for the circulation and capturing of value for the Australian economy. Networks of entrepreneurs and professionals that bridged the divide between a certain Australian economy and the emerging Asian 'tiger' economies was an ideal of the Government's broad economic development goals to turn Australia into a postindustrial trading nation. The reality, as evinced by FDI patterns and Global Value Chain developments, was that Australian productivity was being bought and sold via larger forces and sources of global capital, with many migrant business people and corporate professionals as fragments in a larger mosaic of the globalising market economy.

The shift to a market-oriented citizenship in support of economic restructuring under successive Labor governments was contentious. Their approach however suggests a demarcation between a state-driven idea of

208 Conclusion

the accumulation of capital with a *laissez-faire* approach of their more conservative Liberal party opponents. Both approaches can be considered within a neoliberal critique. Belonging and citizenship remained tenets of Australia's overall population policy, including business and skilled migration policy. The idea of citizenship, however, was itself undergoing transformation as the global market economy took root. This is made plain in the conceptions of business and related recruitment programs over the period of the Hawke–Keating Labour governments from 1983 to 1996.

Productive Diversity has since become redundant as a policy term in part because its goals were subsumed within wider neoliberal policy agendas to enact a social and economic transformation towards a market society. Nevertheless, the conservative Liberal governments that followed Labor from the mid-1990s continued to use the term intermittently, despite a move away from the rhetoric and reality of multiculturalism, and the idea that diversity is essential to productivity prevails. Fundamentally, 'diversity' is a western discourse and largely of the material wealth of the Global North. Theories of diversity and the economy remain divided along progressive and neoliberal lines about agency, economic advantage and material justice. The issue of a global division of labour is centrally important to interpreting these fault lines. If countries such as Australia increasingly recruit global economy professionals, entrepreneurs and business migrants, and increasingly on shorter stay visas, while the country is complicit in Global Value Chain dispersal and segregation of low-cost labour, multicultural rights theory could benefit from renewed thinking that analyses material productive forms globally or beyond nation-state borders. More work on value theory and market economy is warranted to develop a more detailed understanding of 'economic citizenship', beyond the idea of individuals as consumers but as actively engaged in the circulation of capital.[3]

Relatedly, there is a need to examine actual transnational firms and Global Value Chain operations and the circulation of people, migrants, in that process. This would help to understand individual roles and 'agency' for their class relationships but to provide empirical evidence on exactly how migration for the global economy works. There is a compelling reason of social justice to understand a link between the exploitative production in the Global South with the demands of the Global North and to understand the extent to which labour and whole communities are is able to defend their interests globally, and how the interests of capital interact.

More work is needed on Australia's independent professionals migrant category, and those who are long- and short-stay business migrants to better appreciate theories concerning global elites and those that support transnational corporations in the global city milieu. At the micro-level, it is possible to see the recruitment of professional and entrepreneurial talent as part of what Harvey termed 'dispossession by accumulation' – where the social relations of and for production were progressively if inconsistently privatised to strengthen the operation of market capital.[4] In this case,

Conclusion   209

coupled with a winding back of Australia's social contract noted in earlier chapters, the clear attempt by Government from the late 1980s to swell self-employed, independent enterprise via migrants, would likely if loosely fit Harvey's description of a society on the road to dispossession. The class interests of contemporary non-labour migrants to Australia are not thoroughly understood. Theorising the relationship between migrant market actors and their occupational patterns matched with qualitative data gathering on individual political and socioeconomic dispositions presents itself as an area for investigation.

Finally, this book offers some needed detail to theorising the political history of Australia's economic development in relation to the global economy. Understanding the nuances of Australian party-political class interests is a worthy topic given the often-summary dismissal of all actions as neoliberal. The nuances are important for anyone with hope! Labor governments bent on engaging a global free-market economy while deindustrialising still brought with them a statist approach to economic development. A true *laissez-faire* approach appears not to be manifest in the totality of Labor politics despite their ideological abandonment of a collectivist worker-derived social worldview. The role of the bureaucracy is a vital ingredient in shaping policy, although in this case, both politicians and bureaucrats acted within the confines of the global structures and dynamics of market capital. The idea of migrant Productive Diversity was founded upon a concern about how Australia might compete.

Notes

1 Toscano, N. (2019) '7-Eleven operator fined $335,000 in wage scandals', *Sydney Morning Herald*, 18 January, https://www.smh.com.au/business/workplace/7-eleven-operator-fined-335-000-in-wage-scandals-20190118-p50s81.html (accessed 18 February 2020).
2 Clibborn, S. and Wright, C.F. (2018) 'Employer Theft of Temporary Migrant Workers' Wages in Australia: Why Has the State Failed to Act?' *The Economic and Labour Relations Review* Vol. 29, No. 2, June, pp. 207–27. DOI:http://dx.doi.org/10.1177/1035304618765906.
3 Cf. Ben Fine's work: Trentmann, F. (ed.) (2006) *The Making of the Consumer: Knowledge, Ppower and Identity in the Modern World*, Oxford and New York: Berg, chapter 13, pp. 291–311.
4 Harvey, D. (2003) *The New Imperialism*, Oxford: Oxford University Press; Harvey, D. (2005), p. 178.

References

Interviews

Neil Edwards, Former Director of the Office of Multicultural Affairs, 24 January 2012, University House, Melbourne

Nick Bolkus, Former Minister for Immigration and Ethnic Affairs, 1993–96, 15 January 2012, the Observatory Hotel, Sydney

Tony Fedderson, Former Regional and Research Director, Committee for the Economic Development of Australia (CEDA), 24 January 2012, University House, Melbourne

News Media

Australian Financial Review
Australian Mining
BIPR Bulletin
Business Asia
Chicago Tribune
China Labour Watch
Houston Chronicle
International Herald Tribune
Multicultural Marketing News
PM, ABC Radio (Australia)
The Australian
The Canadian Asia Pacific Foundation (see http://www.asiapacific.ca)
The Globe and Mail (Canada)
The Huffington Post
The Ottawa Citizen (Ottawa)
The Straits Times (Singapore)
The Sydney Morning Herald
The Telegraph (Australia)
The Vancouver Sun (Canada)
The World Today, ABC Radio (Australia)

References 211

Online archives and databases

ASEAN: http://www.Asean.org
Australian Bureau of Statistics: http://www.abs.gov.au
Hansard: http://parlinfo.aph.gov.au/parlInfo/search/search.w3p
IMF Data Mapper: http://www.imf.org/external/Datamapper/index.php
Making Multicultural Australia (MMA): http://www.multiculturalaustralia.edu.au
OECD Stat.Extracts: http://stats.oecd.org
OECD TiVA (Trade in value Added) database, May 2013 release: http://stats.oecd.org/Index.aspx?DataSetCode=TIVA_OECD_WTO
US Department of Labor: Bureau of Labor Statistics: http://www.bls.gov/fls/data.htm

Australian government statistical reports and legislation

ABS (1985) and ABS (1981) *Weekly Earnings of Employees (Distribution) Australia*, Catalogue 6310, Canberra: Commonwealth of Australia.

ABS (1990) *Average Weekly Earnings, States and Australia*, November 1989, Catalogue No. 6302.0, Canberra: AGPS.

ABS (1990) *Average Weekly Earnings, States and Australia*, November 1996, Catalogue No. 6302.0, Canberra: AGPS.

ABS (2000) *Australian Social Trends, 2000*, Catalogue 4102.0, Canberra: AGPS.

ABS (2002) *Small Business in Australia 2001*, Catalogue 1321.0, Canberra: Commonwealth of Australia.

ABS (2004) *Economic Activity of Foreign Owned Businesses in Australia, 2000–01*, Catalogue 5494.0, Canberra: Commonwealth of Australia.

ABS (2008) *Australian Historical Population Statistics: 1991 Census*, Canberra: AGPS.

ABS (2009) *3416.0 – Perspectives on Migrants*, Canberra: Commonwealth of Australia.

ABS (2006) *Labour Force, Australia*, Catalogue 6202.0, Canberra: AGPS.

Australian Fair Work Act.

Census of Population and Housing (1981) *Summary Characteristics of Persons and Dwellings*, 30 June.

Commonwealth of Australia Industrial Relations Act, 1993; s3(a).

DIAC (2012) *Subclass 457 State/Territory Summary Report: 2010–11 to 30 June 2011*, n.p., Canberra: Commonwealth of Australia.

DIC (1997) *DIMA Annual Report 1996–97 Sub-program 2.1: Economic Entry*, Canberra: Commonwealth of Australia.

DIEA (1982) *Migrant Entry Handbook*, Canberra: AGPS.

DILGEA (1986) *Australian Immigration Consolidated Statistics, No. 14*, Canberra: AGPS

DIMA (1997) *Australian Immigration – Consolidated Statistics No. 19, 1995–1996*, May. Canberra: Commonwealth of Australia.

DIMIA (2002) *Australian Immigration Consolidated Statistics No. 21*, Canberra: Commonwealth of Australia.

DIMIA (2003) *Settler Arrivals 1995–96 to 2005–06 Australia, States and Territories* Canberra: Commonwealth of Australia.

FIRB (1985–96) *Foreign Investment Review Board Annual Report* (annual reports), Canberra: Commonwealth of Australia.

212 *References*

Scholarly and secondary sources

Adams, M., Brown, N. and Wickes, R. (2014) *Trading Nation: Advancing Australia's Interests in World Markets*, Sydney: NewSouth Books.

Aislabie, C., Lee, J. and Stanton, J. (1994) *Australian Cultural Diversity and Export Growth*, Canberra: AGPS.

Allen, R. and Busse, E. (2016) 'The Social Side of Ethnic Entrepreneur Breakout: Evidence from Latino Immigrant Business Owners', *Journal of Ethnic and Racial Studies*, Vol. 39, No. 4, pp. 653–70.

Alibhai-Brown, Y. (2001) *Imagining the New Britain*, New York: Routledge.

Ang, I. and Stratton, J. (1998) 'Multiculturalism in Crisis: The New Politics of Race and National Identity in Australia', *TOPIA Canadian Journal of Cultural Studies*, No. 2, Spring.

Aronczyk, M. '"Living the Brand": Nationality, Globality and the Identity Strategies of Nation Branding Consultants', in Steger, M. (2012) (ed.) *Globalisation and Culture*, Cheltenham, UK: Edward Elgar.

Arrighi, G. (2009) *Adam Smith in Beijing: Lineages of the Twenty-First Century*, London and New York: Verso.

Australian Council of Population and Ethnic Affairs (1982) *Multiculturalism for All Australians: Our Developing Nationhood*, Canberra: AGPS.

Baeyertz, K. 'Four Uses of Solidarity', in Baeyertz, K. (ed.) (1999) *Solidarity*, Dordrecht: Kluwer.

Banting, K. and Kymlicka, W. (2006) *Multiculturalism and the Welfare State Recognition and Redistribution in Contemporary Democracies*, Oxford, UK and New York: Oxford University Press.

Barbalet, J. (1988) *Citizenship: Rights, Struggle and Class Inequality*, Milton Keynes: Open University Press.

Barnes, T. (2018) *Making Cars in the New India*, Cambridge: Cambridge University Press.

Barnett, N. (2003) 'Local Government, New Labour and "Active Welfare": A Case of "Self Responsibilisation"', *Public Policy and Administration*, Vol. 18, No. 25.

Barwick, Sir G., Cairns, J.F. Crawford, Sir J., Roces, A. and Kojima, K. (1963) *Living with Asia: A Discussion on Australia's Future*, Sydney: Australian Institute of International Affairs, NSW Branch.

Bates, S. 'The Foreign Economic Policies of the Hawke and Keating Governments', in Lee, D. and Waters, C. (eds) (1997) *Evatt to Evans: The Labor Tradition in Australian Foreign Policy*, St. Leonards, NSW: Allen & Unwin, in association with the Dept of International Relations, Research School of Pacific and Asian Studies, Australian National University, Canberra.

Bauder, H. (2008) 'Explaining Attitudes Towards Self-employment Among Immigrants: A Canadian Case Study', *International Migration*, Vol. 46, No. 2.

Bauder, H. 'The Regulation of Labor Markets Through Migration', in Phillips, N. (2011) *Migration in the Global Political Economy*, Boulder, CO: Lynne Rienner Publishers.

Baum, T. (2012) *Migrant Workers in the International Hotel Industry*, International Labour Office, International Migration Branch, Sectoral Activities Department, Geneva: ILO.

Bauman, Z. (2000) *Liquid Modernity*, Cambridge: Polity Press.

Bauman, Z. (2002) *Society Under Siege*, Cambridge: Polity Press.

References 213

Beck, U. (1992) *Risk Society: Towards a New Modernity*, trans. Mark Ritter, London: Sage.

Becker, G.S. (1975) *Human Capital*, 2nd edn, New York: Columbia University Press.

Bertone, S. 'Precarious Bystanders: Temporary Migrants and Multiculturalism', in Jakubowicz A. and Ho, C. (2014) *For Those Who've Come Across the Seas: Australian Multicultural Theory, Policy and Practice*, Melbourne: Australian Scholarly Publishing.

Bertone, M and Leahy, M. 'Social Equity, Multiculturalism and the Productive Diversity Paradigm: Reflections on their Role in Corporate Australia', in Phillips, Scott K. (ed.) (2001) *Everyday Diversity: Australian Multiculturalism in Practice*, Altona, Germany: Common Ground Publishing.

Bertone, S. and Leahy, M. (2003) 'Multiculturalism as a Conservative Ideology: Impacts on Workforce Diversity ', *Asia Pacific Journal of Human Resources*, Vol. 41, No. 1. DOI:10.1177/1038411103041001026.

Bertone, S., Esposto, A. and Turner, R. (1998) *Diversity and Dollars: Productive Diversity in Australian Business and Industry*, Melbourne: Workplace Studies Centre, Victoria University.

BIMPR (1995) *Australian Immigration Consolidated Statistics No. 18, 1993–1994*, Canberra: AGPS.

BIMPR (1996) *Immigration Update*, December quarter, April, Canberra: AGPS.

BIMPR (n.d., c.1995) *Skilled and Business Migration: An Annotated Bibliography*, Library Bibliography Series, Canberra: AGPS.

BIPR (1993) *Australian Immigration Consolidated Statistics No. 17*, Canberra: AGPS.

Birrell, B. (2000) 'The Business Skills Program: Is It Delivering?' *People and Place*, Vol. 8, No. 4.

Birrell, B. and Hawthorne, L. (1997) *Immigrants and the Professions in Australia*, Melbourne: Centre for Population and Urban Studies, Monash University.

Birrell, B., Rapson, V., Dobson, I.R. and Smith, T.F. (2004) *Skilled Movement in the New Century: Outcomes for Australia*, Canberra: Department of Immigration, Multicultural and Indigenous Affairs (DIMIA).

Blainey, G. (1984) *All for Australia*, Sydney: Methuen Haynes.

Borjas, G.J. (1989) 'Economic Theory and International Migration', *International Migration Review*, Vol. 23, No. 3.

Boucher, A. (2016) *Gender, Migration and the Global Race for Talent*. Manchester: Manchester University Press.

Boucher, A. and Gest, P. (2014) 'Migration Studies at A Crossroads: A Critique of Immigration Regime Typologies', *Migration Studies*, Migration Studies Advance Access, published 25 August 2014.

Bourdieu, P. (1986) 'The Forms of Capital', in Richardson, J. (ed.) *Handbook of Theory and Research for the Sociology of Education*, New York: Greenwood, pp. 241–58, http://www.marxists.org/reference/subject/philosophy/works/fr/bourdieu-forms-capital.htm (accessed 18 February 2020).

Bowles, S. and Gintis, H. (1993) 'The Revenge of Homo Economicus: Contested Exchange and the Revival of Political Economy', *Journal of Economic Perspectives*, Vol. 7, No. 1.

Brahm Levey, G. 'Multicultural Political Thought in Australian Perspective', in Brahm Levey, G. (ed.) (2008) *Political Theory and Australian Multiculturalism*, New York: Berghahn Books.

214 References

Bramston, T. 'The Hawke Leadership Model', in Ryan, S. and Bramston, T. (2003) *The Hawke Government: A Critical Retrospective*, Sydney: Pluto Press.

Broinowski, A. (2003) *About Face: Asian Accounts of Australia*, Melbourne: Scribe Publications.

Brooks, C. (1996) *Understanding the Labour Market*, Canberra: Bureau of Immigration, Multicultural and Population Research.

Brownlee, P. (2016) 'Global Capital's Lieutenants: Australia's Skilled Migrant Intake and the Rise of Global Value Chain Production', *Journal of Australian Political Economy*, Vol. 77.

Brownlee, P. and Mitchell, C. (eds) (1998) *Migration Research in the Asia Pacific: Australian Perspectives*, APMRN Working Paper No. 4. Papers presented at a workshop sponsored by the Academy of the Social Sciences of Australia, Wollongong University, April. Wollongong: Institute of Social Change and Critical Inquiry.

Bryan, D. (2010) 'The Duality of Labour and the Financial Crisis', *Economic and Labour Relations Review*, Vol. 20, No. 2, July.

Bryan, D. 'Bridging Differences: Value Theory, International Finance and the Construction of Global Capital', in Westra, R. and Zuege, A. (eds) (2003) *Value and the World Economy Today: Production, Finance and Globalization*, Basingstoke and New York: Palgrave Macmillan.

Bryer, R.A. (1997) 'The Mercantile Laws Commission of 1854 and the Political Economy of Limited Liability', *The Economic History Review*, Vol. 50, No. 1, February.

Burnley, I. 'Immigration and Globalisation? Affluence and Poverty Among Immigrants from Asia in Metropolitan Sydney', in Brownlee, P. and Mitchell, C. (eds) (1998) *Migration Research in the Asia Pacific: Australian Perspectives*, APMRN Working Paper No. 4. Papers presented at a workshop sponsored by the Academy of the Social Sciences of Australia, Wollongong University, April. Wollongong: Institute of Social Change and Critical Inquiry.

Business Skills Assessment Panel (1994) *Migration of Business People to Australia: Directions for Change*, Canberra: Department of Immigration and Ethnic Affairs. March 1994 (aka The Deveson Review).

Button, J. (1994) *Flying the Kite: Travels of an Australian Politician*, Milson's Point, NSW: Random House.

CAAIP Report (1988) *Immigration: A Commitment to Australia – Committee to Advise on Australia's Immigration Policies*, Committee to Advise on Australia's Immigration Policies (Fitzgerald, S. chair). Canberra: AGPS.

Carney, T. and Hanks, P. (1994) *Social Security in Australia*, Australia: Oxford University Press.

Carney, T. and Ramia, G. (2010) 'Welfare Support and "Sanctions for Non-Compliance" in a Recessionary World Labour Market: Post-Neoliberalism or Not?' *International Journal of Social Security and Workers Compensation*, Vol. 2, No. 1.

Carpenter, T. (1986) 'Pursuing a Strategic Divorce: The U.S. and the Anzus Alliance', *Cato Institute Policy Analysis*, No. 67. Washington, DC: Cato Institute, http://www.cato.org/pubs/pas/pa067.html (accessed 18 February 2020).

Carroll, W. 'Capital Relations and Directorate Interlocking: The Global Network in 2007' in Murray, G. and Scott, J. (eds) (2012) *Financial Elites and Transnational Business: Who Rules the World?* Northampton, MA: Edward Elgar.

References   215

Carroll, W. 'Whither the Transnational Capitalist Class?' in Panitch, L., Albo, G. and Chibber, V. (2014) *Socialist Register 2014: Registering Class*, Vol. 50.

Carter, A. (2001) *The Political Theory of Global Citizenship* New York: Routledge.

Cashin, P. and McDermott, C.J. (2002) 'Riding on the Sheep's Back: Examining Australia's Dependence on Wool Exports', *The Economic Record*, Vol. 78, No. 242.

Cashmore. E. (ed.) (2004) 'Surplus Value', in *Encyclopaedia of Race and Ethnic Studies*, London: Routledge.

Cass, B., Wilkinson, M. and Webb, A. (1992) *Economic, Labour Market and Social Circumstances of Sole Parents of Non-English Speaking Background*, Canberra: OMA, DPM&C, AGPS.

Castells, M. (1990) *The Informational City: The Informational City: Information Technology, Economic Restructuring, and the Urban Regional Process*, Oxford, UK and Cambridge, MA: Blackwell.

Castells, M. (2000a) *The Information Age: Economy, Society and Culture – Vol. I: The Rise of the Network Society*, 2nd edn, Malden, MA, Oxford, UK and Carlton, VIC: Blackwell.

Castles, S. and Collins, J. 'Restructuring, Migrant Labour Markets and Small Business', in Cope, B. (ed.) (1992) *Policy into Practice: Essays on Multiculturalism and Cultural Diversity in Australia*, Paper No. 20, Wollongong: Centre for Multicultural Studies, University of Wollongong.

Castles, S., Cope, B., Kalantzis, M. and Morrissey, M. (1992) *Mistaken Identity: Multiculturalism and the Demise of Nationalism in Australia*, 3rd edn, Leichhardt: Pluto Press.

Castles, S., Foster, W., Iredale, R. and Withers G. (1998) *Immigration and Australia: Myths and Realities*, St Leonards, NSW: Allen & Unwin.

Castles, S., De Haas, H. and Miller, M.J (2014) *The Age of Migration: International Population Movements in the Modern World*, 5th edn, Basingstoke and New York: Palgrave Macmillan.

CEDA (1969) *Supplementary Paper*, No. 22, Melbourne: CEDA.

CEDA (1993) *Productive Diversity: Winning Business Through Australia's Multicultural Competitive Advantage* (conference proceedings), Brisbane: CEDA.

Cederberg, M. and Villares-Varela, M. (2018) 'Ethnic Entrepreneurship and the Question of Agency: The Role of Different Forms of Capital, and the Relevance of Social Class', *Journal of Ethnic and Migration Studies*, Vol. 45, No. 1, pp. 115–32.

Chang, H.-J. (2007) *Bad Samaritans: Rich Nations, Poor Policies and the Threat to the Developing World*, London: Random House and Cornell University Press.

Chester, L. 'The Australian Variant of Neoliberal Capitalism', in Cahill, D., Edwards, L. and Stilwell, Frank (eds) (2012) *Neoliberalism: Beyond the Free Market*, Cheltenham, UK: Edward Elgar.

Chomsky, N. (2004) *Hegemony or Survival: America's Quest for Global Dominance*, Crow's Nest, NSW: Allen & Unwin.

Clibborn, S. and Wright, C.F. (2018) 'Employer Theft of Temporary Migrant Workers' Wages in Australia: Why Has the State Failed to Act?' *The Economic and Labour Relations Review*, Vol. 29, No. 2, June. DOI:10.1177/1035304618765906.

Colic-Peisker, V. (2011) 'A New Era in Australian Multiculturalism? From Working-Class "Ethnics" to a "Multicultural Middle-Class"', *International Migration Review*, Vol. 45, No. 3, Fall.

216 References

Colic-Peisker, V. and K. Farquharson (2011) 'Introduction: A New Era in Australian Multiculturalism? The Need for Critical Interrogation', *Journal of Intercultural Studies*, Vol. 32, No. 6.

Collins, J. (1991) *Migrant Hands in a Distant Land: Australia's Postwar Immigration*, 2nd edn, Leichhardt, NSW: Pluto Press.

Collins, J. (1995) *Immigration and the Labor Government in Australia: 1983–95*, Working Paper No. 45, March. Sydney: School of Finance and Economics, University of Technology.

Collins, J. (1996) *Ethnic Small Business and Employment Creation in Australia in the 1990s*, Working Paper No. 71, December, Sydney: School of Finance and Economics, University of Technology.

Collins, J. 'Asian Small Business in Australia', in Brownlee, P. and Mitchell, C. (eds) (1998) *Migration Research in the Asia Pacific: Australian Perspectives*, APMRN Working Paper No. 4, papers presented at a workshop sponsored by the Academy of the Social Sciences of Australia, Wollongong University, April. Wollongong: Institute of Social Change and Critical Inquiry.

Collins, J. (2003a) 'Cultural Diversity and Entrepreneurship: Policy Responses to Immigrant Entrepreneurs in Australia', *Entrepreneurship and Regional Development*, Vol. 15, No. 2, April–June.

Collins, J. (2003b) 'Cosmopolitan Capitalists Down Under', in Kloosterman, R. and Rath, J. (eds) *Immigrant Entrepreneurs: Venturing Abroad in an Age of Globalisation*, Oxford, UK and New York: Berg.

Collins, J., Gibson, K., Alcorso, C., Castles, S. and Tait, D. (1995) *A Shop Full of Dreams: Ethnic Small Business in Australia*, Annandale, NSW: Pluto Press.

Committee to Advise on Australia's Immigration Policies (FitzGerald, S. chair) (1988) *Immigration: A Commitment to Australia – Committee to Advise on Australia's Immigration Policies*, Canberra: AGPS.

Connell, J. (1993) *Kitanai, Kitsui and Kiken: The Rise of Labour Migration to Japan*, Sydney: Economic & Regional Restructuring Research Unit, University of Sydney.

Connell, R. (2013) 'The Neoliberal Cascade and Education: An Essay on the Market Agenda and Its Consequences', *Critical Studies in Education*, Vol. 54, No. 2.

Connell, R. and Dados, N. (2014) 'Where in the World Did Neoliberalism Come From? The Market Agenda in a Southern Perspective', *Theory, Culture and Society*, Vol. 43, pp. 117–38. DOI:10.1007/s11186-014-9212-9.

Cooper in Garnaut, R. and Drysdale, P. (eds) (1994) *Asia Pacific Regionalism: Readings in International Economic Relations*, Sydney: Harper Educational Publishers in association with the Australia–Japan Research Centre, the Australian National University.

Cope, B. and Kalantzis, M. (1997) *Productive Diversity: A New Australian Model for Work and Management*, Annandale, NSW: Pluto Press.

Cope, B. and Morrissey, M. (1986) '*The Blainey Debate and the Critics of Multiculturalism*', paper presented to the Australian Institute for Multicultural Affairs National Research Conference, Melbourne University, May. Annandale, NSW: Common Ground.

Cotton, J. and Ravenhill, J. 'Australia's "Engagement with Asia"', in Cotton, J. and Ravenhill, J. (eds) (1997) *Seeking Asian Engagement: Australia in World Affairs 1991–1995*, Melbourne: OUP, in association with Australian Institute of International Affairs.

References 217

Crock, M. (1998) *Immigration and Refugee Law in Australia*, Annandale, NSW: The Federation Press.

Dalrymple, R. (2003) *Continental Drift: Australia's Search for a Regional Identity*, Aldershot, UK: Ashgate.

David, A. and Wheelwright, T. (1989) *The Third Wave: Australia and Asian Capitalism*, Sutherland, NSW: The Left Book Club Co-Op.

Delanty, G. 'Theorising Citizenship in a Global Age', in Hudson, W. and Slaughter, S. (eds) (2007) *Globalisation and Citizenship: The Transnational Challenge*, London: Routledge.

De Lepervanche, M. 'Immigrants and Ethnic Groups', in Encel, S. and Bryson, L. (eds) (1984) *Australian Society*, Melbourne: Longman Cheshire.

Devinney, T. and Kirchner, S. (1997) 'Perspectives on Growth: Implications for Asia, Australia and New Zealand', *Agenda*, Vol. 4, No. 4.

DFAT-East Asia Analytical Unit (1995) *Growth Triangles of South East Asia*, Canberra: Commonwealth of Australia.

Dibb, P. (1986) *Review of Australia's Defense Capabilities: Report for the Minister for Defense*, Canberra: AGPS.

Docquier, F. and Lodigiani, E. (2010) 'Skilled Migration and Business Networks', *Open Economic Review*, No. 21.

Donaldson, M. and Donaldson, T. (1983) 'The Crisis in the Steel Industry', *Journal of Australian Political Economy*, Vol. 14.

Drago, R. (1995) 'Divide and Conquer in Australia: A Study of Labor Segmentation', *Review of Radical Political Economics*, Vol. 27.

Duleep, H.O. and Regets, M.C. (1999) 'Immigrants and Human Capital Investment', *The American Economic Review*, Vol. 89, No. 2. Papers and Proceedings of the One Hundred Eleventh Annual Meeting of the American Economic Association (May).

Duménil, G. and Lévy, D. (2011) 'Unproductive Labor as Profit-Rate-Maximizing Labor, Rethinking Marxism: A *Journal of Economics'*, *Culture & Society*, Vol. 23, No. 2, April.

Durkheim, E. (1997) *The Division of Labor in Society*, trans. L.A. Coser. New York: Free Press.

Duvall, T. 'The New Feudalism: Globalization, the Market, and the Great Chain of Consumption', in Steger, M. (2012) (ed.) *Globalisation and Culture*, Cheltenham, UK: Edward Elgar.

Edwards, L., Cahill, D. and Stilwell, F. 'Introduction: Understanding Neoliberalism Beyond the Free Market', in Cahill, D., Edwards L. and Frank Stilwell (eds) (2012) *Neoliberalism: Beyond the Free Market*, Cheltenham, UK: Edward Elgar.

Edwards, S. (1993) 'Openness, Trade Liberalization and Growth in Developing Countries', *Journal of Economic Letters*, Vol. 31, No. 3, September.

Evans, G. (1995) 'Australia in East Asia and the Asia-Pacific: Beyond the Looking Glass', *Australian Journal of International Affairs*, Vol. 49, No. 1, May, p. 105.

Farazmand, A. (1999) 'The Elite Question: Toward a Normative Elite Theory of Organisation', *Administration and Society*, Vol. 31, No. 3, July.

Fine, B. (2007) 'Eleven Hypotheses on the Conceptual History of Social Capital: A Response to James Farr', *Political Theory*, Vol. 35, No. 1.

Fine, B. (2008) 'Social Capital versus Social History', *Social History* Vol. 33, No. 4, November.

218   References

Fine, B. (2010a) *Theories of Social Capital; Researchers Behaving Badly*, London: Pluto Press.

Fine, B. (2010b) 'Locating Financialization', *Historical Materialism*, Vol. 18, No. 2.

FitzGerald, S. and Drysdale, E. (1980) *Asia in Australian education: Report of the Committee on Asian Studies to the Asian Studies Association of Australia*, August 1980 Canberra: Asian Studies Association of Australia, Committee on Asian Studies.

FitzGerald, S. (1997) *Is Australia and Asian Country?* St Leonards, NSW: Allen & Unwin.

Foster, D. and Stockley, L. (1990) 'The Construction of a New Public Culture: Multiculturalism in an Australian Productive Culture', *ANZJS*, Vol. 26, No. 3.

Foster, L.E. and Stockley, D. (1998) *Australian Multiculturalism: A Documentary History and Critique*, Avon and Philadelphia: Multilingual Matters.

Frank, A.G. (1969) *Latin America: Underdevelopment or Revolution*, New York: Monthly Review Press.

Frank, A.G. (1998) *ReOrient: Global Economy in the Asian Age*, Berkeley: University of California Press.

Frankel, B. (1992) *From the Deserts Prophets Come: The Struggle to Reshape Australian Political Culture, Melbourne*: Arena Publications.

Freeman, G. (1992) 'Migration Policy and Politics in the Receiving States', *International Migration Review*, Vol. 26, No. 4.

Freeman, G. and Jupp, J. (eds) (1992) *Nations of Immigrants: Australia, the United States, and International Migration*, Melbourne: Oxford University Press.

French, S., Leyshon, A. and Wainwright, T. (2011) 'Financializing Space, Spacing Financialization', *Progress in Human Geography*, Vol. 35, No. 6.

Galbally, F. (1978) *Review of Post Arrival Programs and Services for Migrants* (The Galbally Report) Migrant Services and Programs, Canberra: AGPS.

Garnaut, R. (1989) *Australia and the Northeast Asian Ascendancy*, Canberra: AGPS.

Gereffi, G. (2019) 'Global Value Chains and International Development Policy: Bringing Firms, Networks and Policy-Engaged Scholarship Back In', *Journal of International Business Policy*, Vol. 2, No. 3, September.

Gereffi, G. and Lee, J. (2016) 'Economic and Social Upgrading in Global Value Chains and Industrial Clusters: Why Governance Matters', *Journal of Business Ethics*, Vol. 133, No. 1, pp. 25–38.

Gereffi, G., Korzeniewicz, M. and Korzeniewicz, R. (1994) 'Introduction: Global Commodity Chains', in Gereffi, G. and Korzeniewicz, M. (eds) *Commodity Chains and Global Capitalism*, Westport, CT: Praeger, pp. 1–14.

Giddens, A. (1998) *The Third Way: The Renewal of Social Democracy*, Cambridge, UK: Polity Press.

Gilding, M. (1999) 'Superwealth in Australia: Entrepreneurs, Accumulation and the Capitalist Class', *Journal of Sociology*, Vol. 35, No. 2, August.

Gillespie, P. (2012) Tax Troubles: How TNCs Enhance Profits by Avoiding Taxes', Third World Resurgence, No. 268, December, http://www.twnside.org.sg/title2/resurgence/2012/268/cover01.htm.

Goh, B.H. and Wong, S. (2004) *Asian Diasporas: Cultures, Identities, Representations*, Hong Kong: Hong Kong University Press.

Goldring, L and Landolt, P. (2011) 'Caught in the Work-Citizenship Matrix: The Lasting Effects of Precariousness Legal Status on Work for Toronto Immigrants', *Globalizations*, Vol. 8, No. 3.

References 219

Greene, P.G. (1988) 'Dimensions of Perceived Entrepreneurial Obstacles', cited in Baughn, C.C. and Neupert, K.E. (2003) 'Culture and National Conditions Facilitating Entrepreneurial Start-ups', *Journal of International Entrepreneurship*, Vol. *1*.

Griffin-Warwicke, J. (1992) *Australian Economic Indicators, ABS 1350.0, November*, Canberra: AGPS.

Hadrt, M. and Negri, A. (2000) *Empire*, Cambridge, MA and London: Harvard University Press.

Hage, G. (2000) *White Nation: Fantasies of White Supremacy in a Multicultural Society*, New York and Annandale, NSW: Routledge, in association with Pluto Press.

Hage, G. (2003) *Against Paranoid Nationalism: Searching for Hope in a Shrinking Society*, Annandale, NSW: Pluto Press.

Hardt, M. and Negri, A. (2000) *Empire*, Cambridge, MA and London: Harvard University Press.

Harris, J. (2012) 'Outward Bound: Transnational Capitalism in China', *Race & Class*, Vol. *54*, No. 13.

Harvey, D. (2003) *The New Imperialism*, Oxford, UK: Oxford University Press.

Harvey, D. (2005) *A Brief History of Neoliberalism*. Oxford, UK: Oxford University Press.

Hawke, Bob (1991) '*Statement by the Prime Minister*' *(Budget), Building a Competitive Australia*, Canberra: AGPS.

Hawthorne, L. (1995) 'Productive Diversity: Reality or Rhetoric', paper presented at Local Diversity, Global Connections: Communication, Culture and Business, conference, 9–11 November, Sydney.

Hay, I. (1996) *Managing Cultural Diversity: Opportunities for Enhancing the Competitive Advantage of Australian Business*, Canberra: AGPS.

Heinrich, M. (2013) 'Crisis Theory, the Law of the Tendency of the Profit Rate to Fall, and Marx's Studies in the 1870s', *Monthly Review*, Vol. *64*, No. *11*, April.

Held, D. (2013) *Cosmopolitanism: Ideals and Realities*, Oxford, UK: Wiley.

Hiebert, D., Collins, J. and Spoonley, P. (2003) *Uneven Globalization: Neoliberal Regimes, Immigration, and Multiculturalism in Australia, Canada, and New Zealand*, Research on Immigration and Integration in the Metropolis, Working Papers series, No. 03–05.

Higgot, R.A. and Nossal, K.R. (1997) 'The International Politics of Liminality: Relocating Australia in the Asia Pacific', *Australian Journal of Political Science*, Vol. *32*, No. 2.

Hilmer, F. (chair) (1993) *National Competition Policy*, Canberra: AGPS.

Hiscox, M.J. 'The Domestic Sources of Foreign Economic Policies' on the Plaza Accord in Ravenhill, J. (ed.) (2005) *Global Political Economy*, Oxford, UK and New York: Oxford University Press.

Ho, C. 'From Social Justice to Social Cohesion: A History of Australian Multicultural Policy', in Jakubowicz, A. and Ho, C. (2013) *For Those Who've Come Across the Seas: Australian Multicultural Theory, Policy and Practice*, Melbourne: Australian Scholarly Publishing.

Ho, C. and Alcorso, C. (2004) 'Migrants and Employment', *Journal of Sociology*, No. *40*, Vol. 3.

Horverak, O. (1988) 'Marx's View of Competition and Price Determination', *History of Political Economy*, Vol. *20*, No. 2.

220 References

Howard, M.C. and King, J.E. (2008) *The Rise of Neoliberalism in Advanced Capitalist Economies: A Materialist Analysis*, Basingstoke and New York: Palgrave Macmillan.

Howe, B. (chair) (2012) *Lives on Hold – The Independent Inquiry into Insecure Work in Australia*, Melbourne: ACTU.

Hugo, G. (2006) 'Temporary Migration and the Labour Market in Australia', *Australian Geographer*, Vol. 37, No. 2.

Hugo, G., Rudd, D. and Harris, K. (2001) *Emigration from Australia: Economic Implications*, Melbourne: CEDA.

Ibrahim, G. and Galt, G. (2003) 'Ethnic Business Development: Towards a Theoretical Synthesis and Policy Framework', *Journal of Economic Issues*, Vol. 37, No. 4, December.

ILO (2013) *Global Wage Report 2013/13: Wages and Equitable Growth*, Geneva: International Labour Office.

IMG Consultants-Australia New Zealand Business Council Ltd. (1985) *The Role of Australia and New Zealand in the Asia and Pacific Region*, Canberra: Department of Trade.

Inglis, C. 'Australia: Educational Changes and Challenges in Response to Multiculturalism, Globalization, and Transnationalism', in Luchtenberg, S. (ed.) (2004) *Migration, Education and Change*, London and New York: Routledge.

Inglis, C. and Wu, C.-T. (1991) *'Business Migration to Australia'*, conference on International Manpower Flows and Foreign Investment in Japan, 9–12 September, conference proceedings, Paper #21. Tokyo: Nihon University and East West Centre, Hawaii.

Inglis, C., Gunasekaran, S., Sullivan, G. and Wu, C.-T. (eds) (1992) *Asians in Australia: The Dynamics of Migration and Settlement*, Singapore: ISEAS.

Iredale, R. (2001) *Skilled Migration: The Rise of Temporary Migration and Its Implications*, CAPSTRANS/CEDA Policy Papers Series, Issue 6, Wollongong: Committee for Economic Development of Australia and Centre for Asia Pacific Social Transformation Studies, University of Wollongong.

Iredale, R. and Appleyard, R. (eds) (2001) 'International Migration of the Highly Skilled', *International Migration*, Vol. 39, No. 5, Special Issue.

Jakubowitz, A. (1984) 'Ethnicity, Multiculturalism and neo-Conservatism', in Bottomley, G. and de Lepervanche, M. (eds) *Ethnicity, Class and Gender in Australia*, Sydney: George Allen & Unwin.

Jakubowicz, A. (2011) 'Chinese Walls: Australian Multiculturalism and the Necessity for Human Rights', *Journal of Intercultural Studies*, Vol. 32, No. 6.

James, M.L. (1995) *Engineering Effective Innovation to Asia*, Research Paper No. 23, 1994/95, Canberra: Department of Parliamentary Library.

Jamrozik, A., Boland, K. and Urquhart, R. (1995) *Social Change and Cultural Transformation in Australia*, Cambridge, UK and New York: Cambridge University Press.

Javorcik, B., Ozden, C., Spatareanu, M. and Neagu, C. (2011) 'Migrant Networks and Foreign Direct Investment', *Journal of Development Economics*, Vol. 94.

Jayasuriya, L. (1983) *'Multiculturalism: Fact, Policy or Rhetoric?' The Nation is People*, Nedlands, Perth: The University of Western Australia, The Extension Service.

Jones, B. (1981) *'Technological Change Seminar Carnarvon, W.A.'* 2 August, keynote speech delivered to Geraldton-Gascoyne A.L.P. Electorate Council.

References   221

Jones, E. (1994) *'Asia's Fate: A Response to the Singapore School'* The National *Interest*, Spring, Washington, DC: The Nixon Center.

Joseph R.A. (1994) 'New Ways to Make Technology Parks More Relevant', *Prometheus: Critical Studies in Innovation*, Vol. *12*, No. *1*. DOI:10.1080/08109029408629377 (accessed 15 July 2013).

Junakar, P.N. and Mahuteau, S. (2005) 'Do Migrants Get Good Jobs? New Migrant Settlement in Australia', *The Economic Record*, Vol. *81*, No. *255*, August.

Jupp, J. (2002) *From White Australia to Woomera: The Story of Australian Immigration*, Cambridge: Cambridge University Press.

Jupp, J. (2007a) *From White Australia to Woomera: A History of Australian Immigration*, 2nd edn, Cambridge, UK, New York and Melbourne: Cambridge University Press.

Jupp, J. (2007b) 'Immigration and National Identity', in Stokes, G. (ed) *The Politics of Identity*, Cambridge, UK: Cambridge University Press.

Jupp, J. (2008) *Social Cohesion in Australia*, Port Melbourne: Cambridge University Press.

Kallenberg, A.L. (2009) 'Precarious Work, Insecure Workers: Employment Relations in Transition', *American Sociological Review*, Vol. *74*, February.

Karpin, D. (1995) *Enterprising Nation: Renewing Australia's Managers to Meet the Challenges of the Asia-Pacific Century*, Canberra: AGPS.

Keating, P. 'Statement by the Treasurer The Honorable P.J. Keating MP: Building a Competitive Australia – Taxation Measures', in Bob Hawke, Paul Keating and John Button (1991) *Building a Competitive Australia*, 12 March. Canberra: Department of Prime Minister and Cabinet/AGPS.

Keating, P. (1996) 'Speech by The Prime Minister, The Hon. P.J. Keating MP, The Singapore Lecture 'Australia, Asia and the New Regionalism', Singapore, 17 January, p. 6, https://pmtranscripts.pmc.gov.au/sites/default/files/original/00009905.pdf (accessed 13 April 2020).

Keating, P. 'Securing Our Future', address to Corowa Shire Council centenary, Corowa, 31 July 1993, in Ryan, M. (ed.) (1995) *Advancing Australia: The Speeches of Paul Keating, Prime Minister*, Sydney: Big Picture Publications.

Keating, P. (2000) *Engagement: Australia Faces the Asia Pacific*, Sydney: Macmillan.

Kee, Poo-Kong (1992) *Home Ownership and Housing Conditions of Immigrants and Australian-Born*, Canberra: AGPS.

Kelly, P. (1992) *The End of Certainty*, St Leonards, NSW: Allen & Unwin.

Kelly, P. (2009) *The March of Patriots: The Struggle for Modern Australia*, Melbourne: Melbourne University Publishing.

Kelty, B. 'The Accord, Industrial Relations and the Trade Union Movement', in Ryan, S. and Bramston, T. (2003) *The Hawke Government: A Critical Retrospective*, Sydney: Pluto Press.

King, R. (1997) 'Australians Studying Asia: The ASAA 1976–1997', Honours dissertation, University of New South Wales, http://coombs.anu.edu.au/SpecialProj/ASAA/King/King01.html (accessed 18 February 2020).

Kingston, P. (2001) 'The Unfulfilled Promise of Cultural Capital Theory', *Sociology of Education*, Vol. *74, Extra issue*.

Kivisto, P. (2002) *Multiculturalism in a Global Society*, Oxford, UK: Blackwell.

Klein, N. (2002) *No Logo: No Space, No Choice, No Jobs*, New York: Picador.

222 References

Kloosterman, R., Van Der Lun, J, and Rath, J. (1999) 'Mixed Embeddedness: (In) formal Economic Activities and Immigrant Businesses in the Netherlands', *International Journal of Urban & Regional Research*, Vol. 23, No. 2.

Kloosterman, R., Van Der Lun, J., and Rath, J., (1998) 'Across the Border: Immigrants' Economic Opportunities, Social Capital and Informal Business Activities', *Journal of Ethnic and Migration Studies*, Vol. 24, No. 2.

Konings, M. (2012) 'Neoliberalism and the State' in Cahill, D., Edwards, L. and Stilwell, Frank (eds), *Neoliberalism: Beyond the Free Market*, Cheltenham, UK: Edward Elgar.

Koffman, E. and Raghuratnum, P. (2017) *Gendered Migrations and Global Social Reproduction*, Basingstoke: Palgrave Macmillan.

KPMG/Salt, B. (2011) *Australian Taxi Industry Association – Demographic Analysis of the Australian Taxi Industry*, Melbourne: KPMG.

Kuhn, R. (2006) 'Introduction to Henryk Grossman's Critique of Franz Borkenau and Max Weber', *Journal of Classical Sociology*, Vol. 6. No. 2.

Kymlicka, W. 'The New Debate on Minority Rights (and Postscript)', in Laden, A.S. and Owen, D. (eds) (2007) *Multiculturalism and Political Theory*, Cambridge: Cambridge University Press.

LaFeber, W. (1983) *Inevitable Revolutions: The United States in Central America*, New York: W.W. Norton.

Landau, A. (2001) *Redrawing the Global Economy: Elements of Integration and Fragmentation*, Basingstoke and New York: Palgrave Macmillan.

Landstrom, H. (2008) 'Entrepreneurship Research: A Missing Link in our Understanding of the Knowledge Economy', *Journal of Intellectual Capital*, Vol. 9, No. 2.

Lassalle, P. and Scott, J.M (2018) 'Breaking-Out? A Reconceptualisation of the Business Development Process Through Diversification: The Case of Polish New Migrant Entrepreneurs in Glasgow', *Journal of Ethnic and Migration Studies*, Vol. 44, No. 15, pp. 2524–43. DOI:10.1080/1369183X.2017.1391077.

Lauter, P. 'Multiculturalism and Immigration', in Rubin, D. and Verheul, J. (2009) *American Multiculturalism After 9/11: Transatlantic Perspectives*, Amsterdam: Amsterdam University Press.

Le, M. (2001) Migrants, Refugees and Multiculturalism: The Curious Ambivalence of Australia's Immigration Policy, 2001 Alfred Deakin Lecture.

Leigh, A. (2002) 'Trade Liberalisation and the Australian Labor Party', *Australian Journal of Political History*, Vol. 48, No. 4.

Lentin, A. and Titley, G. (2011) *The Crises of Multiculturalism: Racism in a Neoliberal Age*, London and New York: Zed Books.

Lever-Tracy, Constance, Ip, David; Kitay, Jim, Phillips, Irene and Tracy, Noel (1991) *Asian Entrepreneurs in Australia – Ethnic Small Business in the Chinese and Indian Communities of Brisbane and Sydney*, Canberra: Australian Government Publishing Service.

Lewins, F. (1987) 'The Blainey Debate in Hindsight', *Australia and New Zealand Journal of Sociology*, Vol. 23, No. 2.

Ley, D. (2003) 'Seeking Homo Economicus: The Canadian State and the Strange Story of the Business Immigration Program', *Annals of the Association of American Geographers*, Vol. 93, No. 2, June.

Ley, D. (2010) *Millionaire Migrants: Trans-Pacific Life Lines*, Malden, MA: Wiley-Blackwell.

References 223

Lim, H. 'Regional Trade Agreements and Conflict: The Case of Southeast Asia', in Rafi, S. (ed.) (2009) *Regional Trade Integration and Conflict Resolution*, Abingdon, UK and New York: Routledge, in association with the International Development Research Centre, Ottawa.

Lister, R. (2003) 'Investing in the Citizen-Workers of the Future: Transformations in Citizenship and the State under New Labour', *Social Policy & Administration*, Vol. 37, No. 5.

London, H. (1970) *Non-White Immigration and the 'White Australia' Policy*, Sydney: Sydney University Press.

Lopez, M. (2000a) *The Origins of Multiculturalism in Australian Politics 1945–1975*, Melbourne: Melbourne University Press.

Lopez, M. (2000b) '*The Politics of the Origins of Multiculturalism: Lobbying and the Power of Influence*', paper delivered at the 10th Biennial Conference of the Australian Population Association, Population and Globalisation: Australia in the 21st Century, Melbourne, 28 November–1 December 2000, http://www.apa.org. au/upload/2000-5A_Lopez.pdf (accessed 15 August 2014).

Love, D. (2008) *Unfinished Business: Paul Keating's Interrupted Revolution*, Carlton, VIC: Scribe.

Lowe, P. (2012) '*The Changing Structure of the Australian Economy and Monetary Policy*', address to the Australian Industry Group 12th Annual Economic Forum, Sydney, 7 March. Reserve Bank of Australia, http://www.rba.gov.au/speeches/ 2012/sp-dg-070312.html (accessed 8 April 2020).

Lu, X. (2012) Who Drives a Taxi in Canada, Research and Evaluation section, Citizenship and Immigration Canada, http://www.cic.gc.ca/english/pdf/research-stats/taxi.pdf (accessed 18 February 2020).

Lukács, G. (2000) *History and Class Consciousness: Studies in Marxist Dialectics*, Cambridge, MA: The MIT Press.

Marin, E. (2013) 'Precariousness at Work: An International Problem', *International Journal of Labour Research*, Vol. 5, No. 1.

Markus, A. (2001) *Race: John Howard and the Remaking of Australia*, Crows Nest, NSW: Allen & Unwin.

Markus, A. and Ricklefs, M.C. (eds) (1985) *Surrender Australia?* Sydney: George Allen & Unwin.

Martin, P. (1996) 'Migrants on the Move in Asia', *AsiaPacific Issues*, No. 29, http:// hdl.handle.net/10125/3795 (accessed 18 February 2020).

Marx, K. (1945) *Value, Price & Profit*, Adelaide: People's Bookshop.

Marx, K. (1976) *Capital: A Critique of Political Economy*, Vol. 1. Harmondsworth: Penguin.

Marx, K. (1977) 'Preface', in *A Contribution to the Critique of Political Economy*, Moscow: Progress Publishers.

Marx, K. (1986 [1954]) *Capital: A Critique of Political Economy*, Vol. 1, Moscow: Progress Publishers.

Marx, K. (1986 [1959]) *Capital: A Critique of Political Economy*, Vol. 3, chapter 27, New York: International Publishers.

Matthews, T. and Ravenhill, J. 'Australian Policy and Northeast Asian Economic Growth', in Robison, R. (1996) *Pathways to Asia: The Politics of Engagement*, St Leonards, NSW: Allen & Unwin.

224 *References*

Mayer, E. (1990) '*Immigration: Some Issues for Discussion*', EPAC Discussion Paper 90/05, Canberra: AGPS.

Mazzucato, M. (2018) *The Value of Everything: Making and Taking in the Global Economy*, London: Allen Lane.

McCracken, G. (1986) 'Culture and Consumption: A Theoretical Account of the Structure and Movement of the Cultural Meaning of Consumer Goods', *Journal of Consumer Research*, Vol. 13, No. 1.

McKinsey & Co. (1993) *Emerging Exporters: Australia's High Value-Added Manufacturing Exporters*, Melbourne: McKinsey & Company.

McKinsey and Co. (1994) *The Wealth of Ideas: How Linkages Help Sustain Innovation and Growth - Report by the Australian Manufacturing Council Secretariat and McKinsey & Company to the Australian Manufacturing Council*. Melbourne: AMC.

Meagher, G. and Cortis, N. (2009) 'The Political Economy of for-Profit Paid Care: Theory and Evidence', in King, D. and Meagher, G. (eds) *Paid Care in Australia*: Politics, Profits, Practices, Sydney: Sydney University Press.

Milberg, W. (2008) 'Shifting Sources and Uses of Profits: Sustaining US Financialization With Global Value Chains', *Economy and Society*, Vol. 37, No. 3, August.

Millar, D. (2009) *Principles of Social Justice*, Cambridge, MA: Harvard University Press.

Miller, T. (2007) *Cultural Citizenship: Cosmopolitanism, Consumerism, and Television in a Neoliberal Age*, Philadelphia: Temple University Press.

Milne, F. and Shergold, P. (eds) (1985) *The Great Immigration Debate*, Sydney: FECCA.

Milner, A. 'The Rhetoric of Asia', in Cotton, J. and Ravenhill, J. (eds) (1997) *Seeking Asian Engagement: Australia in World Affairs 1991–1995*, Melbourne: OUP, in association with Australian Institute of International Affairs.

Milner, A. and Johnson, D. (2002) The Idea of Asia, Faculty of Asian Studies, Australian National University, Canberra, http://dspace.anu.edu.au/bitstream/1885/41891/1/idea.html and https://digitalcollections.anu.edu.au/bitstream/1885/41891/1/idea.html (accessed 18 February 2020).

Milner, A. and Quilty, M. (1996) *Comparing Cultures*, Melbourne and New York: Oxford University Press.

MSJ Keys Young Planners Pty Ltd (1989) *Expectations and Experiences: A Survey of Business Migrants*, Canberra: AGPS.

Mulholland, K. and Stewart, P. (2014) 'Workers in Food Distribution: Global Commodity Chains and Lean Logistics', *New Political Economy*, Vol. 19, No. 4.

Muller, T. (2003) 'Migration, Unemployment and Discrimination', *European Economic Review*, No. 47.

Murray, G. 'Australia's Ruling Class: A Local Elite, a Transnational Capitalist Class or Bits of Both?' in Murray, G. and Scott, J. (eds) (2012) *Financial Elites and Transnational Business: Who Rules the World?* Northampton, MA: Edward Elgar.

Neuman, K. (2006) 'Our Own Interests Must Come First – Australia's Response to the Expulsion of Asians from Uganda', *History Australia*, Vol. 3, No. 1, June. DOI:10.2104/ha060010 (accessed 23 February 2020).

Norman, N. and Miekle, K. (1983) *Immigration: The Crunch Issues*, Melbourne: Committee for Economic Development of Australia.

References 225

Norman, Neville R. and Meikle, Kathryn F. (1985) *The Economic Effects of Immigration on Australia*, Vols 1 and 2; and *The Economic Effects of Immigration on Australia: Booklet of Summaries*, Vol. 3. Melbourne: Committee for Economic Development of Australia.

Norton, A. (2006) *'Disliking Making a Fuss'*, Policy, Autumn, Sydney, Centre for Independent Studies.

O'Brien, J. (1994) 'McKinsey, Hilmer and the BCA: The 'New Management' Model of Labour Market Reform', *Journal of Industrial Relations*, December.

OECD, WTO, UNCTAD (2013) *Implications of Global Value Chains for Trade, Investment, Development and Jobs*, Prepared for the G-20 Leaders' Summit, St. Petersburg (Russian Federation), September, npp: OECD, WTO, UNCTAD, 6 August.

Office of Multicultural Affairs (1989), *National Agenda for a Multicultural Australia: Sharing Our Future*, Canberra: Commonwealth of Australia.

Oksenberg-Rorty, A. (1994) 'The Hidden Politics of Cultural Identification', *Political Theory*, Vol. 22, No. 1.

Oksenburg-Rorty, A. (1995) 'Rights: Educational Not Cultural', *Social Research*, Vol. 62, No. 1.

OMA (1995) *Our Nation: Multicultural Australia and the 21st Century: The Government's Response to the Report of the National Multicultural Advisory Council's 'Multicultural Australia: The Next Steps, Towards and Beyond 2000*, Canberra: OMA.

OMA and CEDA (1992) *Productive Diversity in Business: Profiting from Australia's Multicultural Advantage Conference Outcomes*, Canberra: CEDA & OMA.

Ongley, P. and Pearson, D. (1995) 'Post-1945 International Migration: New Zealand, Australia and Canada Compared', *International Migration Review*, Vol. 29, No. 3, Autumn.

Otis, E.I (2008) 'Beyond the Industrial Paradigm: Market-Embedded Labor and the Gender Organization of Global Service Work in China', *American Sociological Review*, Vol. 73 No. 1, February. DOI:10.1177/000312240807300102.

Ozawa, T. (2007) *'Professor Kiyoshi Kojima's Contributions to FDI Theory: Trade, Structural Transformation, Growth, and Integration in East Asia'*, paper presented at the 2006 Annual Conference of the Japan Society of International Economics (JSIE), Nagoya University, Japan, 14–15 October 2006, https://pdfs. semanticscholar.org/1a7b/a50f46364ffa8bcfacc943f2960a06cd7016.pdf (accessed 23 February 2020).

Pages, E.R., Freedman, D., and Von Bargan, P. 'Entrepreneurship as a State and Local Economic Development Strategy', in Hart, D.M. (2003) (ed.) *The Emergence of Entrepreneurship Policy*, Cambridge: Cambridge University Press.

Parekh, B. (2000) *The Future of Multi-Ethnic Britain: The Parekh Report*, London: Profile Books.

Parliamentary Joint Committee of Public Accounts (1991) *Report 310: Business Migration Program, Seventeenth Committee*. Canberra: Commonwealth of Australia.

Pearson, J., Fawcett, S. and Cooper, A. (1993) 'Challenges and Approaches to Purchasing from Minority-Owned Firms: A Longitudinal Examination', *Entrepreneurship Theory and Practice*, Winter.

Peck, J. (1996) *Workplace: The Social Regulation of Labor Markets*, New York: Guilford Press.

226 References

Pe-Pua, R., Mitchell, C., Iredale, R. and Castles, S. (1996), *Astronaut Families and Parachute Children: The Cycle of Migration between Honk Kong and Australia*, Canberra: Bureau of Immigration, Multicultural and Population Research.

Peters, J. (2011) 'The Rise of Finance and the Decline of Organised Labour in the Advanced Capitalist Countries', *New Political Economy*, Vol. *16*, No. *1*. DOI:10.1080/13563461003789746.

Peterson, W.C. (1980) 'Stagflation and the Crisis of Capitalism', *Review of Social Economy* Vol. *38*, No. *3*, December. DOI:10.1080/00346768000000034.

Pettman, J. (1988) 'Learning about power and powerlessness: Aborigines and white Australia's Bicentenary', *Race and Class*, No. *29*, pp. 69–85.

Pink, B. and Jamieson, C. (2000) *A Portrait of Australian Exporters: A Report Based on the Business Longitudinal Survey*, Canberra: Commonwealth of Australia.

Piore, M.J. (1979) *Birds of Passage: Migrant Labor and Industrial Societies*, New York: Cambridge University Press.

Polanyi, K. (1944) *The Great Transformation*, New York: Farrar & Rinehart.

Polanyi-Levitt, K. (2013) *From the Great Transformation to the Great Financialization*, London: Zed Books.

Pookong, K. 'Australia's Business Migrants from Taiwan', in Zhuang, G. (ed.) (1998) *Ethnic Chinese at the Turn of the Centuries*, Fujian, China: Fujian Peoples Publishing House.

Pusey, M. (1991) *Economic Rationalism in Canberra: A Nation-Building State Changes Its Mind*, Cambridge, UK and Melbourne: Cambridge University Press.

Putnam, R. (2000). *Bowling Alone: The Collapse and Revival of American Community*, New York: Touchstone.

Putnis, P. (1989) 'Constructing Multiculturalism: Political and Popular Discourse', *Australian Journal of Communication*, No. *16*, December.

Pyke, J. (2005a) 'Productive Diversity: Which Companies are Active and Why', paper delivered at the Australian Social Policy Conference, University of New South Wales, July.

Pyke, K. (2005b) 'Productive Diversity: Which Companies are Active and Why?' Master's thesis, Victoria University, Australia. http://vuir.vu.edu.au/386 (accessed 23 February 2020).

Ram, M., Jones, T. and Villares-Varela (2016) 'Migrant Entrepreneurship: Reflections on Research Practice', *International Small Business Journal: Researching Entrepreneurship*, Vol. *35*, No.*1*.

Ramsay, T. and Battin, T. (2005) 'Labor Party Ideology in the Early 1990s: Working Nation and Paths Not Taken', *Journal of Economic and Social Policy*, Vol. *9*, No. *2*, Article 9, http://epubs.scu.edu.au/jesp/vol9/iss2/9 (accessed 9 April 2020).

Rath, J. 'Introduction: Immigrant Businesses and their Economic, Politico-Institutional and Social Environment', in Rath, J. (ed.) (2000) *Immigrant Business: The Economic, Political and Social Environment*, Basingstoke and New York: Palgrave Macmillan.

Rath, J. and Kloosterman, R. 'The Netherlands: A Dutch Treat', in Kloosterman, R. and Rath, J. (eds) (2003) *Immigrant Entrepreneurs: Venturing Abroad in an Age of Globalisation*, Oxford, UK and New York: Berg.

Reay, D. Hollingworth, S., Williams, K., Crozier, G., Jamieson, F., James, D. and Beedell, P. (2007) 'Inner City Schooling "A Darker Shade of Pale?" Whiteness, the Middle Classes and Multi Ethnic', *Sociology*, Vol. *41*, No. *6*, December.

References 227

Reay, D., Crozier, G., James, D., Hollingworth, S., Williams, K, Jamieson, F. and Beedell, P. (2006) 'Re-invigorating Democracy?: White Middle Class Identities and Comprehensive Schooling', *The Sociological Review*, Vol. 56, No. 2.

Reserve Bank of Australia (1997) 'Australian Economic Statistics 1949–1950 to 1996–1997', Occasional Paper No. 8, http://www.rba.gov.au/statistics/frequency/occ-paper-8.html#section_3 (accessed 5 March 2010).

Rizvi, F. and Lingard, R. (2010) *Globalizing Education Policy*, Abingdon, UK: Routledge.

Robbins, S. P. (1991) *Organizational Behaviour: Concepts, Controversies and Applications*, Upper Saddle River, NJ: Prentice Hall.

Robinson, W.I. (2009) *Global Capitalism Theory and the Emergence of Transnational Elites*, Working Paper 2010/02, Finland: UNU World Institute for Development Economics Research (UNU-WIDER), http://www.soc.ucsb.edu/faculty/robinson/Assets/pdf/WIDER.pdf (accessed 26 July 2013).

Robinson, W.I. (2010) 'Beyond the Theory of Imperialism: Global Capitalism and the Transnational State', in Anievas, A. (ed.) *Marxism and World Politics: Contesting Global Capitalism*, Abingdon, UK and New York: Routledge.

Robison, R. 'Looking North: Myths and Strategies', in Robison R. (ed.) (1996) *Pathways to Asia: the Politics of Engagement*, St Leonards, NSW: Allen & Unwin.

Rodan, G. (ed.) (1996) *Political Oppositions in Industrialising Asia*, London and New York: Routledge.

Rodan, G. and Hewison, K. 'Clash of Cultures or Convergence of Political Ideology', in Robison, R. (1996) *in Pathways to Asia: the Politics of Engagement*, St Leonards, NSW: Allen & Unwin.

Ronen, P. (2006) *The Offshore World: Sovereign Markets, Virtual Places, and Nomad Millionaires*, Ithaca, NY: Cornell University Press.

Rorty, R. 'Solidarity or Objectivity', in Wray, K.B. (ed.) (2002) *Knowledge and Inquiry: Readings in Epistemology, Peterborough*, ON and New York: Broadview Press.

Saad-Fihlo, A. (2014) 'The "Rise of the South": Global Convergence at Last?' *New Political Economy*, Vol. 19, No. 4.

Sanger, M.B. (2003) *The Welfare Marketplace: Privatization and Welfare Reform*, Washington, DC: Georgetown University Press.

Sassen, S. (1996) 'New Employment Regimes in Cities: The Impact on Immigrant Workers', *New Community*, Vol. 22, No. 4.

Sassen, S. (2001) *The Global City; New York, London, Tokyo*, 2nd edn, Princeton, NJ: Princeton University Press.

Seccombe, W. and D.W. Livingstone. (2000) *Down to Earth People: Beyond Class Reductionism and Postmodernism*. Aurora, ON: Garamond Press.

Sheridan, G. (1997) *Tigers: Leaders of the New Asia-Pacific*, St Leonards, NSW: Allen & Unwin.

Sherrington, G. (2002) 'The Big Brother Movement and Citizenship of Empire', *Australian Historical Studies*, No. 120.

Simpson, L., Purdam, K., Tajar, A., Fieldhouse, E., Gavalas, V., Tranmer, M., Pritchard, J. and Dorling, D. (2012) *Ethnic Minority Populations and the Labour Market: An Analysis of the 1991 and 2001 Census*, London: Department for Work and Pensions.

Skeggs, B. (2004) *Class, Self, Culture*, London: Routledge.

228 References

Slavnic, Z. (2010) 'The Political Economy of Informalisation', *European Societies*, Vol. *12*, No. *1*.

Smith, A. (1937 [1776]) *An Inquiry into the Nature and Causes of the Wealth of Nations*, New York: Random House, reproduced in part in Argyrous, G. and Stilwell, F. (eds) (2011) *Readings in Political Economy: Economics as a Social Science*, 3rd edn, Prahran, VIC: Tilde Press.

Smith, A., Rainnie, A., Dunford, M., Hardy, J., Hudson, R. and Sadler, D. (2002) 'Networks of Value, Commodities and Regions: Reworking Divisions of Labour in Macro-Regional Economies', *Progress in Human Geography*, Vol. 26, No. 1.

Smith, N. (2004) *'Investigating the Consumption of "Asianness" in Australia: Culture, Class and Capital'*, paper presented to the 15th Biennial Conference of the Asian Studies Association of Australia, Canberra, 29 June–2 July 2004.

Steil, B. (2013) *The Battle of Bretton Woods: John Maynard Keynes, Harry Dexter White, and the Making of a New World Order*, Princeton, NJ: Princeton University Press.

Strahan, K. and Williams, A. (1988) *Immigrant Entrepreneurs in Australia, Canberra: Office of Multicultural Affairs*. Department of the Prime Minister and Cabinet.

Stratton, J. 'Multiculturalism and the Whitening Machine, or How Australians Become White', in Hage, G. and Couch, R. (1999) *The Future of Australian Multiculturalism: Reflections on the Twentieth Anniversary of Jean Martin's The Migrant Presence*, Sydney: Research Institute for Humanities and Social Sciences, University of Sydney.

Sturgeon, T.J. and Memedovic, O. (2011) *Mapping Global Value Chains: Intermediate Goods Trade and Structural Change in the World Economy*, Development Policy and Strategic Research Branch Working Paper 05/2010, Vienna: UNIDO.

Syed, J. (2007) 'Employment Prospects for Skilled Migrants: A Relational Perspective', *Human Resource Management Review*, Vol. 18.

Taksa, L. and Groutsis, D. (2010) 'Managing Diverse Commodities?: From Factory Fodder to Business Asset', *The Economic and Labour Relations Review*, Vol. 20, No. 2, July.

Taylor, C. (1992) *Multiculturalism and the Politics of Recognition: An Essay*, Princeton, NJ: Princeton University Press.

Theocarakis, N.J. (2010) 'Metamorphoses: The Concept of Labour in the History of Political Economy', *Economic and Labour Relations Review*, Vol. 20, No. 2, July.

Thompson, G. (1998) 'Globalisation versus Regionalism?' *Journal of North African Studies*, Vol. 3, No. 2.

Throsby, D. (1993) 'Cultural Capital', *Journal of Cultural Economics*, Vol. 23.

Trewin, D. and Australian Bureau of Statistics (2001) *Small Business in Australia*, ABS Catalogue No. 1321.0, Canberra: Commonwealth of Australia.

Turner, D.E. and Norman, N. (1984) *Managers' Perceptions of the Migrant Worker: A Survey Contribution to the Economics of Immigration Project*, Melbourne: Committee for Economic Development of Australia.

UNCTAD (2013) *World Investment Report: Implications of Global Value Chains for Trade, Investment, Development and Jobs*, New York and Geneva: UNCTAD.

UNCTAD (2018) *World Investment Report: Investment and New Industrial Policies*, New York and Geneva: United Nations. US Army (1946) *Pamphlet No. 4*,

References 229

Pillars of Peace – Documents Pertaining to American Interest in Establishing a Lasting World Peace: January 1941–February 1946, Carlisle Barracks, PA: Book Department, Army Information School, May, http://www.ibiblio.org/pha/policy/1944/440722a.html (accessed 18 February 2020).

Vaille, Mark, 'Australia as a Trading Nation', Speech to Business Club of Australia, Former Australian Government Minister for Trade, Sydney, 15 September 2000, http://www.trademinister.gov.au/speeches/2000/000915_trading_nation.html (accessed 15 September 2014).

Van Fossen, A. 'The Transnational Capitalist Class and Tax Havens' in Murray, G. and Scott, J. (eds) (2012) *Financial Elites and Transnational Business: Who Rules the World?* Northampton, MA: Edward Elgar.

Vertovec, S. (2004) 'Migrant Transnationalism and Modes of Transformation 1', *The International Migration Review*, Vol. 38, No. 3, Fall.

Wacqant, L. (2009) *Punishing the Poor: The Neoliberal Government of Social Insecurity*, Durham, NC and London: Duke University Press.

Wacquant, L. (2012) *'Keynote Address'*, 27 November 2012, 12th Conference of The Australian Sociological Association (TASA), Brisbane: University of Queensland.

Waldinger, R., Aldrich, H. and Ward, R. (eds) (1990) *Ethnic Entrepreneurs: Immigrant Business in Industrial Societies*, London: Newbury Park.

Walker, B. and Con Walker, B. (2001) *Privatisation: Sell Off or Sell Out: the Australian Experience*, Sydney: ABC Books.

Wallerstein, I. (1989) *The Modern World-System III: The Second Era of Great Expansion of the Capitalist World-Economy, 1730–1840*. New York: Academic Press.

Walters, R. (1990) *Recent Developments in Asia Pacific Investment*, Canberra: DFAT.

Walton-Roberts, M. (2009) *India–Canada Trade and Immigration Linkages: A Case of Regional (Dis)advantage?*, Metropolis Working Paper Series, No. 09–04, June, Vancouver: Metropolis British Columbia-Centre of Excellence for Research on Immigration and Diversity.

Warby, M. (1994) *From There to Back Again?: Australian Inflation and Unemployment 1964 to 1993*, Background Paper Number 9, Canberra: Department of the Parliamentary Library.

Watts, N., White, C. and Trilin, A. (2004) *The Cultural Capital Contribution of Immigrants in New Zealand*, Palmerston North, NZ: Massey University.

Weber, M. (2009) *The Protestant Ethic and the Spirit of Capitalism with Other Writings on the Rise of the West*, trans. Stephen Kalberg, New York: Oxford University Press.

Wei, H. (2004) *Measuring Human Capital Flows for Australia: A Lifetime Labour Income Approach*, Canberra: Commonwealth of Australia.

Wennekers, S. and Thurik, R. (1999) 'Linking Entrepreneurship and Economic Growth', *Small Business Economics*, Vol. 13.

Westra, R. and Zuege, A. (eds) (2003) *Value and the World Economy Today: Production, Finance and Globalization*, Basingstoke and New York: Palgrave Macmillan.

Whitlam, G. Speech at the Inaugural Meeting of the Ethnic Communities' Council of NSW, Sydney, 27 July 1975.

WI (2004) *A Theory of Global Capitalism: Production, Class, and State in a Transnational World, Baltimore*, MD: Johns Hopkins University Press.

230 References

Wilkinson, J. (2000) *Changing Nature of the NSW Economy – Background Paper No 1.* Sydney: NSW Parliamentary Library Research Service.

WIPO (2013) '*World Intellectual Property Indicators – 2013*'. Geneva: World Intellectual Property Organization, http://www.wipo.int/ipstats/en/wipi (accessed 18 February 2020).

WIPO (2019) '*World Intellectual Property Indicators 2019*'. Geneva: World Intellectual Property Organization, http://www.wipo.int/ipstats/en/wipi (accessed 18 February 2020).

Wiseman, J. (1998) *Global Nation? Australia and the Politics of Globalisation,* Cambridge: Cambridge University Press.

Wrench, J., Rea, A. and Ouali, N. (eds) (1999) *Migrants, Ethnic Minorities and the Labour Market: Integration and Exclusion in Europe,* Basingstoke and New York: Palgrave Macmillan.

Yu, H. (2010) 'Global Migrants and the New Pacific Canada', *International Journal,* Vol. *64,* No. *4,* Autumn.

Zang, X. and Hassan, R. (1996) 'Residential Choices of Immigrants in Australia', *International Migration,* Vol. *34,* No. *4,* October.

Zimmerman, K.F. (2007) 'The Economics of Migrant Ethnicity', *Journal of Population Economics,* Vol. *20.*

Index

agency: class interests 74–8, 86; concept of 6–7, 9, 16, 19–22, 41, 206; productive diversity 17; and social capital 46, 52; migrant entrepreneurs 82–5, 87; *see also* migrant entrepreneurs and mixed embeddedness

APEC 116–7, 120, 130, 136;

ASEAN 97, 132; ASEAN Free Trade Agreement (AFTA), 128–30; Australia and 116–117, 121; economic growth 108, 109–112

Asian Studies Association of Australia 106

Asian Values 122–23, 130–34, 140

Australia and Asia: Hawke and Keating 105–7, 114, 119, 128, 134, 139, 141, 181, 194; Blainey Debate 116, 126n2, 131, 135–37, 149; Fitzgerald, Stephen 124n1, 129, 142n6; *Garnaut Report* 119–20; *see also* APEC; Asian Values

Bauder, H. 9, 78

Blainey Debate *see* Australia and Asia

BMP, *see* Business Migration Program (BMP)

Bolkus, Nick: Immigration Minister xi, 154, 192; on productive diversity 195

Bowles, S. and Gintis, H: 'contested exchange' 5, 21

Bourdieu, P. 9, 22, 39–40, 42–3, 47–8; *see also* agency; *see also* cultural capital

BSC *see* Business Skills Category

Bureau of Immigration Research (BIR) 147, 158, 160

Business Migration Program (BMP) 173, 175–180, 183–85, 190, 197;

1991 Joint Parliamentary Inquiry 153–54, 182, 188; 189; comparisons with Canada 186–7; import substitution, 154, 170n76, 178–9; Labor politics, 177, 181; *see also* Business Skills Category

Business Skills Assessment Panel *see* Deveson Report

Business Skills Category: successor to Business Migration Program 178, *185*, 188–191, 197

Business Skills Program (BSP): successor to Business Migration Program 184–5, 189, 193,

CAAIP Report: skilled migration and productivity 105, 136–7, 142, 160, 166, 177, 183, 190, 193; politics of multiculturalism, 138–9, 147, 150

Castells, M.: *informationalism* 52, 64, 66, 83, 89n20

CEDA *see* Committee for the Economic Development of Australia

Committee to Advise on Australia's immigration Program *see* CAAIP

Committee for the Economic Development of Australia 151–3; *see also* OMA: productive diversity

Cope, B. and Kalantzis, M: *Productive Diversity* theory 4–5, 21, 40, 206,

cultural capital 6, 8–10, 20–26, 26–8, 34, 39–41, 82, 181, 187; exchange value 42–8, 85, 173, 206; Productive Diversity policies 162, 192, 194–5

Deveson Report 185, 187–93

Duménil, G. and Lévy, D.: unproductive labour 6

232 Index

Economic Restructuring: import substitution 178; Paul Keating 114–15, 188; unemployment 1, 3, 23n9, 94, 133, 157–8; *see also* Australia and Asia: Hawke and Keating

Edwards, Neil xi, 11, 210; on business migration programs, 184; Office of Multicultural Affairs, 151; on neoliberalism 156–7; on Productive Diversity 17, 148, 152–4, 157, 160, 164, 166

entrepreneurs *see* migrant entrepreneurs

ethnic surplus value 6–8, 26–30, 36, 206–7; *see also* cultural capital: exchange value

exchange value 27, 63–4; *see also* cultural capital: exchange value

Fedderson, Toni xi, 11, 210; migrant skills 41; on Productive Diversity 151–2, 157

Fine, B. 52, 66

Fitzgerald Report *see* CAAIP

Foreign Direct Investment (FDI): Australia 67, 111, 123, **112**, 114, 207; *see also* Global Value Chains

Galbally Report 98–100, 105, 149

Garnaut Report *see* Australia and Asia

gendered division of labour 3, 16, 93

Global Value Chains 9–10, 53, 55–6, 58–64, 69, 142; Australia 54, **62**; Financialisation 66–7; and Foreign Direct Investment 53, 65–6, 68, 81–2; intellectual property 57–8

Grassby, A. *see* Multiculturalism

GVCs *see* Global Value Chains

Hage, G. *see* ethnic surplus value; *see also* Productive Diversity: whiteness

Hawke, B. 121; *see* Australia and Asia: Hawke and Keating

Hayden, B. 116–17, 121

Hayek, F.: visit to Australia 100

Howard, J.: comments on Asia 138, 181; *see also* Blainey debate

import substitution *see* Business Migration Program (BMP): 1991 Joint Parliamentary Inquiry

Japan: economic relations 106–10, **108**, **112**, 113, 141, 164; business migrant program intake **179**; *see also* Global Value Chains

Keating, P.: Asia and Australia 106, 120–22, 134; Treasurer 111, 114; *see also* economic restructuring; *see also* protectionism

Lee Kuan Yew, (Singaporean Prime Minister) *see* Asian Values

manufacturing: economic significance of 1, 3; 23n9, 53, 61–2, 67, 97, 110, 113, 122, 141–42, 178; and New International Division of Labour, 92–3; *see also* protectionism, tariffs

migrants: Canada comparison 148, 156, 180, 184, 186–87; commoditised 162–3; entrepreneurs 78–9, 82, 153–54, 156, 165, 172–6; exchange value 6, 10, 27, 43, 45, 63, 75, 85, 206; ethnic breakout theory 7, 83; ethnicity 37n25, 135; mixed embeddedness theory 83–4; networks 45–6, 48, 148; self-financing and investment 159–60, 180, 188, 192–4; *see also* Business Migration Program

migration: *passim*; 3D jobs theory 32; Human capital theory 32–4; effect on economy 150; Howard Government 19, 190, 195–6; racism 158; mixed embeddedness theory *see* migrants: entrepreneurs; reserve army of labour theory 92; skilled 2, 7, 9, 11, 91, 173–4; statistics, Australia 30, 79, 81, 93, **94**, **95**, *174*, *175*, *176*, *179*, *185*; tertiary students 205

multiculturalism x, 2–5, 98–100, 134; *passim*; and Anti-Discrimination Act 1975 (Australia), 95, 98, 136, 149; Al Grassby 94–5; *Big Brother Movement*, 99; Fraser government (Australia) 98–9, 180; Gareth Evans on 134; Mainstreaming 137–9; Malcom Fraser on 137; National Agenda for a Multicultural Australia 15, 138–9, 146–9, 183, 193–6; Neil Edwards on 17; Paul Keating and 17, 133, 148; Peter Shergold on 139, 147–8; Whitlam government 94–96, 98; *see also* CAAIP neoliberalism 17, 35, 40, 78, 86, 100, 113, 115, 119, 208–9; Economic Restructuring, 118; Fraser government 100; Labor governments, 18, 124, 137, 157; migrant settlement policies, 194; Productive Diversity 22, 156; Regionalism 117, 120

non-productive labour 2, 4, 6, 8–9, 15, 29, 82, 87, 163 *passim*;

Numerical Multi-factor Assessment System (NUMAS) 93

Office of Multicultural Affairs (OMA) x, xi, 10–11, 17, 137, 146, 150–51, 155–61, 164–5; and human capital theory 41; Neil Edwards 148; Peter Shergold 139, 147; *see also* Productive Diversity

Productive Diversity x, 2–8, 11, 15, 17–18, 21, 166, 193, 195–7; *passim*; and cultural capital 39, national conference on 39; Nick Bolkus on 195; whiteness 206–7; theory *see* Cope, B. and Kalantzis, M.; *see also* Edwards, N. *see also* Fedderson T. *see also* ethnic surplus value; *see also* Office of Multicultural Affairs

protectionism 3, 115, 129; tariffs 96, 98, 117

Small and Medium Enterprise: definition 89n32; migrant 82–83, 85, 87, 152, 172, 174; sector growth 23n9, 58, 84, 153, 164–66; SME *see* Small and Medium Enterprise

Taksa, L. and Groutsis, D. 7, 85, 162–3

transnational capitalist class 75–8, 82–3

temporary migration 2, 10, 19–20, 80–81, 183, 190–1; 195–6; TNC executive personnel 193–4

value 2–3, 5, 8–10, 20, 35, 39, 206–8; *passim*; theory (Karl Marx) 5, 26–28; *see also* migrants: exchange value; *see also* Global Value Chains; *see also* ethnic surplus value

White Australia Policy 96, 106, 121

Whitlam, G. 95; government 96–100, 111, 115

World Intellectual Property Organization (WIPO) 58